THE WINCHESTER

THE WINCHESTER

THE GUN THAT BUILT AN AMERICAN DYNASTY

BY

Laura Trevelyan

Yale

UNIVERSITY

PRESS

NEW HAVEN & LONDON

First published 2016 in the United States by Yale University Press
and in the United Kingdom by I.B. Tauris & Co. Ltd.

Yale University Press books may be purchased in quantity
for educational, business, or promotional use. For information, please e-mail
sales.press@yale.edu (U.S. office) or sales@yaleup.co.uk (U.K. office).

Typeset by Data Standards Ltd, Frome, Somerset.
Printed in the United States of America.

Library of Congress Control Number: 2016938152
ISBN 978-0-300-22338-5 (hardcover: alk. paper)

A catalogue record for this book is available from the British Library.

This paper meets the requirements of ANSI/NISO Z39.48-1992 (Permanence of Paper).

10 9 8 7 6 5 4 3 2 1

This book is dedicated to Mary Foote Rounsavall – custodian of the Winchester flame and beloved New England matriarch.

CONTENTS

ACKNOWLEDGMENTS

THIS BOOK HAS many godparents, as is the way with projects which are a long time in the making. The first godparent is Igor Webb, who one blustery day on Martha's Vineyard a quarter of a century ago remarked what an interesting family history I had. You know, the story of the family behind the Winchester Rifle would be a terrific read, said Igor, encouragingly, as the waves crashed against the rocks. Intimidated by the knowledge that Igor himself was a formidable writer and family historian, I nonetheless lodged the thought for future reference.

The second godparent is my cousin Mary Foote Rounsavall, scion of New England and Kentucky, and matriarch supreme in the fine tradition of some of the characters you'll meet, chiefly Jane Winchester, and Jennie and Susan Bennett. Mary has been unfailingly encouraging, and has directed me towards many sources of information, within the family and without. What's more, she and her niece Katie Haddock welcomed my husband and our boys to these shores with open arms in 2004 – and we have never wanted to leave, having made our lives here, in a country we find so dynamic and endlessly invigorating. Thank you also to my father George Trevelyan and my uncle Tom for their helpful researches, and to all the Winchester Bennett cousins who reminisced about their happy and sunlit childhoods at Johnson's Point. And for my cousin Ted Lovejoy, cheerleader-in-chief of Johnson's Point and all matters Winchester, mere thanks are inadequate.

Godparent the third is the long-suffering Iradj Bagherzade, publisher of I.B.Tauris, who must wonder how I can survive as a reporter, given how many book deadlines I have missed along the way. All I can say is thank you for this opportunity, and for your patience – heartfelt thanks which must be extended to the truly wonderful Azmina Siddique and Joanna Godfrey, my editors at

I.B.Tauris. Azmina and Joanna have been so helpful and supportive, believing against the odds that the book would eventually materialize.

The fairy godmother is undoubtedly Sue Fox, my indomitable researcher, who has traversed America, delving into archives in search of material for this book. No request has been too taxing for Sue, and it is she who has unearthed the detail which is the spine of this book. Thank you to Mary Robinson of the McCracken Research Library at the Buffalo Bill Center of the West, Carol Peterson at the San Mateo County History Museum, Sierra Dixon at the Connecticut Historical Society, Frances Skelton, Betsey Goldberg and Bonnie Campbell at the New Haven Historical Society, Mary Warnement at the Boston Athenaeum, Jeannie Sherman at the Connecticut State Library, and Jim Reed at History San Jose for being so helpful to Sue Fox as she researched my many and varied requests. Thanks must also go to Elizabeth Stone and Linsey Hague for meticulously proofreading the book.

Thanks are due too to my three boys, Isaac, Toby, and Ben, and my dear, accommodating, forbearing husband James Goldston. And finally, any errors in the text are unintentional, and most certainly mine.

LIST OF ILLUSTRATIONS

INTRODUCTION

T
HE ROCKY PINK granite of the Connecticut coastline between Branford and the Thimble Islands is not a particularly famous part of America's eastern seaboard, despite its undeniable beauty and timeless charm. Vacationers heading towards the popular summer holiday spots of Cape Cod and Maine drive past with barely a backward glance. Here, where the rocks of ages jut out into Long Island Sound and the ospreys swoop overhead, grappling with fish in their talons, is Johnson's Point. Once the grand summer residence of the Winchester Bennett family, now both a beloved year-round home and a seasonal playground for their descendants, this compound was built with the profits from the Winchester Repeating Rifle, known as "The Gun That Won The West." The peninsula, with wide-open views of the gateway to the Atlantic Ocean, appealed to one Thomas Gray Bennett in the early 20th century. As the millionaire son-in-law of Oliver Winchester, founder of the Winchester Repeating Arms Company in nearby New Haven, Bennett wished to build a summer home, Islewood, where he and his family could sail and swim to their heart's content. It was on Johnson's Point some 85 years later that I was introduced to my Winchester relatives and the famous repeating rifle.

As a teenager visiting this most captivating stretch of Connecticut, I had my first encounter with the Great Aunts and their elderly elephant gun, which had been adapted to fire tennis balls – woe betide the intruder who came too close to the family property. This weapon had quite the kick, and you had to be careful to hold it close to your shoulder when firing, or risk injury from the recoil. The results were most satisfactory – tennis balls would arc above the water, over the granite of the pleasing shoreline, before splashing harmlessly into the Long Island Sound. The peace of the kayakers and the ospreys were briefly disturbed, and one might get an odd look from the fishermen combing the Sound for oysters, but that was about it in terms of consequences. The Great Aunts were a characterful bunch, fond of tennis, family, and cocktail hour: one was known to shoot squirrels from her bedroom. Few outsiders dared risk the wrath of the Great Aunts and their tennis ball gun by attempting to penetrate their summer compound – but as a family member visiting from far-flung England, I was welcomed with warmth and kindness. Only later did I ask why we were firing tennis balls around with such jollity, and learn the link between our family and the bloody history of the Winchester repeating rifle in settling the American West. Having seen Jimmy Stewart's Western movies as a child, I had only the dimmest of ideas about cowboys and Winchesters. This book is my attempt to follow the historical thread from an idyllic afternoon in Branford back to 19th-century New England.

This spirited Connecticut branch of my family were all descendants of my great-great-great-grandfather Oliver Winchester, a penniless farm boy who became a shirtmaker, entrepreneur, and one of the most successful weapons manufacturers in 19th-century America. My approach is to tell the story of the rise and fall of the Winchester Repeating Arms Company as a family concern, through the lens of the individuals themselves. An important disclaimer: I should apologize to gun enthusiasts in advance, since this isn't a technical history of the most successful Winchester models. I shan't deal at length with calibers, range, magazines, or sight specifications. Others have done so far more successfully than this decidedly non-technical writer ever could. Even after researching this book, I am still hazy on the merits of the Model 94 versus the 86. Read no further if you wish to learn more about octagonal barrels, or precisely why the Winchester '73 was the favorite longarm of the Old West.

This book will focus instead on history and human interest, telling the story of the family behind the rifles. The popularity of Winchester arms mirrored American expansion at a time of rugged individualism and the opening up of the Western Frontier. From the Civil War era until World War I, larger-than-life characters ran the Winchester Repeating Arms Company with great success. The war led to a precipitous decline in the company's fortunes, and eventually the end of the family's involvement with the business. My ancestor Oliver Winchester would almost certainly have frowned on this project. Earlier attempts by others to write a history of the company were deemed impolitic. As Edwin Pugsley, my great-great-uncle and Winchester's chief engineer, opined, "We want a company history, and do not want to kill a number of Indians and Buffalo on every page."[1] There is an excellent history of the company by the distinguished writer Harold F. Williamson, written more than half a century ago, and I have drawn upon that as well as other comprehensive histories by R. L. Wilson, George Madis, and Herbert G. Houze. Henry Brewer, a Winchester official, believed the company's chronological history should be written "interestingly" with the "picturesque and salient features" presented in "entertaining form."[2] Therein lies the challenge.

The Winchester repeating rifle was revolutionary because it was one of the first commercial guns to fire continuously, without having to be reloaded after each round was fired. Oliver Winchester tried to sell this newfangled weapon to the Union side during the US Civil War, but distrust of the new from the Army's bureaucracy prevented him from making much headway. Yet Oliver persevered and lived to see the Winchester became a favorite of presidents, pioneers, and outlaws. Everyone from Annie Oakley to Ernest Hemingway had one. As Harold F. Williamson wrote, firearms, the axe, and the plow were "the three cornerstones upon which the pioneer Americans built this nation. Of the three, firearms were the most dramatic and appealed most to the popular imagination."[3]

The very mention of the Winchester rifle conjures up images of the American West – a cowboy galloping across the plains on his trusty steed, his Winchester close at hand. His progress is tracked by Native Americans, who are also armed with the rifle they called the spirit gun. A confrontation is looming. Jimmy Stewart's movie *Winchester '73* captures the rugged, romantic, and lawless spirit of American expansion. Photographs from that era show both settlers and Native Americans posing proudly with their Winchesters. Buffalo Bill was a devoted Winchester fan, as was President Teddy Roosevelt, who had

Winchesters delivered to the White House for his big game hunting trips in Africa.

Yet the tale of the rifle's success is really one of the man behind the company, and his vision. Oliver Winchester, who was born into poverty and expected to work on a farm aged only six, grew up to be a canny entrepreneur who assembled the best designers and gun-makers and sold his rifles around the world. This far-sighted businessman saw the potential in the repeating rifle immediately. A shirtmaker by trade, he astutely invested his spare cash in rifles – a trade he knew nothing about initially.

Oliver Winchester believed in keeping the business in the family – but his son and heir William Wirt Winchester died young. Wirt's wife Sarah Winchester became a wealthy widow, who moved to California and built the extraordinary house which is now a tourist attraction, due to be immortalized by Hollywood – the Winchester Mystery House. According to the myth, Sarah Winchester was ridden with guilt because her fortune came from Native Americans killed by settlers of the West with their Winchesters. As the story goes, Sarah was haunted by images of death and destruction. After consulting a medium, she was told that if she would only keep building, then the spirits of the dead Native Americans would be satisfied. This supposedly explains why Sarah's house in San Jose is vast and unfinished, with staircases which lead nowhere – the tortured woman engaged in a whirlwind of construction, to appease those killed with the rifles which had produced her immense wealth. Or did she?

Oliver Winchester cultivated his son-in-law Thomas Gray Bennett as a prospective leader of the company. Mr Bennett was another impressive New Englander, though from a very different background to Oliver's hardscrabble one. Bennett was a Yale University man, and a commander of one of the few units in the American Civil War which had both black and white soldiers. As they were fighting for the abolition of slavery, the North had to set an example by showing African American soldiers fighting alongside white. Thomas Bennett's war diaries reveal both the practical difficulties of integration and the triumphs it produced on the battlefield.

Oliver Winchester sent Thomas Bennett around the world to sell rifles – and Bennett's letters back to his long-suffering wife Jennie are a fascinating portrait of the geopolitics of the time. Bennett wrote from Paris and Istanbul, waiting around endlessly to see defense officials and sultans, in search of the lucrative contracts which would make Winchester a household name. A man of great business acumen and tremendous integrity, Thomas Bennett stepped on a train to Utah in the 1880s and hired three young Mormons in the gunmaking business – the Browning brothers, as it turned out, famous names in the history of American gun-making. As the Winchester Repeating Arms Company went from strength to strength, the Winchester factory in New Haven, Connecticut came to dominate and define the town – New Haven was Winchester. Connecticut became the gunmaking capital of the East Coast in the 19th century – the rival Colt company was based in nearby Hartford.

Thomas Bennett's son Winchester Bennett was the final family member to be involved in the company. Winchester (known to the family as Win) suffered from various ailments throughout his life, and was not as vigorous a force in the company as his father T. G. Bennett and his grandfather Oliver Winchester had been. Win was a gentleman and a sportsman, devoted to family, sailing, fishing, and shooting. This genteel character summered with his clan at Johnson's Point in Branford, Connecticut, in a summer residence called Islewood with majestic views of Long Island Sound. My grandmother Molly, Win's daughter, was born in Islewood on Johnson's Point with its sweeping veranda, a home built by her grandfather Thomas Gray Bennett. Although Molly married an Englishman, Humphry Trevelyan, son of the historian G. M. Trevelyan, Molly returned to Connecticut with her children every other summer – which is how my father came to take me to Johnson's Point as a teenager. There, I learned to fire the tennis ball gun, just as previous generations had done. My grandmother was hardly weighed down by Sarah Winchester's supposed level of guilt about the origins of her wealth – yet she was an active member of the Campaign for Nuclear Disarmament, and would take me to rallies in Cambridge, England. There she would nod sagely as speakers railed against the evils of the arms trade. Only in later years did the memory of the Winchester heiress tut-tutting about the unpleasantness of the weapons business strike me as paradoxical.

Fig. 1 Molly Trumbull Trevelyan, the author's grandmother, on the rocks at
Johnson's Point with her mother-in-law Janet Trevelyan, *c.*1936.

By the time I was learning about Hiroshima and Nagasaki at
Molly's side, the glory days of Winchester were long gone. The
company's massive expansion to deal with the demands of World War
I was to be its undoing – it was crippled by interest on the loans which
financed that increase in production, and undermined by fixed price
contracts paid by the government. The fear of an increase in taxes on
those perceived to have profited from the bloody business of war
loomed large. The family-owned company staggered on after the war,
diversifying into Winchester-themed products such as ice-skates,
razor blades, and washing machines. But by 1931 the game was up,
and Winchester went into receivership.

The period in which the Winchester Repeating Arms Company
came into being and prospered is a dynamic one in American
history. As the era of the frontier recedes, it seems even more
daring and dramatic than ever, full of adventure and risk, primal and

brutal. Survival was all. Men relied upon their Winchester rifles to keep them alive. Native Americans, first overpowered by the rifle they called the spirit gun, soon adopted it in their battle against the encroaching settlers. During the violent Reconstruction period after the Civil War, when African Americans were regularly lynched by mobs furious about the abolition of slavery, the Winchester rifle was used by black men to defend their families and their property. "The Winchester Rifle deserves a place of honor in every black home," declared the schoolteacher and early civil rights campaigner Ida B. Wells.[4] At a turbulent time in the new country's early years, the story of Oliver Winchester and his rifles reflects the very history of America.

My great-great-grandfather Thomas Gray Bennett loved John Greenleaf Whittier's poem *Snow-Bound*, keeping it in his Yale yearbook, and I have found his favorite quote to be inspiring while writing this book.

Clasp, Angel of the backward look
And folded wings of ashen gray
And voice of echoes far away,
The brazen covers of thy book;
The weird palimpsest old and vast,
Wherein thou hid'st the spectral past[5]

If our spectral past can be illuminated by faraway echoes, then time spent burrowing through weird palimpsests these past few years will not have been in vain.

Laura Trevelyan, The Writer's Room, New York City, 2016

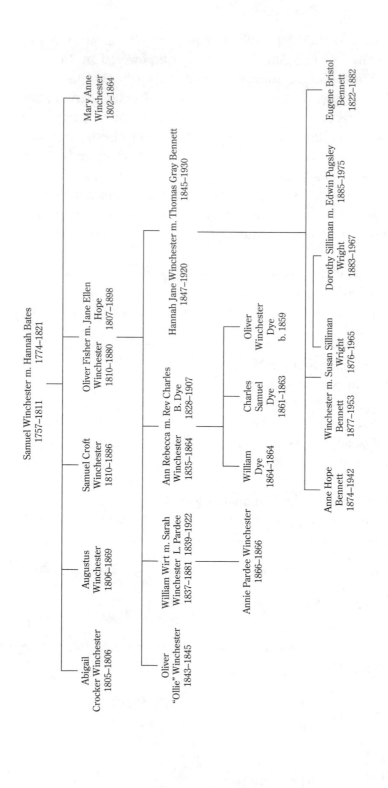

Samuel Winchester m. Hannah Bates
1757–1811   1774–1821

Abigail
Crocker Winchester
1805–1806

Augustus
Winchester
1806–1869

Samuel Croft
Winchester
1810–1886

Oliver Fisher m. Jane Ellen
Winchester   Hope
1810–1880   1807–1898

Mary Anne
Winchester
1802–1864

Oliver
"Ollie" Winchester
1843–1845

William Wirt m. Sarah
Winchester L. Pardee
1837–1881 1839–1922

Ann Rebecca m. Rev Charles
Winchester   B. Dye
1835–1864   1828–1907

Hannah Jane Winchester m. Thomas Gray Bennett
1847–1920   1845–1930

Annie Pardee Winchester
1866–1866

William
Dye
1864–1864

Charles
Samuel
Dye
1861–1863

Oliver
Winchester
Dye
b. 1859

Anne Hope
Bennett
1874–1942

Winchester m. Susan Silliman
Bennett   Wright
1877–1953   1876–1965

Dorothy Silliman m. Edwin Pugsley
Wright
1883–1967   1885–1975

Eugene Bristol
Bennett
1822–1882

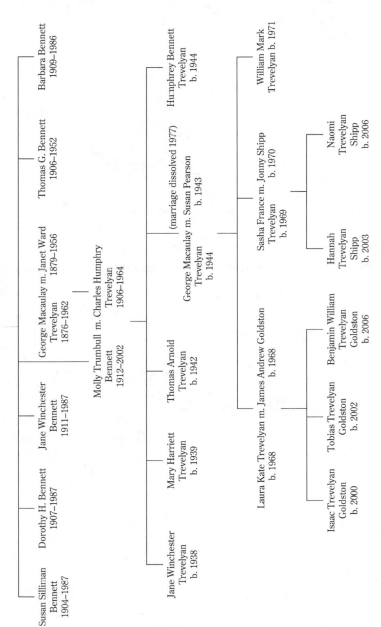

Winchester Bennett m. Susan Silliman Wright
1877–1953   1876–1965

Susan Silliman
Bennett
1904–1987

Dorothy H. Bennett
1907–1987

Jane Winchester
Bennett
1911–1987

George Macaulay m. Janet Ward
Trevelyan   1879–1956
1876–1962

Thomas G. Bennett
1906–1952

Barbara Bennett
1909–1986

Molly Trumbull m. Charles Humphry
Bennett   Trevelyan
1912–2002   1906–1964

Jane Winchester
Trevelyan
b. 1938

Mary Harriett
Trevelyan
b. 1939

Thomas Arnold
Trevelyan
b. 1942

George Macaulay m. Susan Pearson
Trevelyan   b. 1943
b. 1944

(marriage dissolved 1977)

Humphrey Bennett
Trevelyan
b. 1944

Laura Kate Trevelyan m. James Andrew Goldston
b. 1968   b. 1968

Sasha France m. Jonny Shipp
Trevelyan   b. 1970
b. 1969

William Mark
Trevelyan b. 1971

Isaac Trevelyan
Goldston
b. 2000

Tobias Trevelyan
Goldston
b. 2002

Benjamin William
Trevelyan
Goldston
b. 2006

Hannah
Trevelyan
Shipp
b. 2003

Naomi
Trevelyan
Shipp
b. 2006

CHAPTER 1

The Damn Yankee Rifle

RURAL MASSACHUSETTS in the early 19th century was a quiet place, before the first stirrings of the industrial revolution began to change the landscape and the lives of America's early settlers. Colonial Boston was still a small town, though the Revolutionary War had been forged here in the 1770s, when tension between the British king and the colonists erupted. Oliver Fisher Winchester was born on November 30, 1810 in Boston, into a new century where the reign of King George III was still a powerful memory for the young America. Weapons had helped the colonists throw off British rule, and they were to propel Oliver into the history books as the founder of the Winchester Repeating Arms Company. From impecunious farm boy to wildly successful arms manufacturer, Oliver was born on the cusp of the era of mechanization. His ability to capitalize on all the promise and progress of the industrial age was to bring him riches indeed. As he left the humble farmstead of his birth far behind, this son of New England made the Winchester rifle a household name. Oliver wasn't an inventor of guns – but he was a supremely talented salesman, businessman, and investor, and an indefatigable believer in his own rifles. Driven and determined, he took advantage of the new country's eagerness for firearms. During the Civil War, Oliver met with only with only partial success, but as the United States expanded westward, his business flourished.

For the pioneers who were settling America, a rifle was a necessity, a utility like water and fire – it was a way to get food and to protect your family from attack. As a visiting Englishman wrote in 1774:

There is not a Man born in America that does not Understand the Use of Firearms and that well [...] It is Almost the First thing they Purchase and take to all the New Settlements and in the Cities you scarcely find a Lad of 12 years that does not go a Gunning.[1]

This was the world Oliver was born into, and the one which made him rich beyond the wildest dreams of his ancestors. The Winchesters were descended from English immigrants, and until Oliver's sweeping success they had lived a meager life in their new world.

Oliver's relative John Winchester left England's shores as a teenager, and made the long and uncomfortable voyage over the Atlantic to Boston in 1635, five generations before Oliver was born. Whether John was seeking freedom of religious worship, or the opportunity for a better life, or indeed fleeing problems at home, history does not record. Life did not proceed smoothly for the new resident at first – John joined the Ancient and Honorable Artillery Company of Boston in 1638, and in the military disturbance of 1644–5 was fined for the trouble he and his neighbors had caused. John's fine was remitted since he did not have enough money to pay it. His outlook improved considerably upon moving to the Muddy River district of Boston, now the town of Brookline, where John, despite being unable to pay a fine, was nonetheless able to purchase a 140-acre farm. John was now the proud owner of salt marsh and swampy fresh meadow. As was the way of the pilgrims and early settlers from England, John worked hard, lived a simple life, and became one of the first members of his local church. He was a "well known citizen, his sons and grandsons were among the most prominent and useful people of the community."[2]

John lived out his days on the Ronton farm, reaching the fine age of 82. His estate was valued at £307 10s. The farm that he had bought nearly 40 years before was by 1694 worth a princely £267. John's children John, Mary, Jonathan, and Josiah were positioned comfortably, and the Winchesters became steady if unspectacular members of their New England community. Alongside the hard graft, some fun was occasionally allowed. Hannah, John's widow, was the happy recipient of his largesse. John's will reads that Hannah shall be allowed; "one barrel of Cyder [. . .] every year so long as she shall live and brought in place where she shall order." [3]

The descendants of John Winchester took a break from farming and drinking cider when the uprising against British rule began – a few served in the Revolutionary War of 1776, on the side of the rebels against the King of England, George III. But by and large the Winchesters were salt of the earth folk, living quotidian, uneventful lives. As a family genealogist noted:

> I do not find that they were men of note or known for their great deeds to mankind, but I do realize that they were men of strong character, earnest purpose, and deep religious conviction, upright and useful citizens, holding many offices of trust in the communities of which they were members, and helpful in building up the towns they selected for their homes, showing both ability and public spirit. [4]

Oliver was to combine this fundamental uprightness with an entrepreneur's flair and flourish, making the name of Winchester known across the new nation.

For all that the Winchesters had sailed the ocean in search of new beginnings, Oliver was born into circumstances even less auspicious than those of John Winchester's children more than 100 years earlier. Life was harsh for the young Oliver. His father Samuel died a year after his birth, which left his mother with several toddlers and no means of support. Samuel had known much misery in his life – his first wife Martha died leaving four children, while his second wife Theodora died after only three years of marriage, having given birth to two babies. Hannah, Samuel's third wife, survived him with five children. Fate's cruelty deprived Oliver of his father, and left him as just one of Samuel Winchester's eleven children, all struggling to survive. These straitened childhood years instilled drive and ambition into Oliver, who never sat still for a moment and wasted no time in leaving his youthful poverty far behind. He was not the only shining star in his generation – one of his half-brothers, Samuel, became a successful furniture manufacturer in Keene, New Hampshire, and later moved to Grand Rapids, Michigan with another of Oliver's half-brothers Enoch. Samuel pioneered the use of assembly line methods in furniture production, much as Oliver was to mass-produce rifles. The Winchester brothers Samuel and Enoch and their outstanding craftsmanship helped create Grand Rapid's reputation as the furniture capital of America.

Samuel was a full 25 years older than Oliver, his half-brother, and the two lived separate lives in different parts of the new country. Oliver and his twin brother, also named Samuel after the deceased father, started working on a farm near Boston when they were aged just six, to bring in much-needed income for their penniless mother. Only in the winter, when farm work dried up, were the boys allowed to attend school. Oliver remembered that in his childhood days he was "always hungry and always cold." [5] At 14, Oliver was apprenticed to a carpenter, and after buying out the final year of his apprenticeship, in 1830 he became a master builder. Unusually for one so young, Oliver secured a contract to build a church in Baltimore. Church-building in America was booming in the early 19th century. The new nation had been founded by the Pilgrim Fathers escaping religious persecution, and seeking freedom of worship; so places to gather and pray, the centerpiece of these new communities, were sought after. To this day we see the signature New England white wooden church on the village green, with the spire visible from afar. The New England settlers modeled their churches on the English style – and the art of constructing trusses necessary to support a church roof was highly specialized. When the leaders of the Connecticut town of Branford (named by the pilgrims after Brentford in Middlesex) built a new church on the village green, the commissioners had to ship over a specialist builder from England just to build the trusses.

Oliver excelled at church building yet abruptly changed course in 1833, switching from master building to haberdashery after only a few years. His training in the intricate, delicate architecture of building trusses was to prove an invaluable grounding in the importance of accuracy, which applied equally to his later careers of shirtmaking and manufacturing rifles. The impatient entrepreneur did not want to work for others in the sleepy world of constructing houses of worship – he wished to run his own show and make his own destiny. Buoyed by his marriage to Jane Ellen Hope from Maine in 1834, Oliver opened what has been described as both a haberdashery store in Baltimore and "the first gentleman's furnishing goods store in Maryland."[6] Though the store opened during the depression year of 1837, Oliver wasn't daunted by the poor economic climate, and his store on Baltimore Street close to Barnum's hotel flourished, selling everything from dry goods to men's clothes. Oliver's men's shirts won prizes in Baltimore – he was awarded a silver medal by the Maryland Institute for the quality of his shirts, bosoms, and collars. O. F. Winchester and Company were marketed as "manufacturers of the patent shoulder seam shirts, which they make to order and warrant to fit."[7]

Jane and Oliver had three children while they were living in Baltimore – Ann Rebecca, William Wirt, and Hannah Jane, known as Jennie. A second son, Oliver, was born in 1843, but became ill and died before his second birthday. Oliver's wife Jane was from a hard-up, flinty background, just like her husband – she too had grown up in poverty, raised by a widow. Jane and Oliver had lost parents and siblings in their own childhoods, and while the early death of their own toddler must have been tragic, such miseries were all too common in those days. There was nothing for it but to focus on providing for the Winchesters' three surviving children. Only one, Jennie, was to outlive her parents.

When the Winchesters were raising their family, Baltimore was a city trying to cope with a huge influx of German and Irish immigrants, who frequently clashed as the two ethnic groups tried to secure better lives for their extended clans. Factories mass-produced flour, textiles, and canned oysters – there was plenty of money being made, and enough cash in the pockets of the menfolk for Oliver's gentlemen's furnishings store to thrive. After ten years of the store on Baltimore Street, the 37-year-old Oliver was restless once again. He had been actively involved in the civic life of Baltimore, lobbying the Mayor and City Council to build the Baltimore and Ohio railroad, thus opening up the city for more trade. Now he was interested in investing in the manufacture of men's dress shirts, designed by his good self. Quite what lay behind this switch from haberdashery is not altogether clear. Maybe Oliver couldn't abide uncomfortable shirts, and often discussed this topic with his gentleman customers; or, more likely, did the astute businessman see a gap in the market? Given the prizes he had won for the quality of his shirts, this was a chance for him to combine his flair for invention with his entrepreneurial skills. The ever energetic Oliver applied for a patent to make what he believed would be the perfect men's dress shirt.

In his patent application, Oliver wrote about how he intended to overcome the pull on the neckband which bedeviled those who had to cut shirts:

> The object of my invention is to remedy this evil, and this I effect by making a curved seam on top of and corresponding with the curve of that part of the shoulder which extends from the arm to the neck so that the shirt shall be supported on the shoulder and thereby avoid a pull on the neckband. The bosom is also curved out on each side which aids the effect produced by so cutting the shirt and also serves to make it fit better.[8]

The drawings accompanying the patent application are quite ingenious, and suggest a creative, practical, problem-solving mind at work. Oliver invented and perfected that curved seam which makes modern men's shirts sit comfortably.

Shortly before Oliver was granted patent number US 5421 on February 1, 1848, he sold the Baltimore business. His various successors boasted of their connection to him. William P. Towles, a former partner, promised to continue Oliver's good work, giving particular attention to the "manufacture of the patent shoulder seam shirt [. . .] Gentlemen at a distance can have their Shirts made to order and forwarded to them, to any part of the Union."[9] C. Brett also claimed to be Oliver's successor, selling "Gentlemen's linen made to order in superior style." Oliver left Towles and Brett to exploit their association with him, and moved Jane and the family north to the bright lights of New Haven.

Settled by pilgrims in 1638, New Haven enjoyed a strategic position on the banks of the natural harbor of Long Island Sound. The nine original squares of the community were the focus of the city, with Yale College, then an institute of religious education, having moved nearby in 1718.[10] Goods were shipped to and from the West Indies and the south of the country, with the harbor and the waterfront the center of commercial life at the time Oliver arrived. Buildings were made of wood, the streets weren't paved, and there were no street lamps for those riding or walking at night. New Haven's now famous Green had just been planted with the double row of graceful elm trees, hence the name of the Elm City.

In this bustling city, in the old Garfield factory on State Street, Oliver embarked upon the business of making and selling shirts to the gentlemen of New Haven. The well-to-do from the carriage and clock factories in town must surely have flocked to his store. An advertisement in the *Hartford Daily Courant* read: "Shirtmakers wanted, to whom constant employment will be given and cash paid. Also, two or three capable women between 20 and 30 years of age (Americans) as ironers, to whom high wages will be paid. O.F. Winchester." [11] Oliver needed workers, and fast, as he had timed his arrival at a time of tremendous growth in both the population and the economy of New Haven. By the late 1840s this once somnolent New England settlement was flourishing. The population was approaching 30,000 as the newly built railways delivered Irish immigrants escaping the famine and Germans and Italians in search of a better life.[12] There were three railroad terminals in town by 1849, with a fourth to follow in the 1850s. Taverns, grog shops, and bowling saloons sprung up alongside the graceful church spires.[13]

In the course of his new business Oliver met John M. Davies of New York, an importer of men's furnishing goods, and in 1849 the pair formed the company of Winchester and Davies to make men's shirts. Davies was to become Oliver's ally, collaborator, and lifelong friend. In the early days of their partnership, Oliver oversaw the making of the shirts while Davies handled marketing and distribution – the shirts were sold up and down the coast from New Haven to New York, to the growing middle class of men keen to buy dress shirts as a sign of their new-found status. In New Haven itself, likely customers would have included the bold-faced names of the day – men such as James Brewster the wealthy carriage-maker, Henry and Wooster Hotchkiss, the lumberyard owners on Long Wharf, James E. English, the shipping magnate, Leverette Candee, the manufacturer of rubber clothing, and Ezra C. Read, the ivory piano key manufacturer.[14] The Winchester–Davies partnership was to be profitable in all ways, and formed the basis for a close personal friendship – Winchester and Davies built matching mansions in New Haven later in the century, and lived cheek by jowl.

The two men mass-produced shirts on a grand scale, cutting the material in the factory, and initially sending the pieces out to be sewed by women in their homes. In the days when work outside the home was not considered ladylike, several hundred women were employed in this fashion, and the delivery routes covered hundreds of miles of roads around New Haven.[15] But the nature of the business changed dramatically with the invention of the sewing machine in 1852. Oliver was initially skeptical about the gadget, which had been invented and patented by Nathaniel Wheeler. Wheeler had hoped to interest Oliver in his creation, since Oliver was a mass employer of seamstresses. Wheeler and his partner James Wilson were banking on Oliver purchasing several hundred sewing machines, giving them the money they so badly needed to kick-start production of their prized asset. Wheeler demonstrated the sewing machine to Oliver, and was disappointed by his lack of interest. Then came Wheeler's stroke of genius:

> The next day I returned, with some cloth already cut, and my wife demonstrated to him by sewing a shirt together before his very eyes. At this, Winchester was so surprised that he gave me a large order, and within the week had agreed with us to purchase more machines.[16]

Oliver was evidently extremely impressed by Mrs Wheeler's demonstration, because he and John Davies immediately became investors in the Wheeler and Wilson Sewing Machine Works. Later, Wheeler and Wilson would return the vote of confidence and put their money into the New Haven Arms Company. Oliver was also a sales agent for the sewing machine. An advertisement of the time from Winchester and Davies alerts

> housekeepers, seamstresses, dressmakers, tailors [to the] perfect adaptation and unrivaled excellence of these sewing machines [...] They are simple in construction, efficient and durable in operation,

beautiful in model and finish, fitted to adorn the parlor and suited to the workshop [...] Substituting, as they do, healthful exercise and rational employment for the soul and body, destroying drudgery of hand-sewing, they are hailed as WOMAN'S FRIEND.[17]

The hum of those sewing machines in the company factory was vastly productive – though the machines were not always friendly to the women who operated them. One Ann Farley had her scalp torn off in an accident at the Winchester and Davies shirt factory,[18] and was for evermore dependent on the town for support. According to the Census of 1860, the firm of Winchester and Davies had invested capital of $400,000 and used 1,500,000 yd of cotton cloth, 25,000 spools of thread, 25,000 gross of buttons, 50,000 lb of starch and 18,000 lb of soap. With 500 foot pedal sewing machines, the firm produced 40,000 dozen shirts annually, valued at $600,000.[19] The quiet industry of those ladies and the buying power of New Haven's gentlemen were making Oliver and his partner wealthy. John Davies built a new factory on Court Street, which at the height of its productivity was "one of the largest, if not the largest, shirt manufactory in the world."[20] The name of Winchester and Davies was prominent not only in New Haven but further afield, as Oliver and his partner were credited with introducing a new manufacturing industry to America.

As the farm boy morphed into the well-to-do factory owner, Oliver did not forget those upon whom his fortune had been built. In June 1852 he held a festival at the New Haven shirt manufactory. Strawberries, ice creams, cakes, and iced water (but no alcohol) were served at this summer party thrown for the shirtmaking workforce. Oliver's wife and daughter provided the floral decorations, and the cutters, clerks, washers, sewers, and ironers were the guests of honor. The company account of this affair dwells upon the "gentle rays of a setting sun [...] combined with the pleasurable excitement that sparkled in every eye and glowed on each cheek, fully realized the poet's dream of a glimpse at fairy-land, and touched and softened the hearts of all who witnessed it."[21] Oliver addressed his workforce, urging them to attain still greater heights in the making of shirts:

Perfection belongs only to the Deity; still, while we are short of that point, there is much room for improvement. Let us, therefore, be united in our efforts and purpose, to devote to our several departments, all the energies we possess, nor be satisfied while a stitch is misplaced, a stain unremoved, or a wrinkle unsmoothed; remembering that a shirt, however coarse, is an emblem of purity, and as the work of our hands, which are directed by our minds, it is the index to our character, to which the close observer of human nature requires no more certain key.

Oliver's linking of spiritual satisfaction to good, honest hard work places him firmly in the tradition of America's early settlers. Indeed, he paid tribute to the pilgrims of 200 years earlier in this address to the shirt factory workforce:

Who of us remembers [...] the weariness of passengers, in their sailing craft, that crept lazily along our shores, or through the sinuosities of our mighty rivers, or breasted the adverse storms and winds of the ocean, taking months for a voyage to Europe; who, I ask, but will admit that had these passengers been content therewith, and acted upon the principle of "letting well-enough alone," we should have never known the comfort of a Railroad, at forty miles an hour, the security and splendor of the mighty steamship [...] or the wondrous palaces, that follow, the course of our rivers, with the speed of an arrow.[22]

Oliver, the proud descendant of an English settler, John Winchester, was full of wonder at the "great motive power which propels the world in its present rapid course of improvement."

Oliver was conscious that his world was in the throes of great progress, and he was poised to take advantage of the possibilities his forefathers had worked so hard to create. He was also a shrewd boss who knew that rewarding staff for their arduous work would reap dividends. At the summer festival, he gave out awards to those who had distinguished themselves at the shirt factory. Mrs Phoebe Sanderson of the Washing Department received a Silver Cup for her "untiring assistance." Miss Abiah C. Breed of the Cutting

Department was recognized by Oliver as an "amiable and faithful superintendent." Miss Ellen Stoddard, who joined the shirt factory as a "mere child," was rewarded for her "quiet, indomitable energy" – Oliver recorded that she was leaving to get married, plucked away by the "insatiable foe [...] Matrimony has culled fifteen of our choicest flowers."

As an upstanding citizen of New Haven, in 1854 Oliver was elected to the board of the New Haven Water Company, which was attempting to develop a public water system. The need was vital. Wooden buildings burned to the ground with alarming frequency, as there was no ready supply of water for firefighting. Immigrants lived in squalid conditions in tenements with only outdoor toilets, and there was no public sewage system. Oliver and others knew the city could not continue to grow without bringing water into New Haven in an organized fashion. Relying on public wells and cisterns was simply not adequate. However, the outcry from those who felt the city of New Haven had no business spending huge amounts of public money on this shelved the project for a few years. By 1856, Oliver and the prominent gunmaker Eli Whitney II were among those appointed to a committee to look once again at creating a public water supply in New Haven. Oliver resigned soon after the financial panic of 1857 – and water eventually flowed into the mains of New Haven in 1862. Interestingly, as Oliver departed from the board, Benjamin Silliman Junior, professor of geology and chemistry at Yale and son of the first ever chemistry professor at Yale, joined the enterprise. The grand-children of the two men, Winchester Bennett and Susan Silliman Wright, were to marry in the next century.

As a curious, creative type, Oliver was drawn to experimenting with the array of new varieties of plants and flowers in America. He became a director of the New Haven County Horticultural Society in 1851. The first festival of the horticultural and pomological (fruit-growing) societies was a fine affair. Members of the societies made jellies from their home-grown fruit, decorated New Haven's State House with choice flowers they had grown, and the tables groaned under the weight of pears, peaches, grapes, melons, and much else besides.[23] As the Old Gentleman's Band played, Oliver showed off his prize pears, to suitable acclaim.

Despite the crash of 1857, caused by speculative investment in the railroads and the drastic fall off in European demand for American crops as the Crimean War ended, Oliver's shirt business was in rude good health, much like his produce. He had been squirreling money away in his bank account to the point that he wanted more rewarding places to put his cash. This energetic 45 year old began to look around for investment opportunities. The firearms industry at that point was dominated by the likes of Eli Whitney, Eliphalet Remington, and Samuel Colt, inventors and machinists who also had a nose for business. Oliver Winchester knew next to nothing about guns – but he had cash, could recognize a market opportunity when he saw one, and invested in 80 shares of stock in New Haven's Volcanic Arms Company in 1855. Horace Smith and Daniel Wesson, who went on to achieve fame as makers of the revolver that bore their name, had at this point developed a pistol and ammunition which Oliver thought worth a bet. Oliver was also drawn in by the involvement of Courtlandt Palmer, a wealthy financier from New York who controlled some patents on the Jennings rifle – while Smith and Wesson had a patent on a firearm seen as an improvement on the Jennings. From his work on the perfect dress shirt, Oliver knew about the value of patents, and he liked the look of Volcanic's talent and backers.

Oliver became the first president of the Volcanic Arms Company, which came to life in a brick building standing at the center of a triangle formed by the railroad, Orange Street, and Audubon Street in New Haven. There were 33 subscribers to the stock of this new enterprise,[24] the majority were clockmakers, since clockmaking was the most prominent industry in New Haven outside the manufacture of horse-drawn carriages. The roll call of investors' names shows where money was being made in 19th-century New Haven and its environs – Hiram Camp, president of the New Haven Clock Company; Henry Hooker, Silas R. Sperry, and George B. Bishop of the carriage trade; Morris Tyler of the shoe business; and the New York cracker manufacturer William Hustace all put their brass into Oliver's venture. By June 1856, the company had 45 employees on the pay roll – the ammunition was manufactured by four girls, who had been transferred from gun work.[25] Six-inch pistols sold for $16, and the eight-inch version commanded $20.

Equipment and materials for the company came from the four corners of New England. The primers, the components which react chemically to produce heat for igniting and firing ammunition, came from South Coventry, Connecticut; brass components for the rifles originated in Ansonia's Brass and Battery Company, Connecticut; and the factory machinery made its way down from Vermont and Massachusetts. Gunpowder was transported from Henry Tomes and Company in New York, wood from the New Haven Saw Mill. Drill presses, planing machines, lathes, boring machines, spindle drills, polishing stands, and the wonderfully named Hicks vibrating press – every object in the Volcanic Arms Company was dutifully accounted for in the record books. Insurance was taken out for the princely amount of $30,000 – a condition of the policy was that no more than 4 lb of gunpowder could be stored in the ammunition department at any one time, to limit the potential for dangerous explosions.[26]

An important development was taking place in the gun world at this point, which Smith and Wesson were experimenting with. Bullets fired from the traditional muskets were unreliable – to be sure of shooting your opponent, it was necessary to get very close to him, which was clearly high risk and potentially deadly. Rifles were the solution to this problem. Loading bullets into a rifled barrel, which spun ammunition further and with more accuracy than a musket, became much easier after the invention of the Minie ball by the French gunmaker Claude-Etienne Minie. One Horace Smith experimented with the repeating action on a pistol, which would enable it to reload automatically rather than manually. Quite why Smith and Wesson decided to sell their patent rights to the Volcanic Company is unclear, but soon the new venture had firearms which used the repeating action. The *New Haven Journal-Courier* reported enthusiastically in February 1856: "The Volcanic pistol and rifle seem to be the very perfection of firearms, and must be favorites with the public when they are fully known. We understand that orders crowd in upon the Company from all quarters."

The reporter was unfortunately wide of the mark, much like the firearms. The Volcanic Arms Company was not making money, or receiving many orders, and there were problems with the firearms' performance and the ammunition. Edwin Pugsley, later the chief

engineer at Winchester, was scathing about Oliver's first venture into
guns:

> The pistol and ammunition were about what you would expect a shirt-
> maker to grab, as both were about as worthless for the purpose for
> which they were designed as you can imagine [...] reasonable
> ballistics were practically non-existent. With all the strikes against the
> combination it failed, but not before Oliver had put more money into
> the venture and become its president.[27]

The company rapidly began to borrow money from Oliver, and owed
him and Nelson Gaston $20,166.66 by late 1856. On February 6, 1857
an application was made to declare Volcanic insolvent. Cash flow had
dwindled to a measly $97.38.[28]

Undaunted, the irrepressible Oliver bought up the inventory of the
bankrupt venture for a mere $40,000 and persuaded shareholders
from the Volcanic Arms Company to join him in a new venture,[29] the
New Haven Arms Company, formed on April 25, 1857. Leverett
Candee, founder of the Candee Rubber Company, threw his hat into
the ring as a shareholder, joining the clock and carriage-makers from
the Volcanic days. Oliver persuaded the investors it was worth
ponying up extra money to manufacture improved versions of the
firearms and ammunition made by the doomed Volcanic Arms
Company. There was no doubt that the repeating firearms had
promise, Oliver reasoned, but more cash had to be invested before
the things would fire straight. Oliver was the largest single
stockholder, with 800 shares.

The shirtmaker threw himself into arms manufacturing with all the
enthusiasm which had led him to patent the perfect shirt collar,
becoming the president and treasurer of the New Haven Arms
Company. Oliver was also the informal head of marketing, using
circulars to promote his products and break down the gun-buying
public's resistance to machine-made firearms as opposed to those
bought from the gun shop. Endless chit-chat with a friendly gunsmith
was worth missing if you could have a magic repeating rifle from a
factory, according to O. F. Winchester. This letter was among the
"numerous testimonials" Oliver trumpeted to his prospective

customers. Relentless marketing of testimonials was an Oliver Winchester trademark, the advertising of its day.

> Gent:- I consider the Volcanic Repeating pistol the ne plus ultra of Repeating or Revolving Arms, and far superior in many respects to Colt's much extolled Revolver. I have fired, myself, over 200 shots from it without even wiping the barrel – this is an advantage which no other arm I know of possesses. I have had the pistol with me at sea for more than eighteen months, on a voyage around the world, and find that, with the most common care, it will keep free from rust far more so than Colt's. I find the Balls as good now as when I left New York. I have shown the pistol to my friends in San Francisco, Hong Kong, Manila, Canton, and Shanghai, and they were much pleased with it.[30]

Despite this and other glowing testimonials, the guns produced by the New Haven Arms Company were still not of the highest quality. There was a recurring problem with the ammunition used by the Volcanic firearms. Enter Benjamin Tyler Henry, an inspired hire on the part of Oliver Winchester. Legend has it that the two met when Oliver employed him to repair sewing machines at the New Haven shirt factory. However the auspicious meeting came about, Henry became the Superintendent at the gun factory on May 1, 1857, exactly a week after the Volcanic Arms Company was reorganized into the New Haven Arms Company.[31] Grandson of a famous ironmaster, Henry had worked in various gun shops including the Springfield Armory and was an expert on firing mechanisms. He was the right man at the right time, and set about improving the Volcanic firearm and ammunition.

The relationship between the two men was to sour in spectacular fashion, as we shall see, but at the outset Benjamin Tyler Henry was a huge asset. It was he who turned the promise of the repeating rifle into reality. A gun that would fire and fire again, without needing to be reloaded, would transform the way men fought and defended their land. Henry's task was to somehow make this gun from the patents Winchester had purchased, and create the sought-after repeating weapon. Henry lived in the gunshop, with a cot for naps, sleeping for an hour or two and then returning to work, trying to perfect a gun and

Fig. 2 The New Haven Arms Company Factory, *c*.1858.

cartridge that would be reliable and profitable. Oliver was still in the shirt business with John Davies, and kept a beady eye on Henry's work. Those who had to endure Oliver's constant inquiries reported:

> Winchester had very little patience and often couldn't understand that every step in the development of a gun and cartridge took time. He would often come to the shop and ask what progress had been made. When he would see that a project was not completed, he would almost lose his patience and say that we had to get the gun and the cartridge perfected and we had already spent too much time and money on them. Mr Winchester was fine to work with but had little understanding at first of this work.[32]

By October 1860, after the boss's patience had been sorely tried, Henry was at last granted a patent for his new improved repeating rifle.[33]

By 1861 the New Haven Arms Company was virtually bankrupt, but Henry was painstakingly fixing the various problems with his still erratic repeating rifle. This gave Oliver the confidence to keep pouring his personal fortune into the new venture. War was on the horizon, scaring off many investors from making a long-term commitment, but encouraging Oliver in his belief that there could soon be a new market for the repeater. According to Edwin Pugsley, who was Winchester's chief engineer in later years, "the company failed each morning before breakfast, but by noon Mr Winchester had a new set of directors and more money, and kept it going. How he did this was a mystery, but a testimonial to the trust he was able to engender in new capital." [34] As Oliver Winchester wrote to one of his stockholders in October 1862, "from the commencement of our organization, till within the past three months, five years and a half, there has not been a month in which our expenditures have not exceeded our receipts." [35] Oliver's half-brother, George F. Winchester, was a strong supporter of the company in its difficult infancy, selling rifles through an agency he had established in Baltimore, Maryland.

Meanwhile, Benjamin Tyler Henry enlarged and strengthened the rim fire cartridge which French inventors, encouraged by Napoleon, had made great strides in developing. Once he'd made a working cartridge, Henry adjusted the Volcanic repeating mechanism to the use of the new ammunition. It was Henry's ingenuity which created the repeating rifle of great promise – a firearm that would fire again and again, without being reloaded. Naturally enough, the rifle was named for its inventor. The business cards of the New Haven Arms Company proudly proclaimed that Henry's repeating rifle was manufactured in New Haven, Connecticut. Oliver wrote to the Commissioner of Patents, supporting an attempt by Henry to patent changes he made to the metallic cartridge. "The result is now before you in the improvement which he claims. I esteem these to be new and valuable, and trust he may be successful in his application." [36]

The profound disagreement over slavery and states' rights which divided the United States and led to the Civil War provided enormous opportunities for gunmakers. Neither the North nor the South was well armed when the firing began at Fort Sumter in April 1861. Now there were two armies in need of the latest firearms, and Oliver Winchester had a spanking new repeating rifle, accurate and rapid firing, to sell to the Union side. Hopeful as Oliver was of selling his revolutionary repeating rifle to the Union Army, he had not realized how the bureaucracy would react to a newfangled product. The Army's Ordnance Department at the start of the war was wedded to the single-shot muzzle-loading Springfield rifle. This was antediluvian compared to the rifle which could fire over and over again without being reloaded. Soldiers back then had to bite the end off a paper cartridge, pour the powder in the muzzle, "insert the bullet with a ramrod, cock the hammer, and then place a percussion cap on the nipple under the hammer," [37] before taking aim and firing. All this for just one shot.

Oliver confronted a further problem in that there was a rival repeating rifle out there, the Spencer, competing for the attention of the Army bigwigs. Christopher Spencer, the inventor, was a Connecticut native who had worked for Colt firearms. Both Oliver Winchester and Christopher Spencer vied to get their rifles taken seriously by the old-school folk in the Secretary of War's office. Colt, the rifle manufacturer based in Hartford, Connecticut, also had a repeating rifle, though it was deemed inferior to the Spencer and the Henry.

Oliver, knowing all about the competition out there, seized the moment and arranged to have his Henry rifle tested at the earliest opportunity. It surely helped that the Secretary of the Navy, Gideon Welles, was a fellow New Englander from Connecticut. In May 1862 a US navy officer tested the rifle at the Washington Navy Yard. The Henry fired 187 shots in 216 seconds – not including time for reloading the magazine. Compare this with other rifles, which fired 120 rounds in 340 seconds, including reloading. One full 15-shot magazine was fired from the Henry in only 10.8 seconds. The tests showed the Henry rifle to be speedy and accurate, as the official report noted: "it is manifest from the above experiment that this gun may be fired with great rapidity, and it is not liable to get out of order. The penetration, in proportion to the charge used, compares favorably with that of other arms." [38]

However, the US army hierarchy was sniffy about the Henry's merits. Brigadier General James W. Ripley, the elderly Chief of Ordnance, wrote imperiously to the Secretary of War Simon Cameron on December 9, 1861, after tests showed that both the Henry and the Spencer repeating rifle were worthy of further investigation. He was resolutely unconvinced.

> I regard the weight of the arms with the loaded magazine as objectionable, and also the requirement of special ammunition, rendering it impossible to use the arms with ordinary cartridges or with powder and ball. It remains to be shown by practical trial what will be the effect on the cartridges in the magazine of carrying them on horseback [...] In view of the foregoing, of the very high prices already asked for these arms, and of the fact that the government is already pledged on orders and contracts for nearly 73,000 breech-loading rifles and carbines, to the amount of $2,250,000, I do not consider it advisable to entertain either of the propositions for purchasing these arms.[39]

James Ripley detested repeating rifles, which he seemed to regard as unduly expensive – with a repeating rifle, soldiers would simply spend more money and waste good ammunition, according to his logic. Yet no less a figure than President Abraham Lincoln was a fan of the repeating rifle. A special edition Henry, engraved and inscribed, and fitted with rosewood stocks, was presented to the President, as Oliver promoted his product with gifts to the influential.[40] Legend has it that on a fine spring morning in 1861, Lincoln himself tried both the Henry and the Spencer repeating rifles, preferring the weight and feel of the Spencer. Christopher Spencer is said to have walked into the White House himself, carrying his rifle for the President to try out.

Lincoln, a gun buff, realized that a repeating rifle could potentially shorten the war, saving thousands of lives. If you could shoot more quickly than your rival, because you didn't have to reload, then it stood to reason that battles should be concluded more rapidly. However, the Spencer rifle never reached the front line in the volume that Lincoln might have imagined, doubtless generating a sense of schadenfreude in Oliver's breast. As Chris Kyle puts it, "Through the end of 1861 and much of 1862, General Ripley conducted a one-man mutiny of disobedience and delay against President Lincoln. He refused to approve production orders, threw gun inventors out of his office, and repeatedly slow-tracked Lincoln's orders."[41] Brigadier General Ripley summed up his policy on new arms as follows:

> A great evil now especially prevalent in regard to arms for the military service is the vast variety of the new inventions, each having, of course, its advocates [...] The influence thus exercised has already introduced into the service many kinds [...] of arms, some, in my opinion, unfit for military weapons, and none as good as the US musket.

Historians have puzzled over whether the course of the Civil War could have been different had the Army only equipped its troops with more modern rifles rather than Ripley's trusted muskets. This debate has largely centered on the difference that even a modest change could have made, from the faithful musket to a rifle which loaded at the breech. Professor Robert V. Bruce of Boston University developed this counterfactual version of history in his 1956 book *Lincoln and the Tools of War*. Professor Bruce opined that had the Union Army been issued with single shot breechloaders by late 1862, never mind repeating rifles, then

> Gettysburg would certainly have ended the war. More likely, Chancellorsville or even Fredericksburg would have done it, and history would record no Gettysburg Address, no President Grant, perhaps no carpetbag reconstruction or Solid South. Instead, it might have had the memoirs of ex-President Lincoln, perhaps written during retirement during the administration of President Burnside or Hooker.[42]

If this could have been achieved by breechloaders, which eliminated all the fuss of loading muskets, then just imagine what Union troops equipped with a 16-shot Henry repeating rifle could have accomplished. Most soldiers in the Civil War shot at ranges of not much over 100 yds, where the Henry's firepower would have been at its most effective. Even if the Confederate side had been able to manufacture the Henry, they did not have the technology to manufacture the cartridges.

Oliver Winchester himself had made this impassioned appeal for US troops to adopt repeating rifles:

What would be the value of an army of one hundred thousand infantry and cavalry, thus mounted and armed [...] each artilleryman with a repeating carbine slung to his back? Certainly the introduction of repeating guns into the Army will involve a change of the Manual of Arms. Probably it will modify the art of war; possibly it may revolutionize the whole science of war. Where is the military genius that is to grasp this whole subject [...] the exclusive control of which would enable any government (with resources sufficient to keep half a million men in the field) to rule the world?[43]

There was no changing the mindset of the obdurate military planners on the Union side. Inasmuch as they trusted the repeating rifle at all, they preferred the Spencer to the Henry. The Ordnance Department bought 1.5 million muzzle-loading rifles during the war – and 130,000 Spencer repeating rifles.[44] The men of the 72nd Indiana regiment were amongst the few fighting units that tried out both the Spencer and the Henry, and they preferred the Spencer,[45] finding it more reliable, much to Oliver's chagrin. In June 1863 the Army did finally authorize a government order for 250 or so of Oliver Winchester's Henry rifles, for the 1st District of Columbia Cavalry – small beer compared to the musket orders. Still, Oliver was at last in correspondence with the chief creator of Army resistance to the Henry, Brigadier General Ripley. Mr Winchester wrote enthusiastically: "if these arms are used as efficiently by the men who are to receive them as they have been by our union friends in Kentucky, the country will have no cause to regret the expenditure."[46] The federal government purchased 800 more Henrys to equip the eight companies of Maine cavalry assigned to the 1st District of Columbia Cavalry. The regimental chaplain, Samuel H. Merrill, wrote glowingly of the Henry's superiority:

After having witnessed the effectiveness of this weapon, one is not surprised at the remark, said to have been made by the guerilla chief Mosby, after an encounter with some of our men, that "he did not care for the common gun, or for Spencer's seven shooter, but as for these guns that they could wind up on Sunday, and shoot all the week, it was useless to fight against them."[47]

Even though the Army only ever ordered the Henry rifle in small numbers, word of the gun's potential spread. Oliver worked hard to secure testimonials from those who did use the weapon and like it. He was not above writing to the newspapers himself, under an assumed identity, to generate publicity for the Henry repeater. Versions of the following alarmist letter appeared in various newspapers between 1861 and 1863.

I would like to call the editor's and the reader's attention to the fact that, in the hands of the Rebel, the repeating rifle (sixteen shooters) as now made in New England, could cause terrific losses among gallant fighting men, causing this conflict to drag on eternally, and cause loss of spirit. Already we have discontent among the ranks, and if these terrible weapons fall into the wrong hands, the hurt will be too great to bear. Our boys, who are willing to sacrifice all, must be provided with the latest and most modern arms. Nothing else will satisfy the Union and all loyal citizens.

Signed
L.W.W.[48]

When not penning letters under a pseudonym, Oliver was promoting endorsements for his rifles. This testimonial in a Henry catalogue was from an abolitionist who lived below the Mason–Dixon line, and was suspected by his neighbors of being active in the underground railroad which freed slaves. One morning six of the abolitionist's irate neighbors showed up at breakfast and began shooting at him, one bullet breaking the tumbler in his wife's hand. As Edwin Pugsley writes:

He remonstrated with his callers, suggesting they not shoot him in the presence of his family as it would be a messy job [...] they all repaired to the yard behind the barn [...] On the way out there our hero reached inside the door of the corn crib, grabbed his loaded Henry and killed five of them, one right after the other [...] He wrote into the company and said he thought it was a very good gun.[49]

Very good gun as it was, Oliver feared the government bureaucracy was never going to deliver the timely bulk orders he was seeking for the Henry. So in 1862 he contracted the firm of John W. Brown of Columbus, Ohio to act as the New Haven Arms Company's general agent. The traveling salesman, a stalwart from the Volcanic era named W. C. Stanton, made good progress in Louisville, Kentucky – Kentucky being a key state during the Civil War because it wasn't firmly in the Union camp. Early sales of the Henry were also brisk in the border states of Illinois, Missouri, and Indiana. Oliver knew how successful his rival Samuel Colt had been with his publicity seeking methods, and presentation of revolvers to key officials, so he authorized his agents to do the same. The pro-Union editor of the *Louisville Journal*, George D. Prentice, received a gift of a Henry from Stanton and was so impressed that he wrote favorably about the rifle in his newspaper. This was free advertising, indeed. He even helpfully named the hotel where Stanton was staying, so prospective customers could find him over breakfast. Prentice lauded the Henry as "the simplest, surest and most effective weapon that we know of," which could be fired so rapidly that one man with a Henry was the equivalent of "fifteen armed with (an) ordinary gun."[50] Prentice himself became an agent for the rifle, and purchased 280 Henrys for $7,000.

Communication between John W. Brown's firm and New Haven show how important it was for Oliver, a staunch New Englander, to arm the Union side and not the rebellion – especially after the War Department issued a warning about Henrys ending up in Rebel hands. A few Henry rifles did make their way to the Rebel side, and after the War Department received complaints, Oliver had to make a public statement declaring that his New Haven Arms Company would sell "no guns and ammunition to the Southerners or Southern sympathizers."[51] Oliver's half-brother George, manager of the Baltimore agency of the New Haven Arms Company, was under strict instructions to be watchful and check on who was buying the guns. So, "We have promised to sell no goods to parties on the Mississippi, from Cairo down," Oliver wrote to John Brown, adding, "we hope to hear of an improvement in your sales; but presume trade rather follows with the advance of our armies; it will be most stirring near the scenes of active movements and hostilities." [52] When the advance of the Union side didn't seem to bring a rush of orders from Brown, the company secretary of the New Haven Arms Company wrote despairingly to him in late 1862:

> For several weeks past we have refrained from reading extracts from the Western papers, fearing that we might find an obituary notice of you among them. Our anxiety has become so great that one cannot longer endure the suspense; and accordingly we write to enquire if you are alive [...] If you still live, can you not tell us about the rifle business; and if there is no business, could you not give us some facts [...] opinions in relation to our rifle [...]?[53]

Brown was indeed alive amid a period of great drama in the mid-West, and selling rifles. Brown's advertising flier claimed the Henry was "The Most Effective Weapon In The World, Sixty Shots Per Minute [...] A resolute man, armed with one of these Rifles, particularly if on horseback, CANNOT BE CAPTURED." [54] There was good reason to buy a rifle in these turbulent times. The invasion of Kentucky by Confederate forces made it seem as though Louisville might be captured by the South or abandoned by Union troops. George Prentice, who was griefstricken because his beloved son had been killed while fighting on the Confederate side, feared that Louisville was indeed about to fall. Prentice sold his supply of Henry rifles below cost, to enable the people of Louisville to defend themselves. Unfortunately for the Union side, of which Prentice was a supporter, some of these rifles ended up with Confederate supporters, because of Kentucky's divided loyalties. For Oliver Winchester, the flooding of the market with cheap Henry rifles was a commercial disaster, which infuriated the other dealers he was trying to woo. A chastened Oliver wrote to an irate customer:

We regret the actions of Mr Prentice in selling the rifles (as he did under the influence of a panic when Louisville was threatened by the rebels) at less than cost. It was a matter beyond our control [...] We trust its effect will soon wear away.[55]

However, Oliver was to be rescued by George Prentice later in the year when he secured a valuable order from the Kentucky Cavalry.

Price cutting was not the only hurdle Oliver had to contend with – the early shipments of the Henry threw up innumerable obstacles. The new rifle did not always fire reliably, as there were problems with the cartridges. And the New Haven Arms Company was having difficulty in producing rifles rapidly enough. In May 1863 the New Haven Arms Company cartridge factory was accidentally blown up, when explosives stored at the plant were somehow ignited. This didn't help Oliver's problems with the cartridges, which were a further setback in his attempts to sell the Henry rifle to the US Army.

Despite these issues, there were glowing reports for the Henry from those fighting on the Union side who had managed to procure the weapon. Captain James Wilson of the 12th Kentucky Cavalry wrote in 1863:

When attacked by seven guerrillas I found it to be particularly useful, not only in regard to its fatal precision, but also in the number of shots held in reserve for immediate action in case of an overwhelming force [...] In my opinion, the Henry rifle is decidedly the best gun in the service of the United States.[56]

But the issuing of special arms for Union regiments was against official War Department policy. Assistant Secretary of War Peter Watson wrote a warning letter to Oliver in the summer of 1862:

companies arming themselves with Henry's repeating rifle, will (not) be allowed to retain them in the field [...] as great inconvenience has resulted from promises heretofore given in other cases to furnish companies of troops with special arms. If you choose to arm and equip a whole regiment at your own expense, or the regiment chooses to arm itself, it will be accepted with the condition that it shall be at liberty to use its own arms and equipments exclusively.[57]

The indefatigable Oliver glossed over such warnings and tried to persuade the Assistant Secretary of War that he had found armories which would enable him to increase production of the Henry – he offered to deliver 40,000 Henry carbines in eight months at $26 each, only to be rebuffed. Two years before the end of the Civil War, the new head of the Army Ordnance Department, Brigadier General George D. Ramsay, was not dead set against the repeating rifle per se, as his predecessor General Ripley had been. Unfortunately, Ramsay preferred the competition, writing:

> Repeating arms are the greatest favorite with the Army, and could they be supplied in quantities to meet all requisitions, I am sure that no other arm would be used. Colt's and Henry's rifles and the Spencer carbines are the only arms of this class in the service. Colt's is both expensive and a dangerous weapon to the user. Henry's is expensive and too delicate for service in its present form, while Spencer's is at the same time the cheapest, most durable, and most efficient of any of these arms.[58]

Just as President Lincoln had preferred the feel of the rival Spencer repeating rifle, so too did the Army's top brass. A total of 1,731 Henry rifles were supplied to the US government during the Civil War, at a cost of $69,953.26 – an average of a little less than $37 a rifle.[59] The government bought more Henry ammunition than the number of rifles warranted – 4,610,400 cartridges at a cost of $107,352.05. This discrepancy, observes Professor Williamson, is explained by the numbers of individual soldiers who purchased their own Henry rifles, which the government then supplied with ammunition.[60] Anecdotal evidence suggests that by the end of the Civil War, the Henry had come to rival the Spencer. Major D. S. Curtiss of the 1st Maine Cavalry wrote that his men had used both repeating rifles:

> I am fully satisfied that the Henry rifle is far superior in all respects, so that I would by no means use any other if it could possibly be

procured. [I] believe the government would realize a great saving of life, money and time in its warfare if all the men were armed with [the] Henry rifle.[61]

Oliver was not deterred by the obduracy of the Army bureaucracy, and used a network of dealers to sell the Henry direct to besieged Union soldiers desperate to keep the rebels at bay. War was an opportunity, and there were enough individual soldiers using the Henry and raving about its prowess for a rigorous word of mouth campaign. Stories about the "sixteen shooter" which could fire cartridges continuously spread far and wide, and towards the end of the war even more tales were in circulation. Oliver was his own enthusiastic press agent, writing to the Chaplain of the 12th Kentucky Cavalry to ask for a plug for the Henry rifle:

I have [...] heard that some very remarkable feats have been accomplished with them by the brave men of your Regiment in their use [...] An authentic narrative of such feats that could publish would be not only an act of justice to the men, but would also be very valuable to me as the best testimony to the power and efficiency of the weapon [...] May I ask the favor of you to make up a narrative of these stirring events.[62]

Lieutenant John Brown of the 23rd Illinois Volunteer Infantry bought his own Henry rifle, and was so pleased with its performance that he ordered thirty for his company. The success of these rifles in combat led the 23rd Illinois's Lieutenant Colonel to write to the New Haven Arms Company in February 1865 asking how much it would cost to arm the entire battalion with the Henry. The 10th West Virginia Mounted Infantry and the 64th and 66th Illinois (the Western Sharpshooters) privately purchased Henry rifles for their regiments. The 32nd Illinois, the 68th Ohio, and the 14th West Virginia Volunteers asked the government for Henrys but were rebuffed.

Soldiers who knew the Army would never buy them Henry rifles were actually prepared to use their hard-won pay to arm themselves, as previously mentioned. Take this testimonial from John H.

Ekstrand of the 51st Illinois Infantry, who reported that his regiment in besieged Chattanooga, Tennessee was using twelve Henry rifles and wanted more:

> In the 51st Illinois it is many that will buy them, and the brigade and division both requested me to write you for information and a price list [. . .] and how many we can get, or when. We now have four months pay due us, and the boys will have the money to send by express to you when we can know how many we can get [. . .] I would like to be able to get as many of Henry's rifles [. . .] so we could drive the Rebs from Chattanooga [. . .] and get something to eat.[63]

Desperate times led to desperate measures. Soldiers of the 7th Illinois Volunteer Infantry all bought Henrys at a cost of $41, or three months' pay. In October 1864, the regiment took part in the Battle of Allatoona Pass, in Georgia. The Federal troops, even though they were outnumbered three to two, defeated the Confederate forces in a battle for control of the Union's supply lines. About 5,500 soldiers were engaged in the firefight at a railroad depot and over 1,600 were killed or wounded,[64] making the casualty rate second only to Gettysburg – the Henry's superior firepower unquestionably helped the Union side.

The only regiment of the Army of the Potomac to be equipped with Henry rifles was Colonel Lafayette C. Baker's 1st Washington D.C. Cavalry. In May 1863 the regiment was part of General Kautz's cavalry division during a raid on Petersburg, Virginia. Rebel troops on their way to Petersburg were ambushed and overwhelmed by a hail of bullets from the Union side, something which amazed the Confederate side. One of the prisoners recalled in horror, "The Northerners must have had a whole army, from the way the bullets flew." [65]

The best praise of all came from a former prisoner of war, Major Joel Cloudsman of the 1st D.C. Cavalry, who wrote that while imprisoned he had often heard the enemy discuss the merits of the Henry. "They all fear it more than any arm in our service, and I have heard them say, "Give us anything but your damn Yankee rifle that can be loaded on Sunday and fired all week." [66] General Lee's men on the Southern side also paid grim tribute to the rifle which made their

Fig. 3 The 7th Illinois Volunteer Infantry with their Henry repeating rifles, *c.*1863.

lives so perilous. As one correspondent wrote, "We never did secure the Winchester (Henry) whose repeating qualities made the enemy's cavalry so formidable towards the end of the war."[67]

The "damn Yankee rifle" was also popular with civilians who armed themselves against the rebels – sales were strong in Kentucky, but also in the neighboring states of Ohio, Indiana, Illinois, and Missouri. Unfortunately, Oliver found "the border states give us more than we can do."[68]

He was referring to his difficulty in producing enough rifles to meet the demand, because the New Haven Arms Company simply didn't have the factory space required for a bigger operation. There was a physical limit imposed by the size of the plant, located at 9 Artizan Street in New Haven. When Colonel J. T. Wilder of the First Brigade Fifth Division, 14th Army Corps, in Murfreesboro, Tennessee, wrote to Oliver asking for a price on 900 rifles, it was impossible for the factory to produce this many. The Tennessee brigade ordered Spencer carbines instead.[69] Without major government contracts, Oliver Winchester was unwilling to take the risk of expanding the

company's facilities. His caution is a fascinating historical footnote –
for it was fixed price government contracts agreed upon during
World War I which were to spell the end of the Winchester Repeating
Arms Company. Not even massive US Army orders during World
War I could protect Winchester against the rising cost of material and
labor. But that was all to come – for now, Oliver's reluctance to
expand without guaranteed orders was understandable. The sales
agent John W. Brown suggested a move into larger premises; Oliver
replied, "We shall go into an Armory, as you have in your eye, but we
must creep a little longer. By and by we hope to walk and then we
shall soon be in a position to drive." [70]

There was to be no driving until after the Civil War was over. Swivels,
jigging machines, barrels of steel, shipments of cartridge blanks,
powder, priming mixtures – the correspondence between the New
Havens Arms Company and its suppliers shows how technical and
complicated increasing production was, as Oliver and his staff of about
65 relied upon so many outside suppliers, including some in far-flung
England. And the orders from civilians and a few regiments weren't
enough, as Oliver wrote, to justify getting "our machines made at big
prices and hire hands at extravagant prices." [71]

There were other hurdles too for Oliver as he managed the
company. Unlike the docile female employees of the ironing
department at the New Haven Shirt Factory, who would leave only
when marriage beckoned, here he was dealing with savvy gunsmiths
who knew their worth in a competitive market. As the weary Oliver
noted, "the immense increase in the costs (gunsmiths to whom we
used to pay $2 per day are now getting $4.50), has made it imperative
on us to sustain our prices firmly to save us from loss, if not ruin." [72]
Labor costs were rising during the Civil War, since so many men were
fighting that those left behind were a valuable commodity, and so too
were the prices of materials used to make the Henry rifle. Lead,
copper, and steel went up 50 percent during a short period, as
demand outstripped supply, causing Oliver great anxiety. He was
reluctant to increase the price of ammunition, "but with the state of
the market we have no choice, as we are not safe in guaranteeing the
price today to be the price tomorrow." [73] Even so, demand began to
outpace production, as Oliver wrote to one agent in 1863. "Our orders

are now largely in advance of our supply and if you are disappointed in the sale of the Rifles and wish to return any portion of them, we shall receive them with great pleasure."[74]

Another factor in the production difficulties may have been Oliver Winchester's vexed relationship with his master gunmaker and midwife of the eponymous Henry repeating rifle, Benjamin Tyler Henry. Henry had been hired in 1858 for $1,500 a year. In 1859 this was changed to a contract, under which Henry was to employ the workers and provide the supplies to manufacture 5,000 arms, at a fixed price to be paid by the New Haven Arms Company. This was the inside contract system at work, as Dean K. Boorman has painstakingly explained – a factory foreman would be responsible for production, including all the contracting, while the management provided materials and handled financing and sales.[75] During the five years of Henry's contract, he made about double the amount he would have done compared to his previous salary. But given that Henry's improvements had created the revolutionary repeating rifle, which was to bring tremendous riches to Oliver Winchester, it was hardly great recompense for his creativity. Henry retaliated with a go-slow on production. After all, what incentive did he have to do anything more than meet the 5,000 rifle quota in his contract.

Oliver tried to get round his grumpy production manager by personally leasing a factory in Bridgeport, Connecticut, and purchasing machinery for it so rifle production could be ramped up as soon as Henry's contract ended in 1864. Henry quit at this point, and new foremen were hired for the New Haven and Bridgeport factories – the total workforce was increased from 37 to 100, and one third were women who made the cartridges.[76] The bad blood between Henry and Winchester remained, and Henry later tried to mount a coup against his former boss.

As the Civil War ground on, Oliver displayed great attention to detail as he responded to criticisms about the performance of the Henry in the field. There were many complaints about the ammunition misfiring. One correspondent suggested this was due to overheating during the manufacturing of the rounds. Oliver experimented with how the melting of the tallow affected the gunpowder. He was able to zero in on the duff batch of ammunition, and discovered the culprit. "It is due [...] to the faithlessness of our man employed to put the cartridges together, as he must have put the grease in hot, instead of cold, to save time."[77] The precision with which Oliver had designed first church buttresses and then a comfortable shirt was now being brought to bear on the manufacture of ammunition. By 1863, a better, more powerful, and reliable cartridge had been created.

User feedback, as we would now term it, was all-important to Oliver. Amazon has nothing on Oliver, who was a one-man customer care center back in his day. He studied the correspondence from the rifle's fans and foes avidly. The firing pin in the Henry Rifle was prone to breaking, and the magazine would sometimes become dented. Oliver advised his pen pals not to pull the trigger without ammunition in the rifle's chamber, but warned those asking for telescopic sights that "in the present scarcity of hands, and the hurried demand for our rifle," such developments were out of reach for the New Haven Arms Company at that time. One interested customer wanted to know if the Henry could be equipped with a bayonet, which soldiers used for hand-to-hand combat. Oliver explained gently that the superior power of a repeating rifle eliminated the need for a bayonet. Customers who paid their bills on time received especially glowing letters from Oliver, earning the epithet "esteemed" for helping with the cash flow. Oliver was proud of his rifles, and assured those ordering that the improvements being made would "render the article perfect."[78]

Somewhat after the fact, once the war had ended, the Army finally held a major ordnance test in March 1866 to decide which breech-loading firearm system it should adopt. Only two magazine repeaters, those old rivals the Henry and the Spencer, were tested. The Henry suffered from various problems – burst cartridge casings, a burst cartridge in the magazine, and a locked breech pin which could only be moved by walloping it. Results of the rust test weren't good either. The final report found the Spencer to be "the best service gun of this kind yet offered."[79] Oliver was enraged, and published his own take on the report, including rude remarks about the Spencer. But he was to have the last laugh. The surplus of arms on the market at the end of the Civil War finished off Christopher Spencer's firm, as prices dropped. By 1868 Spencer had gone bust, and as we shall see, Oliver acquired its assets – buying out the competition was to become another of his hallmarks.

Arguing with Army bureaucracies was also an ingrained Oliver trait. Not content with taking on the US Army, Oliver locked horns with the British bean counters too. He submitted the Model 1868 Winchester rifle for a British Army trial, sending it carefully all the way across the Atlantic Ocean. The rifle performed well in the tests, other than when it was exposed to sand. But the committee in England rejected Oliver's great hope, ostensibly because of its complicated mechanism and its weight when loaded. Much like the US Army's Ripley, the British bureaucrats could not see any advantages to using a repeating rifle in general service. Oliver was livid, and once again penned an angry rebuttal of the findings of administrative army folk, this time writing to Edward Cardwell, the Secretary of State for War in England. Steam coming out of his ears, Oliver took aim at the cartridge adopted by the Brits – describing it as "a dose for an adult elephant." [80] Whether it was the US Ordnance Department or the British Army, guardians of military spending were reluctant to allow their troops to have repeating rifles, fearing they would drain their coffers by wasting rounds.

Government bureaucrats aside, the "damn Yankee rifle" which fired all week was about to come into its own. Despite the lack of lucrative military contracts, the New Haven Arms Company had sold more than 10,000 rifles between 1862 and 1865 and was on a less perilous financial footing. Teetering on the brink of bankruptcy in 1860, at the end of 1866 the company was worth $354,000, the rough equivalent of $5.3 million today. Oliver the perpetual salesman went out on the road in Europe, deciding that with the end of the Civil War, foreign markets must be found for his rifles. Otherwise, his factories would become idle and he would lose money, always anathema to Oliver. The novelty of the repeating rifle appealed to the French and the Swiss, and to the south the Chileans were interested. In late 1865 Oliver sailed to Paris to meet the middleman M. de Suzanne, and show off three revised designs of the Henry rifle. After testing the rifle, de Suzanne ordered 1,000 carbines – the majority were shipped

Fig. 4 Oliver Winchester, great-great-great grandfather of the author, 1864.

to Havana, Cuba. The plan was for the rifles to find their way from Cuba to Mexico, where they would be used by forces loyal to the French-backed Emperor Maximilian I, who was facing an uprising. The Winchester Repeating Arms Company sold weapons to both sides of that conflict, though not at precisely the same time.

As his company grew and its factories churned out more and more rifles, so Oliver became more prominent in New Haven. He was one of the founders of the Yale National Bank, served as a city councilman in 1863, and was a presidential elector in 1864, casting his vote for Lincoln. Friends and business partners referred to the once penniless farm boy as "Governor Winchester," after he served as lieutenant governor under Governor Joseph R. Hawley. The paternalistic and yet profit-obsessed Oliver took an interest in the welfare of his employees, and would help them with their personal matters if he could, though he always asked, "Will it interfere in any way with Company work?"[81] The most well-known image of Oliver was taken casually, after he had been sitting for an official photographic portrait in Frank Bowman's gallery on Chapel Street, New Haven. After the sitting was over, Oliver put on his hat and long military cloak, and Bowman snapped him just as he was, in a characteristic pose.[82] Oliver's eyes seem to be scanning the horizon in that photograph.

New frontiers for the company beckoned: as the West of America opened up, hunters and frontiersmen had their eyes on the rapid fire rifle which would provide personal protection and help penetrate new territory.

CHAPTER 2

The Spirit Gun

ONCE THE YOUNG Republic had ensured its own survival with the end of the Civil War, the nation resumed its attempt to conquer the West – with the help of Oliver Winchester and his weapons. The repeating rifle was much easier to fire on horseback, because you didn't need to stop and reload. This was an obvious selling point, to Oliver's mind, making the repeater well suited for life on the fast-moving frontier. "A weapon that promised life and dealt out death" – so goes the dramatic voiceover for the movie *Winchester '73*, a 1950 drama claiming "epic greatness" which glamorized the rifle of the Old West. James Stewart, Rock Hudson, and Tony Curtis star in this classic Western which features shoot-out after shoot-out – the trusty Winchester '73 rifle saves the day after gun runners and an Indian chief meet their grisly end. More than a few bar doors are kicked open, and stetsons are in virtually every frame. This is how Hollywood immortalized Oliver Winchester's repeating rifle – with its very own movie. Thanks to cinema, we can relive a romanticized version of the West through Clint Eastwood and John Wayne, square jawed and quick on the draw. The Winchester Repeating Arms Company was delighted to receive top billing in the conquest of the lands between the Atlantic and Pacific oceans. Though the rival gun manufacturer Colt had an equally valid claim to have made "The Gun that Won the West,"[1] Hollywood gave the cinematic honors to the folks in New Haven.

The myth of the West as America at its greatest – "no frontier uncrossable, no enemy untameable, no mountain too high or forest too dense for conquest"[2] – has been tempered by a more modern view that counts the sobering cost of murdered Native Americans, dead American soldiers and pioneers, and slaughtered buffalo. The philosophy of Manifest Destiny, which justified the subjugation of Native Americans in the name of inexorable progress, has grown ragged at the edges over the years. The settlement of the West can still be seen through the rosy lens of American Exceptionalism – yet from today's vantage point, it's difficult to defend the mass slaughter of Native Americans trying to defend the lands they had occupied for centuries. By 1893 the Sioux and the other tribes of the Great Plains between the Missouri River and the Rocky Mountains had lost their ancestral lands. The buffalo hunted by the Native Americans for centuries were hunted down and replaced by cattle herded by white ranchers. The Winchester rifle was prominent in this grisly rout, as the American frontier moved steadily westwards, making a mockery of the "permanent" Indian frontier which Native Americans had been promised in exchange for moving off their land. As we shall see, folklore has it that a Winchester heiress named Sarah was so haunted by the fate of the fallen Native Americans that she embarked upon a never-ending construction project to appease their spirits. Oliver Winchester, who doesn't appear to have lost a night's sleep over anything, let alone those killed by his guns, simply saw the shifting frontier as an opportunity to sell more rifles. The expansionist years saw Winchester move towards becoming a profitable company, after years of teetering on the edge of financial viability.

As the Civil War ended, settlers and cowboys were squaring off once again against the Native Americans. The Indian wars were underway. Red Cloud, warrior and statesman of the Lakota, said of the white men: "They made us many promises, more than I can remember, but they never kept but one; they promised to take our land, and they took it." [3] The relative peace in which the early settlers and the Native Americans lived had not lasted long. Once more colonists arrived, they wanted to expand into the lands of those who had been there for hundreds of years before them. By 1829, when Andrew Jackson, or Sharp Knife as the Indians called him, was president, thousands of Cherokees, Chickasaws, and Seminoles had perished in this land grab.

Sharp Knife recommended to Congress that the Indians be moved westward beyond the Mississippi – this was to be the permanent Indian frontier, and no white people would be allowed to settle there. War with Mexico led to further incursions and the highfalutin concept of Manifest Destiny soon meant that virtually any breach of the Indian frontier could be justified. This was the idea that the Europeans and their descendants were dominant, and therefore ordained by destiny to rule all of America and make decisions on behalf of Native Americans – which included taking their forests and mountains, buffalo, antelope, and peach trees. With the end of the Civil War, the US government was determined to secure the safety of the westward trade routes, and the railways which were soon to follow. As hostilities between the Union and Confederate sides ended, thousands of Northern veterans were retained for postwar service. Many were ordered West, joining the hundreds of soldiers already on the Plains battling Native Americans. Adventurers joined the migration, following Horace Greely's dictum of 1855: "If you have no family or friends to aid you, and no prospect opened to you there, turn your face to the great West, and there build up a home and Fortune." [4]

With the settlers' territorial expansion, backed up by the US Army, came the need for guns to secure the new lands. Enter the Winchester. For the Native Americans, guns were new and threatening, as Manuelito, Chief of the Navahos, recounted:[5] "When our fathers lived they heard that the Americans were coming across the great river westward [...] we heard of guns and powder and lead – first flintlocks, then percussion caps, and now repeating rifles." Even before the Winchester repeating rifle became the settlers' trusty weapon, its forerunner the Henry made a few telling cameo appearances out West. Late in 1865, Native Americans in the Rocky Mountains experienced the deadly force of the Henry rifle, which rendered a previously fairish fight unequal.

Two former Union soldiers who had kept their Henrys after demobilization began mining borax in the heart of the Blackfoot Indian country of Montana. Some 40 Blackfoot warriors approached the miners' camp, only to be fired at continuously by the ex-soldiers with their Henry rifles. One of the participants told his story to Paul B. Jenkins many years later:

Fig. 5 Mary Fields and her Winchester rifle, *c*.1895. Mary was the first African American woman employed by the United States Postal Service as a mail carrier – she was nicknamed "stagecoach."

> Shot after shot kept pouring from the guns [...] and to the indescribable horror of the warriors who considered themselves already victorious, man after man of their number fell shrieking or silent in the prairie grass as the deadly and unheard-of continuous firing blazed steadily at them.[6]

Such was the full horror – and effectiveness – of the repeating rifle. For good measure:

> they riddled every corpse with innumerable bullets and dragged the whole number to a heap at a distance beyond rifle range of their fort, that the survivors might return and contemplate the fatal results of their terrible encounter with weapons that obviously never need to be reloaded at all.

Only a few of the Native Americans were unhurt, and one of the survivors recalled with shock and amazement the "spirit gun" which kept on firing.[7]

The second legendary tale of the Henry rifle involves that classic Western plot-line, a brush between the law and stagecoach robbers. A stagecoach carrying wads of cash was held up by armed bandits near Nevada City one fine May day in 1866. The dogged former town marshal, one Steve Venard, took his Henry rifle and pursued the robbers into a steep and treacherous canyon, where his trusty Henry did not disappoint. Neill C. Wilson sets the scene, as the rest of the posse in hot pursuit of the robbers come upon Venard,

> sitting on the buckskin bag, communing with his plain, well oiled rifle. The odds had been three to one [...] yet here they were. Three dead men, two of them still clutching cocked revolvers, and one live deputy. But – four expended bullets. The Henry must be getting old. Steve Venard was regretful.[8]

Such was the casual, rugged, romanticized image cultivated by the sharpshooters of the West. But before Oliver's Winchester new rifle could supersede his Henry and become the pin-up of the West, there were a few local difficulties to overcome. The inventor of the eponymous Henry rifle, Benjamin Tyler Henry, had not forgiven Oliver for the poor pay he received while his boss was becoming quite the Connecticut grandee. When Oliver went to Europe in the spring of 1865, in search of new markets for his guns, Henry plotted his revenge. As Oliver enjoyed the scenery of Switzerland, looking forward to a pleasant tour of European spas and reflecting upon a successful business meeting with the French government, he received an extremely unwelcome dispatch. Over breakfast in Zurich, Oliver read that the secretary of the New Haven Arms Company, Charles W. Nott, in collaboration with the resentful Henry, had petitioned the Connecticut State legislature to change the name of the New Haven Arms Company to the Henry Repeating Rifle Company. Cleverly, the men had used a power of attorney signed by Oliver before his departure for Europe.[9]

The livid Oliver cabled his London bankers to call in all the mortgages and liens he and his son Wirt held against the New Haven Arms Company. This made bankruptcy of the new company Henry and Nott hoped to create a very real threat. Oliver abandoned his croissant and coffee in continental Europe, jumped aboard the first ocean liner back to the United States, and on July 1, 1865 he signed the articles of association that were to establish the Winchester Arms Company in Bridgeport, Connecticut. To ward off lawsuits from the disgruntled Benjamin Tyler Henry, the goal of the new company was to develop a new, improved version of the Henry rifle. The New Haven Arms Company limped on, but Henry filed against the venture, alleging that his 1859 contract had not been honored and that he was owed extra money for his 1860 invention.[10] Realizing that the old company would lose vast amounts of cash if Henry's lawsuit was successful, Oliver Winchester and his partner from shirtmaking days John Davies mounted a takeover bid, which the stockholders voted to accept. On July 7, 1866 the New Haven Arms Company's payroll book was formally closed – and on December 30, 1866, the first step towards the formal organization of the Winchester Repeating Arms Company was taken when the books were opened for subscription to the stock.[11] Oliver's eponymous company was the new game in town, and there was no doubt as to who was headlining the new venture. Operations moved from New Haven to larger premises in Bridgeport, Connecticut, under pressure from some of the new stockholders. It was 1871 before Winchester returned to New Haven. Notwithstanding the change of location, Oliver had shown his mettle under pressure and had deftly outmaneuvered his opponents.

After several experimental guns which attempted to remedy the flaws in the Henry, with a great flourish Winchester announced a new rifle – the Model 1866, the first gun issued under the name of the Winchester Repeating Arms Company. This model was to sell well abroad, thanks to Oliver's efforts. A third or more of Winchester's business between 1866 and 1873 came from domestic sales, driven by events on the Western frontier. The Model 1866 had a yellowish tint to its red brass, earning it the nickname "Yellow Boy." Unlike the capricious Henry, the Model 1866 was indeed a model of reliability. When compared to the original American long rifles, the power, range, and repeating action of the Model 1866 made it ideal for hunting buffalo, elk, bighorn sheep, bears, and mountain lions. Whatever the enemy, human or animal, the rifle was equal to the task.

The first domestic sales of the new gun were for two carbines sent to H. G. Litchfield of Omaha, Nebraska. Litchfield was an Army major and an official in the Department of the Platte, the military administrative district which spanned Iowa to Idaho and ensured that settlers could move safely westwards to Oregon. Later, the Department of the Platte included the construction route of the Union Pacific railroad. Major Litchfield was thrilled with his new rifles, writing to Oliver to express his delight:

> The new Winchesters were received yesterday, and upon inspection have proven to be the finest arms I have ever handled. For great strength and light weight they have no equal and upon taking the guns out to be tested, we found that for rapidity of fire and deadly accuracy they are nothing short of amazing. Believe me, this gun will make the land safe for the frontiersman and will have a great effect in settling the land.[12]

This was, as the Winchester historian George Madis noted, "a prophetic letter from the first frontier user of the Winchester."[13] It was Winchester's next rifle, Model 1873, that earned both celluloid fame and the nickname "The Gun That Won the West." This model used a .44–40 cartridge, the same ammunition as the Colt Frontier revolver; thus the settlers could carry both rifle and revolver while on horseback and reload either weapon without changing cartridge. The Model '73 was:

> the rifle that put the name of Winchester on the map of the West, trotting along with the equally formidable Colt gun at the belt of the frontiersman. It killed more game and more Indians, and more United States soldiers when the Indians awoke to its virtues, than any other type rifle.[14]

Little is known about Nelson King, the man who so successfully modified the Henry and created the Winchester legend. King started working for Oliver Winchester in 1864 and left to become super-intendent of the Sharps Rifle Company in 1875.[15] While we have only the barest outline of King's life, we do know that his ingenuity was most productive. He introduced a fifth modification of the Henry rifle, followed by the Model 1866, altering the construction of the cartridge carrier so a cartridge could pass into the magazine more efficiently when the action was closed. King reduced the number of movements necessary for loading, and used a loading aperture which protected the magazine from unwanted foreign matter.[16] The company's board of directors certainly appreciated King's efforts, voting him a bonus of $5,000, and awarding him the second highest salary in the company after Oliver.

The Model 1866 and Model 1873 were to propel Oliver into the plutocratic class – and in keeping with his prosperity, in 1867 he built himself and his wife Jane a splendid white stone mansion on Prospect Street in New Haven. The Winchesters' imposing home was chock full of cupolas, balconies, and Italianate chimneys, with vast gardens full of generous greenhouses. The house of eclectic styles had fine horizon views which swept all the way from Connecticut's Mount Carmel to the sun sparkling off the waters of Long Island Sound. In old photographs of the mansion, you can make out smartly dressed folk playing croquet on the lawn, enjoying a pleasing afternoon of leisure. Oliver wanted gardens with "taste and artistry,"[17] and engaged the celebrated Scottish landscape designer William Saunders to create his elegant fantasy. Saunders landscaped not only Oliver's rolling acres but also the National Cemetery at Gettysburg and Lincoln's Tomb and Monument in Springfield, Illinois.

Jane must have enjoyed her luxurious surroundings and social standing. Her gracious home bore no relation to the childhood poverty she had known as a widow's daughter in Maine, and was a contrast to the early days of her marriage, when the young couple had eked out a living in the haberdashery trade in Baltimore during the depression years. Now, Jane had numerous staff to attend to her every need. Stern looking, and modestly dressed despite her riches,

Fig. 6 Oliver Winchester's Prospect Street home, *c.*1880.

Jane experienced great sadness amid all the financial blessings of later life. Three of her four children predeceased her – baby Oliver, William Wirt, and Ann – and so did two of her grandchildren, infant William Dye and Sarah Winchester's baby daughter Annie. Jane's oldest daughter Ann died at the age of 29 in 1864, of puerperal fever, a complication from childbirth. Ann's son William died when he was only three weeks old, and his gravestone records that his death came 21 days after that of his mother. Ann's marriage to Charles Dye did produce one surviving child, Oliver, named for his grandfather. Unfortunately, Oliver Dye was to become an embarrassment to his grandmother, a playboy who spent his inherited millions all too freely. Jane, who had known so much personal loss, weighed down by grieving for lost children and grandchildren, became concerned by the plight of New Haven's poor. She took an interest in how they might receive medical care.

Jane and Oliver's dominant Winchester residence, a statement of success if ever there was one, sat atop the hill above the Winchester Repeating Arms Company factory. It was as far removed as one could imagine from Oliver's beginnings in the drab and draughty

Massachusetts farmhouse. Oliver used the notable New Haven architect Henry Austin, who designed a sprawling mansion in what was then the wildly popular French Second Empire style. The local newspaper devoted an entire column to what was described as "one of the finest French villas that has been built in this country." The handsome carriage porch was praised as "elaborately carved and fluted [...] will be one of the features of the building." Oliver's front door was made of black walnut and the entry hall tiles were black and white, a theme echoed in the principal hallway, which was finished "with black walnut and white oak wainscotting , of beautiful design." The parlor was finished with stunning white gloss moldings, while the library overflowed with bookcases "richly ornamented with carved cornices and brackets," finished in yet more black walnut, a mighty expensive wood in those times just as it is today. The dining room was the crowning glory of Oliver and Jane's expansive home – it received the full *Architectural Digest* treatment in the *Norwich Aurora* newspaper, since it was finished "in solid white oak, in the Elizabethan style of architecture [...] The work is beautiful and will attract much attention. The mantels, mirror-frames and side-board, are all made of solid white oak." This was the most enormous and luxurious home New Haven had ever seen:

> all furnished with every convenience desirable. The upper floor is reached by a fine oaken stair case, with black walnut hand-rail, and carved marble post [...] The view from the tower is magnificent, and must be seen to be appreciated [...] It is one of the best residences in the State, and is well worthy of a visit when the grounds are thrown open to the public.[18]

The house was later demolished, and the Yale Divinity School now stands on the site.

Oliver's original shirtmaking partner and pal John Davies also used the architect Henry Austin to design a near identical home right next door on Prospect Street. Yale University tried to demolish this mansion many years later, only to back down when faced with an outcry from students and preservationists. Looking at the former Davies home today, one can imagine it twinned with Oliver's equally grand mansion, both ostentatious symbols of their owners' wealth and status. Here the two former shirt manufacturers must have toasted their timely investment in guns. The Winchester factory would have been clearly visible from the front lawns of the Prospect Street mansions up to Highland Park. As the grimy munitions workers made their exit at the day's end, in the clean air up above, the Winchester ladies enjoyed cucumber sandwiches on the croquet lawn. Oliver's surviving children William Wirt and Jennie were coming of age in luxurious surroundings, utterly divorced from their father's hardscrabble upbringing. How Oliver must have reveled in the contrast, while keeping a weather eye on his factory below. His personal income in 1865 was recorded as $33,649,[19] a fortune by the standards of the day. Only "ninety seven persons" in New Haven paid taxes on incomes above $5,000 that year. Meanwhile, down in the Winchester factory, the workers wore brass tags because of the "garnishee laws" of the time. So many of the employees were in debt, and had money deducted from their wages to pay off what they owed, that the brass tag was used by New Haven's deputy sheriff to identify a man before serving him a writ for unpaid debts.

Although the profitability of the Winchester Repeating Arms Company had improved since the early days when it would flirt with bankruptcy on a regular basis, only to be bailed out by Oliver, the company was far from being on a firm financial footing. Enter one larger than life character, Thomas Emmett Addis, who was to prove an intrepid foreign salesman for Winchester's guns. He was a mysterious figure thought to have changed his name from O'Connor,[20] thanks to a troubled background and perhaps also to avoid the anti-Irish sentiment prevalent in America at that time. He ran away from home before he was 13, and harbored an intense bitterness towards the Roman Catholic Church, never mentioning his home or his parents. Oliver Winchester, though, took a liking to Addis after he left the rival gunmaker of Remington, in upstate New York. Oliver once said that "if he had ten men like Addis, success would be assured and Winchester would quickly be the most important arm in the world."[21]

Addis worked his way up from being a workman in Winchester's primer department to become the chief foreign sales representative, "with unlimited territory and unlimited authority to conduct any of the company's business necessary to make sales."[22] He was remembered by fellow Winchester employees as a man "of striking character [...] who although naturally impetuous, endeavored to keep this quality in restraint." In 1866 Addis, who sported an impressive handle-bar mustache, took some 1,000 guns and 500,000 rounds of ammunition to Brownsville, Texas. His notion was to try to sell this hardware to the warring parties across the border in Mexico – where the French were trying to establish a client state and install their own emperor, while the Mexicans strongly resisted this plan. An adventure ensued – as his colleagues recorded, "Mr Addis was a very peculiar man and his experiences were just as peculiar as he himself."[23]

Addis, idiosyncratic and far-sighted as he was, saw opportunity in the chaos and upheaval engulfing Mexico. The French leader Napoleon, whose armies had overthrown the Mexican Republic, had installed Ferdinand Maximilian, Archduke of Austria, as Emperor of Mexico, despite protests from the Americans. What's more, Winchester had previously provided rifles to the forces of the Emperor, via the French government, which had ordered the arms to protect its protégé. With the end of the Civil War, it became clear that the US government was going to put more pressure on the French and Benito Juarez, leader of the opposition to Maximilian, grew in strength as the unrest spread. Juarez, hearing of a wonderful new repeating rifle made by Winchester in America, rapidly placed orders for the guns and ammunition which he hoped would help topple the Emperor.

The intrepid Tom Addis went to Brownsville, Texas and, after waiting there for a month, received word from Juarez's camp that if he would bring the guns to Monterey in Mexico he would be paid for them. Ignoring Oliver Winchester's strict instructions about not going into Mexico under any circumstances, and after taking advice from an ex-Confederate officer whom he had doubtless met in a bar in Brownsville, Addis took the guns and ammunition across the Rio Grande river to Matamoras. One account says Mr Addis's treasure trove was seized by the government temporarily in power. Another version is more heroic. Taking good care to protect himself from the bandits on the highway, Addis took out six carbines and what he deemed to be a sufficient amount of ammunition from the cases. The rest of the guns and ammo he piled up in ox carts and traveled the 240 miles with his six carbines close at hand. Upon arriving unharmed in Monterey, Addis hired the empty storefront next to his hotel, and proceeded to put all his goods in there. He nailed small US flags on the doors and windows and on each case, announcing that the guns and ammunition were under the protection of the US flag and he would shoot anyone who attempted to remove or injure them.[24] Whatever really happened, "For some months Mr Addis had thrilling experiences in Mexico," record the company's historians. "It evidently was necessary for him to travel considerably, as we have his expense accounts covering two trips from Brownsville to Saltillo, Monterey and San Catalina." When agents for Juarez in Monterey started to haggle over the prices, Addis threatened to sell the rifles to the forces of Emperor Maximilian – a threat which worked – and the Mexicans came up with payment of $27,000 (out of the $57,000 owed) in silver dollars.

Meanwhile Oliver was fretting in New Haven, thinking Addis was still in Brownsville – for no sooner had Addis left New England than Oliver ran into Eli Whitney, a rival gunmaker, who laughed at Oliver's gullibility in sending the secretive Addis on such a mission. Whitney predicted that Oliver would never see the guns, ammunition, or money again.[25] As Oliver waited anxiously, Addis was in trouble – stuck in the middle of bandit-infested country, rather than in Texas as he'd promised Oliver, with boxes full of silver dollars. The Mexicans agreed to provide him with an escort back to the border. What happened next has become the stuff of disputed legend, with several stories about Addis's journey from Mexico back to Texas, or variously New Orleans. He's said to have driven his horses furiously day and night, silver dollars on the back seat of his coach, keeping himself awake by running his spurs up and down his shins, tearing his legs. One version has Addis's Army guards revolting and trying to steal the bags full of money, only to find Addis had filled the sacks full of nails. Another tale has Addis ditching all but one of his guards, and since he didn't trust his remaining driver, sitting behind him with a rifle, stabbing a diamond stick pin into his thigh periodically to keep himself from dozing off during the three-day ride to the US border with Mexico. Close to the border, Addis jumped off with his coin boxes, and told his driver to retreat down the road under the penalty of being shot if he even looked back.[26] Disguised as a farmer driving a farmer's cart, Addis reached the US line and eventually arrived in New Orleans with the silver dollars safely about his person. There, he changed his valuable load for US currency and wired Winchester with news of his whereabouts. Addis said his clothes were so clotted with blood from the wounds he'd inflicted on himself with the diamond stick pin that he had to cut them off.

Whatever the truth of the journey, Addis made it home to New Haven by May 28, 1867, and back to a relieved Oliver who gladly took possession of the $27,000. It was a lifeline for Winchester at the time. As a restrained company historian put it judiciously, "money was not as free at that time as might have been desired." [27] Addis claimed to have been made a colonel while in Mexico, presumably for his services to the forces opposed to Maximilian. With his cane, dark clothes, and high-crowned derby hat, a figure both impressive and eccentric, Addis was established as a salesman extraordinaire. He sold rifles throughout South America and Europe on Winchester's behalf for 35 years. He told a colleague Arthur Earle of his contentment with his lot:

> My life, since I came to Winchester, has been just what I wanted, and I have travelled to my heart's content, happy to be a citizen of this great country and to see the world. With Winchesters we have helped greatly to improve, settle and civilize the world. I am proud and will die happy to have had a part in this great change.[28]

His tombstone in New Haven's Evergreen cemetery was inscribed, "In Memory of Thomas Emmett Addis, Traveler." [29]

Thanks in no small part to the efforts of Thomas Addis, 1866 was a respectable year for the Winchester Repeating Arms Company, even though the Civil War had ended. Oliver recorded that total sales equaled $192, 411.12.[30] The company had moved from New Haven to Bridgeport, at the urging of Nathaniel Wheeler and James Wilson, directors of the company and owners of the eponymous sewing machines which had transformed Oliver's fortunes in his shirt manufacturing days. Winchester rented space from the Wheeler and Wilson sewing machine plant for $316 a month, including power.[31] A fire in the storehouse at Bridgeport destroyed the company's entire stock of cartridges, and so terrified were the firemen by the exploding cartridges that they fled, leaving the Winchester workmen to hose down the blaze.

The Winchester brand had been helped by a competition to select a new military rifle that was held by the Swiss government in 1865 and 1866. Reports of the exacting trials were published by newspapers around the world, which gave Oliver's rifles even greater exposure. The accuracy of the guns under rapid-fire conditions surpassed their rivals – the likes of Howard, Martini-Peabody, Remington, Spencer, and Chassepot. In 1866, Oliver made a trip to Europe just so he could enter a Henry rifle in a Swiss trial. The gun came first in the competition, and a commission recommended that it be officially adopted, but the Swiss decided not to buy the weapon in large quantities.[32] The Swiss government did order 200 rifles from Winchester, the Swiss Model 1866 Sharpshooters Rifle, to be made jointly in the United States and Switzerland.[33] Winchester's main contribution was providing the Swiss government with rifle-making machinery, which was shipped across the Atlantic.

Oliver's dominance of the repeating rifle world was aided by the spectacular collapse of the competition. As we have seen, in the Civil War the Spencer rifle had outsold Winchester's Henry – a source of immense irritation to Oliver. Once the war was over, the glut of Spencers on the market meant there was little demand for new rifles – and in 1868 the Spencer Repeating Rifle Company was wound up, owing money all round. Oliver the predator swooped in and bought what was left of Spencer's assets – the machinery, the rifles, and the all-important patents. The rest of the firm's machinery he purchased at auction for a bargain basement price. In hard-headed business terms, buying the company itself didn't seem to make sense based on Spencer's liabilities, and Winchester passed on the opportunity. The Fogarty Repeating Rifle Company of Boston bought the Spencer concern, and less than nine months later the consolidated corporation of Fogarty and Spencer, the American Repeater Rifle Company, went bankrupt. Oliver pounced once again, and licked clean the carcass of his competitors, buying the combined assets of the Fogarty–Spencer firms – including all machinery, completed arms, works in progress, and patents – for $200,000. Oliver flogged the machinery alone at auction in Boston a month later for $138,000.[34] In what must have been a pleasant surprise, Oliver learned that rifles and carbines owned by the American Repeater Rifle Company were being stored in a warehouse in England. Oliver promptly set sail, claimed the merchandise, and sold the lot for yet another tidy profit.

The single-minded Oliver was focused laser-like on increasing Winchester's market share, and could be unapologetically ruthless in pursuit of this goal, especially if it meant eliminating the competition. In 1865, when an India rubber magnate, Isaac Hartshorn, was filing a patent suit against a manufacturer of the Spencer, the Burnside Rifle Company, Oliver secretly purchased Hartshorn's patent. "With pure Machiavellian foresight, Winchester knew that if the matter was decided in Hartshorn's favor, Winchester could then, by proxy, dictate the terms of the settlement."[35] Hartshorn's patent was declared to be valid, and Winchester demanded that Burnside pay the damages in machinery – which forced the company out of business. By keeping his enemies closer than they knew, Oliver had triumphed. Through similarly shrewd deals, the onward march of Winchester continued. Between 1869 and 1899, Winchester's share of the total US firearms and ammunition industry rose from 8 percent to 29 percent.[36] Some 25 New England firms manufacturing firearms disappeared between 1865 and 1870,[37] as the market for guns contracted in the aftermath of the Civil War – but not Winchester. In 1869, the sales of Winchester rifles amounted to $329,511.50. It was time for an expanded gun shop – and a return to Oliver's roots.

The Winchester management decided to move production of the guns out of Bridgeport, Connecticut and back to New Haven, home of the original Volcanic concern. This was much to the disgust of the sewing machine magnates James Wilson and Nathaniel Wheeler. They disposed of their stock and resigned from Winchester's board of directors in protest, wanting to keep manufacturing in Bridgeport where they owned the premises and lucratively leased them back to Winchester. Ignoring their protests, in August 1870 plans were made for a new and bigger factory, made of stone and brick and timber from

Maine, with boilers and steam engines from the Pacific Iron Works in Bridgeport. Oliver himself owned the land upon which the new facility was to be built, and sold it to the company.

Oliver's sleek and efficient business practices were all about maximizing the profit to be made from the chaos and lawlessness which reigned out West. On the frontier, Civil War veterans clashed with Native Americans trying to protect their ancestral lands from invasion and prevent their means of making a living, the buffalo, from being eliminated. The Winchester rifle was key to the settlers' realization of their ambitions. For the settlers, the buffalo represented hard cash – their hides could be sold for $100 each. The animals were yet another raw material in the industrial revolution – leather from the buffalo was used to make belts for commercial sewing machines, of the type Oliver Winchester and his ilk used in shirtmaking factories. The Native Americans had little protection from this onslaught – while the frontiersmen had their repeating arms and a network of forts, manned by 20,000 US Army troops.[38] The soldiers were armed with weapons left over from the Civil War, such as the Spencer carbine. Under government regulations, white traders were supposed to sell nothing but obsolete muzzleloaders to Native Americans – although some Winchesters did change hands. Both Henrys and the Model 1866 have been found with patterns of brass tacks on their stocks, a sign of Native American ownership. One of the first Native Americans who owned a Winchester '66 was High Backed Wolf, a Cheyenne warrior who was killed on July 25, 1865 at the Platte Bridge on the Oregon Trail, in what is now Wyoming.[39]

As well as pioneers and Native Americans, there was the cowboy market, not to mention the California gold rush crowd and the crews building the railroad – all potential enthusiasts for the Winchester repeating rifle. The post-Civil War period saw the start of the great cattle drives from Texas to Kansas, and then further west. Every 2,000 to 3,000 cattle required up to 20 cowboys to manage them on the range. Just how many cowboys could afford Winchesters for hunting game and self-defense is a moot point – a Winchester rifle cost about $40 a month, whereas cowboys earned only about $30 a month.[40] Then there were the outlaws and the sharpshooters who loved their Winchesters. Jesse James, who had ridden with a notorious

Fig. 7 Geronimo, Native American leader, to the far right of the photograph, carrying his Winchester rifle, 1885. By C. S. Fly.

Confederate guerilla group during the Civil War, took to raiding trains and banks with the aid of his Model 1866 Winchester carbine. In total, Winchester sold 100,000 of the Model 1866. Native Americans embraced the spirit gun which had been used against them with such brutality, and they too were captured on celluloid with their trophy rifle. Geronimo, a famed Apache warrior and chief, poses proudly with fellow fighters, one of whom is carrying a Winchester. William Henry Jackson's portraits of Native Americans show them brandishing what they called "heap-firing" guns or "many shots."[41]

In an odd and ultimately unrepresentative twist of fate, it was Native Americans who gained the greatest advantage from the Winchester's firepower in that most famous and bloody of the Indian Wars – Custer's Last Stand. The Battle of Little Bighorn began on June 25, 1876, near a riverside Indian settlement in eastern Montana. At the start of the battle, General George Armstrong Custer, or Long Hair as the Native Americans called him, had command of over 200 mounted troops and scouts of the US Army Seventh Cavalry, armed mostly with Springfield carbines. Remember, the US Army never did like repeating rifles, seeing them as a good way to waste money on ammunition. Less than an hour after the fighting began, Custer and his men were dead, at the hands of Lakota, Cheyenne, Sioux, and Arapaho warriors armed with many Winchesters. It was a scene of carnage, horrific to behold. Major Reno, one of the survivors, said the scene of Custer's battlefield was "beyond description [...] It filled us with horror and anguish." [42] Another soldier recalled that "there the bodies lay, mostly naked, and scattered over a field maybe half a mile square. We went among them to see how many we could recognize." [43] Reno described how "many had their flesh cut in strips the entire length of their bodies, and there were others whose limbs were closely perforated with bullets, showing that the torture had been inflicted while the wretched victims were still alive."

Custer had apparently hoped to take the Native Americans' women and children hostage, thus forcing them to surrender and sue for peace. Instead, Custer and his troops were outnumbered and outgunned. Sitting Bull, Crazy Horse, and other famous warriors had hidden hundreds of their fighters in the ravines, who descended from the hills on both sides as Custer and his men marched below. Kill Eagle, a Blackfoot Sioux chief, described the Native Americans moving towards Custer's men "like a hurricane [...] like bees swarming out of a hive." [44] Many soldiers revised their low opinions of Native American marksmanship that day, as Charles Windolph's account demonstrates:

> It was plumb light now, and the Indian sharpshooters on the knob of the hill south of us and perhaps a thousand yards away were taking potshots at us. Jones said something about taking his overcoat off, and he started to roll on his side so that he could get his arms and shoulders out without exposing himself to fire. Suddenly I heard him cry out. He had been shot straight through the heart. [45]

Native Americans stripped the corpses of Custer's dead troops of their repeating rifles, adding to their already considerable repeating force. At the bitter end, the soldiers dismounted as the Native Americans surrounded them: "the Sioux shot straight and the soldiers fell dead [...] when we came to the hill there were no soldiers living and Long Hair (Custer) lay dead among the rest," recalled Pte-San-Waste-Win, one of the victorious Native Americans. [46]

Jacob Adams found General Custer, "stripped with the exception of his sox. He had a gunshot wound in his head and another in his side, and in his left thigh there was a gash about eleven inches long that exposed the bone." [47]

One historian of the grisly battle estimates that 25 percent of the Native American warriors were armed with repeating Henrys or Winchester 1866 or 1873 models. The Native Americans had obtained these guns through trade, raids, and battlefield pickups. [48] According to Red Horse, towards the end of Custer's Last Stand "these soldiers became foolish, many throwing away their guns and raising their hands, saying 'Sioux, pity us, take us prisoners.' The Sioux did not take a single soldier prisoner but killed all of them." [49] Naturally, the Sioux were careful to collect as many of the discarded rifles as they could, knowing their deadly value.

For those who might interpret Custer's Last Stand as a clear victory for the Winchester repeating rifle over the Army's Springfield, historians urge caution. General Custer and his doomed men were greatly outnumbered – estimates of Native Americans taking part in the battle range from 2,000 to 3,000, against Custer's 200-odd men. As the high priest of Winchester history Harold F. Williamson puts it, "accepting this estimate, the number of Indians armed with Winchesters would have numbered between 500 and 900 against some 220 soldiers, not to mention the number of Indians armed with other weapons. For this reason the Battle of Little Bighorn was not a definitive test of relative combat effectiveness of the firearms used."[50] Such judgments haven't stopped the speculation over how Custer and his men would have fared had they too been armed with Winchesters. "It seems that the rifle's rapid firing capability of 15 shots in the magazine plus one shot in the chamber without reloading would have made up for the ten to one advantage in numbers held by the Sioux," [51] wrote another distinguished Winchester historian, Dean K. Boorman.

One fact stands out from the Battle of Little Bighorn – it was the biggest victory ever achieved by Native Americans over the US Army, in what was otherwise a war in which the odds were stacked against America's original occupants. The Indian Wars finally ended at Wounded Knee, South Dakota in 1890, where troops of the very same

Seventh Cavalry massacred 150 or more Native American men, women, and children. Many more crawled away to die afterwards. "We tried to run," one Native American named Louise Weasel Bear said, "but they shot us like we were a buffalo. I know there are some good white people, but the soldiers must be mean to shoot children and women." [52] A bloody chapter in American history closed at Wounded Knee – and in the same year the Census Bureau announced the end of the frontier, meaning there were no longer huge acres of land unbroken by settlement. The promise of new land and an unexplored, endless wilderness came abruptly to an end. The pledge to create a permanent Indian frontier had proved to be utterly worthless.

Quite what Oliver Winchester back in New Haven made of his rifle being used to massacre the US Army at Little Bighorn, history does not record. Doubtless he would have fumed and railed against the pig-headed US Army bureaucracy and its inexplicable reluctance to order his rifles. The Civil War had convinced Oliver that his repeating rifle was vastly superior to the single shot. Once the Henry's faults had been remedied with the Model 1866, the indefatigable Oliver was promoting his products vigorously once again. The massacre of Custer's troops in Montana did increase pressure on the Army to find a new gun, and in 1872 the government held trials for a repeating rifle. The Winchester company made a new rifle specially for the competition. But after being subjected to a blast of fine sand-dust, the gun was deemed inoperable. Only in 1892 did the Army give up the Springfield rifle for the Krag bolt action. The Army did buy 10,000 lever action Model 1895 Winchester muskets for use in the Spanish American War of 1898, but unfortunately they arrived too late. [53]

Winchester's gross sales for 1877 were $2,802,564.16 and their net profit for the year was $668,381.35. [54] Between 1867 and 1880 US companies sold almost $100 million's worth of weapons and ammunition to customers abroad, close to $2 billion at today's prices. [55] The New Haven factory was humming with orders, and Oliver's latter years were spent overseeing a growing concern. Chile, Haiti, Peru, France, Morocco, and Spain ordered arms and ammunition, while the company's traveling salesman Thomas Addis went to Shanghai in China to establish a sales office there. [56] Even the South Africans were interested in buying the guns. The Royal Canadian Mounted Police purchased the Model 76, which the men on horseback used to defend the building of the Canadian Pacific Railway westward into Alberta. Once again, white men armed with the deadly repeating rifle clashed with the ancient tribes of North America. Winchester's reputation reached as far as Japan – and in 1878 the Japanese government asked the company to produce the machinery necessary to manufacture a rifle designed by Murata Tsuneyoshi. The company's catalog for 1875 reflected this happy state of affairs:

> It has become a household word, and a household necessity on our western plains and mountains. The pioneer, the hunter and trapper, believe in the Winchester, and its possession is a passion with every Indian. They have found their way to every country of the world. In the armament of the explorer in the wilds of Africa, and other countries, they are sure to have a place.[57]

The fame of the Winchester repeating rifle had spread to Istanbul, where the Turkish Sultan was an eager customer. Despite all the guns sold to pioneers and outlaws, it was Turkey's preparations for war with Russia which were to revolutionize Winchester's fortunes, because of the sheer size of the orders. The decline of the Ottoman Empire, or the sick man of Europe, as British cartoonists liked to caricature it, provoked much maneuvering among the European powers. All wished to benefit from the carve-up of land and influence which would follow the end of the status quo. Russia, through a series of wars with Turkey beginning in the 17th century, was gradually extending its frontier southward into Ottoman territory. The Crimean War of 1853–6, which began after the Russian Emperor tried to gain further concessions from Turkey, saw Britain and France enter the conflict on Turkey's side. Starting in the late 1860s, Turkey, egged on by Britain, reorganized her army and began equipping it with modern weapons, in preparation for the next inevitable conflict with Russia.

Thomas Gray Bennett played a pivotal role as Winchester expanded its markets into Turkey. Tom was the man who built on Oliver's success and expanded Winchester into a world-beating franchise. In 1870 Tom joined the Winchester Repeating Arms Company as an apprentice engineer in the gun shop, and in 1872 he married Oliver's diligent and dutiful daughter Jennie. Soon after this auspicious marriage, New Haven was abuzz as Oliver decided to boost production of the Model '73, using his new factory in town to churn out 200 rifles a day. The project became known as "Winchester's folly."[58] Yet Oliver understood mass production far better than his critics, and he was ramping up production not only for the pioneers out West but also for new markets abroad. Tom Bennett was to be Oliver's trusted emissary in Constantinople as the name of Winchester became known across the globe.

Winchester's dealings with Turkey began in May 1869, when Rustan Bey, a Turkish army officer, was dispatched to the United States to buy the necessary hardware. The Turkish Consul General in New York, one Christophus Oscanyan, acted as Bey's guide, interpreter, and interlocutor. Winchester agreed to pay a 10 percent commission on all sales made by Oscanyan of Winchester or Henry arms. The Winchester company was also hoping for a contract directly from the Turkish government – and agreed that the firm of V. Azarian Pere et Fils, of Constantinople, run by Aristokes Azarian, should be Winchester's official representative in all its official transactions with the Ottoman government. Winchester hoped to provide rifles to the Turkish government, either their brand new weapons, or the remaining Spencer rifles which they held following their purchase of that bankrupt concern in 1868. Mr Joseph Azarian, son of Aristokes, lived in Boston and purchased samples of silver-plated, gold-plated, and plain Winchester muskets which he sent to his father in Constantinople in September 1869.

In the early part of 1870, Caleb Huse of the Winchester Repeating Arms Company visited Constantinople and got on swimmingly with the Azarians, so that a "certificate of agency" was issued by the company to Aristokes and Joseph. A transcription error by the Western Union Telegraph Company held up negotiations with the Turks – instead of pricing the carbines at $27 each, a mistake in the telegraph to Constantinople read instead $20 each. The Turkish Minister of War awarded the contract to Winchester based on the lower price, and Winchester tried to sue Western Union for the lost $35,000, a claim which was eventually dropped.[59] Despite the costly error, Oliver was in business with a huge foreign order – Constantinople ordered 46,000 Winchester muskets and 5,000 carbines, plus ammunition.[60]

Oliver, in his characteristic eagerness not to miss a deal, had been pursuing two routes to the Turkish coffers. The Winchester company ultimately refused to pay Oscanyan his 10 percent commission and won the lawsuit the outraged Consul General brought against them. Interestingly, Winchester didn't try and rebut Oscanyan's claim that he was responsible for the Turkish government's adoption of the Winchester rifle, following Bey's recommendation. There was no way Oliver was going to pay a double commission, and that was that – in his eyes, Azarian Pere et Fils of Constantinople had done the lion's share of the work in getting the Turks interested in Winchester rifles. Oscanyan did not give up easily, and brought a second lawsuit in New York, in which there was tremendous interest. Although he ultimately lost that one too, the Winchester company did not welcome the publicity surrounding it, since it shed light on the inner workings of the world of international arms dealing.

Aristokes Azarian, the eponymous father of the firm, had worked hard for his share of the commission – making overtures to the Sultan of Turkey, no less, with a well-timed gift to His Excellency in 1866. Aristokes was undoubtedly well connected in Constantinople. Tom Bennett, sent to Turkey as Winchester's representative, observed him walking

> into the War department in his muddy boots when all others must take off their shoes or go in slippers made expressly. All the ministers and members of the council defer to him and gather round while he speaks. All make to him the most profound salutes. He is old, very short, very fat, wonderfully active. Eats, drinks and sleeps almost never.[61]

Tom Bennett enjoyed doing business with the Azarians in Constantinople, and described the atmosphere in the firm's office in a letter to his wife Jennie back in New Haven. It was very much a family business – Aristokes Azarian, alongside his sons and brother, ran the operation. Tom wrote:

> The firm is a very curious one. No clerks are kept in the office, the business being of an entirely confidential nature [...] When a telegram is to be worded, it is done by all hands at once. They shout, stamp, gesticulate [...] and just as you expect to see them punch each others' heads the noise ceases and the point is settled.[62]

Tom did not entirely trust the family, however, instructing Jennie to warn her father that the correspondence between Oliver and himself "will be more or less open to the Azarians."[63]

Such drama was part and parcel of the murky subculture of selling arms. Entrees to the powerful were highly prized, and middlemen such as the Azarians were falling over themselves to take a cut of the huge sums involved. As Tom dined on roast oysters, went to see dancing dervishes, and toured American gunboats in Constantinople, passing the time in between meetings with the Azarians and being summoned to court, others scurried around competing for the hand of Winchester. Oscanyan, it was revealed in court, didn't actually make an income from his honorary position as Turkish Consul General in New York – he earned a crust receiving brokerage fees for clearing shipments from the United States to Turkey.[64] The personal touch was all important in deal-making, and so Oliver himself travelled to Constantinople in 1870. Aristokes Azarian had arranged for six specially engraved Winchesters to be presented to the Ottoman Empire's Supreme Council of War, as a generous gesture from the American firm. The one gold-plated rifle and five silver-plated ones helped do the trick, and Oliver came home from parts far east of New Haven brandishing an order for 50,000 Model 1866 rifles. By the time war broke out in 1879, there were 39,000 Winchester Repeating rifles in the Turkish arsenals.[65] Huge orders of ammunition were to follow. At the suggestion of the Azarians, the Sultan of Turkey himself was presented with a carbine and a musket with a saber bayonet. The guns were gold plated, with rosewood stocks and gold-plated hilts. They were packed in rosewood boxes lined with crimson velvet, and silver corners were provided on the cases so that the imperial coat of arms could be engraved upon them once the precious cargo had arrived in Constantinople.[66] The Turkish contracts were invaluable to Winchester.

Tom Bennett was charged with helping negotiate Winchester's foreign contracts and collecting accounts, a delicate and often frustrating task which meant weeks of steamer travel and time spent apart from Jennie in European capitals. Tom disliked the endless rain in Paris and London, marveled at the 12th-century churches in Paris, enjoyed baguettes and French coffee immensely, and wrote evocative descriptions of the polluting yellow fog which enveloped industrial London. One London morning it was so dark that Tom didn't arise until 9.30am, since he had no idea it wasn't the middle of the night. His letters back to New Haven contain many amusing observations of the American abroad – London he found an impossible place to do business, since no one could be called upon until 11am and by 2pm all the lawyers were in their chambers, where they were unobtainable. "The English are so rich that they can live without working, I suppose," [67] sighed Tom.

Despite being a churchgoer, Tom was appalled to find the banks in London closed not only on Good Friday but Easter Monday too – "some other kind of good-for-nothing day when no business is done." [68] The strain of being apart from Jennie and their young children for months at a time leaps off the page – Tom is desperate for news of toddler Anne and baby Winchester Bennett, and gently chides Jennie when she neglects to provide long accounts of the baby's first steps. Anxious about Jennie's strength, Tom advises her to "let the reading club and the kettle drums and the concerts go." [69] Outings to buy Jennie an elegant French silk gown pass the time as Tom waits endlessly for an elderly French gentleman to sign a deposition pertaining to patents of guns. "Wouldn't I like to see you in it – or indeed out of it, my dear girl," writes Tom wistfully of his wife's extravagant dress.[70]

Buying expensive dresses was an activity curtailed by the sorry state of Winchester's finances before the majority of the Turkish contracts were signed. Tom's anxiety about this is revealed in a letter he wrote to Jennie in 1875, written from Paris where he was vainly trying to collect payment from the French government for an order of

rifles which hadn't even arrived in the French capital. Jennie confided
that her father Oliver was sick, and Tom replied:

> I hope this may find him better. The numerous failures and very hard
> times have no doubt affected him. I know that we have a great many
> payments to meet during this month and April and if the Turks have
> sent but five thousand it is but a drop in the bucket. My business goes
> very slowly [...] If I am obliged to go to Brussels my funds will
> hardly hold out [...]You will of course say nothing of this.[71]

By April 1876, as Tom was counting out his final pennies, news of
Turkey's ammunition orders from Winchester reached him in dreary
London, where he was still laboring away on patents for guns. The
Ottoman Empire was arming its troops ahead of what became the war
between Russia and Turkey. Oliver Winchester's travels to Turkey
had resulted in an order for his own ammunition and 600,000
Peabody-Martini rifles, not Winchesters. Even if he couldn't sell his
own rifles, the canny Oliver had made a hefty commission brokering
the sale of the Peabody-Martinis, which should have also made a tidy
profit for the Providence Tool Company, manufacturers of the rifle.
But that enterprise was to go bust when the Turkish government
reneged on payment for the remainder of the rifles (442,240 were
shipped to Turkey).[72]

Even though a gigantic order from the Turks for Winchester
ammunition was ultimately going to make the company viable after
years of lurching instability, Tom was worried:

> Your father writes me that we are awarded a new contract from the
> Turkish Government [...] I do so fear we are going to do it on credit.
> Everyone here [in London] seems to think that the Turks are about to
> be divided up in the interests of the various surrounding nations.
> They have ceased to pay upon their bonds at all. Many English
> families are ruined by this.[73]

Far from ruining Winchester, the Turkish contracts were all-
important to the company. In 1874, Turkey ordered 87.5 million
shells for the Martini rifle, followed in 1875 with an order for an

additional 112.5 million shells. During 1876 and 1877, Winchester supplied the Ottoman government with 80.1 million loaded Snider cartridges, which were fired by the Turkish Infantry's British-made Snider rifles, adapted from the Enfield rifle.[74]

As the men at the Winchester plant labored to produce the mammoth Turkish order, Oliver would visit the gun shop, urging his employees to work as fast as possible. When production inevitably slowed towards the end of a long shift, Oliver would have barrels of beer delivered to the men and would share a drink with them. Although he was "highly respected by everyone in the plant and had an awesome dignity, Winchester was very well liked by everyone [...] he had no mechanical ability and machinery was always a mystery to him,"[75] according to one factory superintendent. Oliver expected his men to keep working on the order of Model 1866 rifles for the Turkish Army, even as the company moved from Bridgeport to the new factory in New Haven. The men worked in two ten-hour shifts, with the machines humming 20 hours a day. To avoid delays in production during the move, the machines did not stop until they were loaded onto horse-drawn drays waiting at the factory gates, which took the precious cargo to the train. The Turkish inspectors insisted on every machine being cleaned and painted before being used again in the new factory. After a break of only seven hours, the manufacture of the Model 1866 resumed at the New Haven Armory – the machines had been moved, taken down, cleaned, painted, and were up and running once more.

Appreciating the profits to be made from such industrious work back in New Haven, Tom Bennett soon overcame his hesitation about Winchester accepting the Turkish contracts. He endured much seasickness in order to spend time in Constantinople flattering the Sultan of Turkey, and being feted in return. Tom had never seen anything like the Sultan's spectacular abode:

The palace is more magnificent in decoration and size than any of the palaces of France that I have seen, and it [is)]well kept, a strange thing to see in this country. The flowers splendid in shining wood. The painted ceiling and cut glass candlesticks and candelabras.[76]

The Sultan made a gift of sparkling jewels to Tom, who brought them home where they were set and proudly worn by his wife Jennie and later her daughter-in-law Susan. My older Connecticut cousins still speak reverentially of the Sultan's jewels – now, alas, vanished into the mists of time, believed to have been stolen from an elderly relative on her sickbed.

Thanks in no small part to the efforts of Tom Bennett and those at the Winchester factory in New Haven, the Turks were ready when Tsar Alexander II declared war on Turkey in 1877. Russia and its ally Serbia came to the aid of Bosnia and Herzegovina and Bulgaria in their rebellion against Turkish rule. It was the 12th conflict between Russia and the Ottoman Empire since the 7th century – but this time, the Winchester Repeating Rifle was to play a leading role in a conflict reported around the world. Oliver's rifles helped keep the Russians at bay for over five months and grabbed the attention of military bureaucrats across continents. The new-fangled rifle, which could keep on firing without being reloaded, was in the spotlight during what became known as the Plevna Delay.

Field Marshal Osman Pasha of Turkey was the hero of the hour, even if his forces ultimately surrendered to the Russians. This brilliant tactician was on his way to back up the Turkish forces at Nikopolis in Bulgaria, armed with 15,000 men and at least 8,000 Model 1866 Winchesters,[77] when he heard the troops there had surrendered. Unnoticed by the enemy, Osman Pasha redirected his soldiers and marched to Plevna (known as Pleven today), 75 miles south-west of Bucharest. As a conscientious chronicler of the Plevna Delay has noted,

> Russian intelligence completely failed to notice this force, and had no idea that it was now located at Plevna, busily constructing trenches, redoubts, fortifications and gun emplacements that would soon baffle the Russian Generals and, at the same time, introduce the repeating rifle into European warfare.[78]

Osman Pasha had built a Trojan Horse inside Plevna, cleverly concealing his troops inside houses and barns, unbeknownst to the hapless Russians. The Russians assumed Plevna was barely defended, and sauntered into the middle of town on July 18, 1877. Once enough Russian troops had poured into Plevna, a bugle was the signal for the Turks to leap out from their hiding places and fire on the unsuspecting Russians. At close range, the Turks unloaded their Winchester rifles upon the Russian troops, while the Peabody-Martins were used for what long-range work there was. The Russians had never seen anything like the firepower of the Winchester Repeater. The ammunition kept on coming. After a mere 20-minute battle, the Russians had lost 74 officers and 2,771 men – compared to the Turks, who lost only 12 men with 30 wounded.[79]

Grand Duke Nicholas, the commander in chief of the Russian army, had to decide how to strong-arm Osman Pasha and his Winchesters out of Plevna. Bypassing the Turks was impossible – the euphoric Turkish General Staff in Sophia sent reinforcements to Osman Pasha so he had upwards of 45,000 men. The Grand Duke dispatched Lieutenant General Baron Krudner and his IX Corps, backed up by other divisions, to avenge Mother Russia. The impatient Grand Duke ordered Krudner to "Attack at the earliest possible moment." On July 30, despite reservations about being outnumbered and outgunned, Krudner's troops advanced on Plevna. The results were disastrous for the Russians. Once again the hot lead of the Winchesters was deployed to devastating effect. War reporters wrote, "to find another instance of a corps being so rapidly destroyed as those the Russians used here, one has to go back to some of the frightful slaughters in the wars of the First French Empire." An official Russian report recorded, "Turkish rifle fire was infernal on the flanks and centre and seemed to increase greatly as our men neared the trenches." Plevna's second battle ended with the loss of 169 Russian officers and 7,136 men.

The Romanians suffered most during the third battle of Plevna, in the autumn of 1877. Osman had been expecting an attack from the Romanians for weeks, and he reinforced a redoubt close to the enemy line with Winchester marksmen. He modified the redoubt's layout so it had three tiers of rifle pits, one above the other like a deadly wedding cake. When the Romanians advanced, they faced 20,000 shots a minute from the repeating rifles. After 20 minutes of this onslaught, the Romanians retreated, leaving 1,000 of their dead soldiers behind.

After this third bloodbath of a battle, the Russians and the Romanians sat tight, besieged Plevna, and waited for tens of thousands of reinforcements to arrive. It was this that led newspapers to christen this episode "The Plevna Delay." Correspondents made much of the fact that so few Turks were holding up the mighty Russian advance. But they didn't seem to put two and two together:

> The value of the rapid-firing Winchesters was never properly recognized by the press or non-Turkish military men, but in many war rooms around the world, decisions were later made to replace outdated big bore rifles with faster shooting rifles of smaller calibre and higher muzzle velocity.[80]

The Turkish military, who knew exactly why the Russians were being delayed, immediately ordered another 140,000 Winchester rifles.

By December 1877, the Russians and the Romanians had a combined army of 150,000 – against the 40,000 or so of Osman Pasha's men. It was all over for the gallant Turks – not even the mighty Winchester could get them out of this gigantic hole. The Turks began to withdraw from Plevna – and surrendered when their situation became desperate, with Osman Pasha himself wounded. As the Field Marshal who had held up the Russian advance for five months lay ignominiously in a small cottage, nursing his wounds, General Ganetsky of Russia ordered his interpreter to say how much he admired the tactics and the defensive positions of Osman Pasha. As Osman was ferried back to Plevna in a carriage, Grand Duke Nicholas greeted with generosity the man who had given him such headaches: "I congratulate you on your defense of Plevna. It is one of the most splendid exploits in history." The Grand Duke even returned Osman's sword at a ceremonial breakfast – a mark of respect for a fearsome opponent. Osman sat out the rest of the Russo–Turkish war, which the Russians finally won in 1878.

Plevna was a pivotal moment for the Winchester Repeating Arms Company. With the world watching, "The Gun That Won The West" proved it was more than a rifle for cowboys. Armies could use it too, with devastating effect. Tom Bennett was in Constantinople signing contracts with the Turks for yet more ammunition when the plucky Osman finally surrendered. The rhythms of the court of Sultan Mahmoud were not visibly disturbed by the defeat. "We have no news of the war here as it is not considered best to give it," wrote Tom, "and all the impending disasters in the Balkans if they transpire or not are unknown. The people of Constantinople will know when the Russians come but not before."[81] Instead, Tom shook hands with Sultan Mahmoud and had "the best talk," though clearly not about Plevna. Rather, Tom observed the annual salutation to the Sultan at his palace, where high officials and noblemen were kissing the Sultan's sash.

> At the ceremony splendid music continues during the whole proceedings. They played Mozart and the Andante from the posthumous quartet and many other splendid pieces. I was the only infidel present. It is curious to think that while this is going on here the Russians are surely grinding their army beyond the Balkans.[82]

Tom was handsomely rewarded for his execution of the contracts selling arms and ammunition to the Ottoman Empire. He received the decoration of the Medjidie from the grateful Sultan in 1877,[83] a prestigious military decoration given to British officers who aided the Ottoman Empire during the Crimean War. It was an honor treasured by Tom, and the occasion of many a dinner table story once he was home in New Haven. Despite losing the war, the Turks were seen to have won the first three battles of Plevna and delayed the Russian advance, aided in no small part by the Winchester rifle. As Oliver Winchester declared with great satisfaction, the Turkish orders "put the Company on Easy Street for many years."[84]

At long last, the demand Oliver had dreamed of for many years was no longer the fantasy of a former shirtmaker. What with the Ottoman Empire and the demands of settling the unruly West, business was brisk – and Oliver turned his mind to who would succeed him in running the company. Keen to keep the expanding Winchester business a family concern, Oliver brought his son William Wirt

Winchester into the management as vice-president and appointed
Tom Bennett, his son-in-law, as company secretary. In 1862 William
Wirt had married Sarah Pardee, she who was to build what's now
known as the Winchester Mystery House in California. The family's
hold was strengthened in 1878 when William W. Converse, who had
married the sister of Sarah Winchester, née Pardee, was elected
treasurer. Oliver could not foresee that his son and heir William was
to die young. Winchester's future had actually been secured through
the auspicious marriage of Oliver's daughter Jennie Winchester to
Tom Bennett.

As he concentrated ownership of the company within his family,
Oliver was at the height of his powers. He had become one of the
wealthiest and most high-profile men in New Haven. He was one of
the commissioners who built the town's City Hall, a prominent donor
to the Calvary Baptist church, a director and founder of the Yale
National Bank, and a generous benefactor to the wider community.
Oliver gave $10,000 to the Yale Scientific School, founded scholar-
ships there, and donated almost as much to Yale's theological studies.
He founded the Winchester Astronomical and Physical Observatory
of Yale at a cost of about $100,000,[85] donating 32 acres of land on
Prospect Street for the purpose. The observatory, finally built in 1882,
ordered a heliometer, a divided objective telescope which was the
only one of its kind in America, and was at the time the largest in the
world.[86] Oliver's aim was for Yale to become a center for original
research into the stars above, rivaling the prominent European
observatories. An enthusiast for the modern age, the frontier of space
was clearly as fascinating to Oliver as the possibilities of new sewing
machines and repeating rifles.

Lacking a formal education himself, Oliver was passionately
interested in the pursuit of knowledge – he must have been entirely
self-taught, since his own sporadic schooling had been slotted in
around farmwork, and by the time he was a teenager, he'd been
apprenticed into the church-building trade. Keen to offer the
opportunities he had never had to others, Oliver became president
of the New Haven Young Men's Institute, an educational society
dedicated to the "mutual assistance in the attainment of useful
knowledge" through a shared book collection and weekly meetings.[87]

This precursor to a public library system was highly successful. In 1857, the institute had nearly 500 members and 7,656 books on its shelves,[88] including volumes presented personally by Oliver. There was a ladies' reading room in addition to the young men's cloistered library, and public lectures on subjects as diverse as "Courage," "The Conduct of Life," "Coral Islands," and "Old Europe and Young America." The poet and transcendentalist Ralph Waldo Emerson and the abolitionist Henry Ward Beecher were among the luminaries who lectured there, enhancing New Haven's intellectual life and its reputation as a center of learning. Emerson's lecture on "Country Life" was billed as a "rich treat to his hearers," delivered by one described as "that most strange compound of the nineteenth century Yankee, with the mystical philosophy of Plato's school."[89] Classes in drawing, book-keeping, writing, and arithmetic were offered, and a group of some 40 German men were taught English. It seems probable that they were Winchester employees, since the gun shop employed a number of Germans at the time, skilled engineers who had emigrated to the New World. Professor Benjamin Silliman of Yale University delivered a course of 20 lectures on chemistry to the Institute's Ladies. Women were part of the intellectual life of the institute, showered with periodicals in their reading room, from the *London Quarterly Review* to *The Knickerbocker* – and one Miss Elizabeth Barber provided the Song of Welcome at the opening of the new building:

> Science, here shall spread her treasures,
> Art, her beauteous gifts shall bring,
> Learning, yielding sweetest pleasures,
> Graces, here their flight shall wing.
>
> Joy! joy! Welcomes us here,
> Smiles, smiles our coming shall cheer,
> Crowning these walls to which Learning are reared.[90]

While Oliver "appealed with confidence to the intelligence of New Haven ladies, to sustain, by numerous subscriptions" their reading room, as president of the New Haven Young Men's Institute his strong focus was improving the education of the mechanics – who must surely have worked at his Winchester factory too. Struck by the quality of the European mechanics who had made their lives in New Haven, the board of the institute set about improving the skills of their own young engineers. "The superiority of the European Mechanic over our own, in a knowledge of those branches of Science and Art, which give completeness and thoroughness to his mechanical skill, has long been acknowledged," pronounced the institute's executive committee in 1857:

> This superiority is owing, in a great measure, to the establishment of scientific, or polytechnic schools, which are supported by government [...] In the absence of such institutions [...] we must content ourselves with either educating the mechanic after he has finished his trade, or educating him during his apprenticeship [...] already the mechanics have begun to realize the advantages of this kind of instruction [...] in a pecuniary point of view.[91]

An educated workforce was to Oliver's advantage too, since it would benefit the manufacture and design of his rifles – thus his altruistic actions dovetailed neatly with his commercial imperatives. However, no pushover with his charitable giving, Oliver complained bitterly about the institute's indebtedness in 1857, and called for subscriptions to avoid the sale of its New Haven property.

In their private life, Oliver and his wife Jane were avid horticulturalists, overseeing the cultivation of unusual varieties of flowers and fruits inside the magnificent Victorian greenhouses of their Prospect Street mansion. William Saunders, their landscape designer, had developed the idea of fixed glass roofs for greenhouses, which was a great help to the ardent gardeners. Like so many affluent Victorians, the Winchesters enjoyed experimenting with the new hot houses, growing exotic species from around the world. When Connecticut's agricultural society held its inaugural fair in 1854 on a sunny fall day, not only did Oliver's Isabella grapes receive a special mention, but his foreign variety grapes did too. In the fair's horticultural hall, there was "a large and very beautiful display of hothouse flowers from the conservatory of O. F. Winchester, Esq, who also exhibits several plates of cut flowers, roses, dahlias etc."[92] Oliver's son William Wirt was even more creative, constructing a pretty floral grotto in the style of an open temple, winning praise for his pains and ingenuity. Jane combined her love of family and gardening with generous philanthropy, giving more than $250,000 to Yale University in her lifetime.

When not happily pottering around his greenhouses, growing greengage plums and beets in his gardens, or keeping tabs on Winchester's sales and productivity, Oliver did his civic duty for the state of Connecticut. Politically a Whig who later became a Republican, and a staunch supporter of Abraham Lincoln during the Civil War, as we have seen Oliver was elected lieutenant governor of Connecticut in 1866. Pleading an ever-expanding business empire and the need to travel abroad, he claimed not to have sought re-election. However, he was also disheartened by the turn of events within the Republican Party after the assassination of Lincoln and Andrew Johnson's elevation to president of the United States. Johnson was an old-fashioned Southern Democrat, with Jacksonian views on states' rights. In the southern states during post-Civil War reconstruction, although slavery had been abolished, "black codes" to regulate the supposedly freedmen were being established. Radical Republicans in Congress moved to challenge Johnson, refusing to seat politicians from the old Confederacy and passing measures to ensure freedoms for the former slaves. Johnson vetoed the legislation, and the Radical Republicans vilified him.

Oliver looked on with disapproval at this battle of wills between Congress and the President, and accused the Republican leadership of abandoning its principles:

> The audacity with which they press upon Congress and the Country the most revolutionary doctrines and disorganizing measures is truly alarming. The animus of all this [...] appears to be contempt of the Supreme Court, and personal, vindictive hatred of the President of the United States. The only excuse offered for this abandonment of principle is progress. It is a fearfully declining progress, which, if not soon arrested, threatens us with political anarchy and financial and social ruin.[93]

This might seem an apocalyptic view of the Radical Republicans' attempt to preserve the gains of the Civil War, but it was one that Oliver felt deeply. He fell out with his own party to such an extent that the Republican Convention didn't invite him to accept renomination for the post of lieutenant governor. Did Oliver feel that, after the upheaval of the Civil War, it was strategic to allow the Southern states some leeway over how they treated their former slaves? As a New Englander, he had been a firm supporter of the Union side as it sought to abolish slavery – but on the thorny question of states' rights during reconstruction, Oliver seemed to side with President Jackson and the Southern states. He was pilloried by the Connecticut press for what was seen as his Conservative Republicanism, and for his departure from true Union principles. "The people will not tolerate such base defection," [94] thundered the *Hartford Courant* after Oliver, in his role as lieutenant governor, met with those known as Johnson Unionists, supporters of President Andrew Johnson who would not support federally guaranteed rights for African Americans.

Towards the very end of his life, Oliver suffered a paralytic shock. Though he recovered partially, "his splendid constitution was broken." [95] In April 1880, Oliver asked the board of directors if his salary might be reduced to $5,000 a year, "in view of the present condition of my health and incapacity for taking an active part in the business." [96] On December 10, 1880, shortly after his 70th birthday, Oliver died at his magnificent home on Prospect Street in New Haven, early in the morning. "After a brave struggle, he succumbed and utter physical prostration ensued, resulting at last in death," the *New Haven Daily Morning Journal* informed its readers. The newspaper's obituary paid tribute to "the busy mind of Mr Winchester," which "was never at rest. He was always planning, and no obstacle seemed too great for his indomitable will and enterprise [...] He was a warm friend and genial companion, an untiring worker [...] of great foresight and administrative ability."

The funeral took place at Oliver's home on Prospect Street, where the founder of the Winchester Repeating Arms Company lay in an elegant casket, in the monument to his wealth and social standing. Company employees were given the day off to mourn their leader, and at the service they joined Oliver's friends from Baltimore and

New York and New Haven's finest ladies and gentlemen, "filling important and influential places in the community, in society, business, literature and the sciences."[97] As befitted a keen horticulturalist, there were "numerous floral tributes." One was a pillow bearing the word Father, which was "richly studded with the choicest flowers."[98] The Reverend Dr Gallaher, who conducted the service, spoke of Oliver's "integrity and perseverance [...] and generous deeds."[99] A quartet sang, and the mourners were told that although the shadow of the death angel had passed, its gloom was dispelled by the glory which God's light had shone on Oliver's trusting soul. At the New Haven chamber of commerce, tribute was paid to a man "who was not only able to plan, but to successfully carry out, gigantic enterprises, whose name will be remembered as a conspicuous example of honesty and integrity."[100] Winchester company employees adopted a resolution, saying that they had

> the best of all reasons to know his worth and to lament his death [...] we unite in expressing to the survivors of his family the sense of personal loss and bereavement which we feel in common with them for a true friend to us and a great captain of industry gone.[101]

Oliver's story was an early version of the American Dream – the rags to riches life, from privation to privilege, a tale of pennies turned into millions of dollars. He left the bulk of his fortune to his wife Jane, and when she died in 1898, her estate was estimated to be worth $40 million.[102] "Richest Woman in New England is Now Dead" proclaimed the banner headlines. Jane died unexpectedly, according to the newspapers, which rebuked her physician Dr B. H. Cheney for not anticipating that Jane's paralysis could be the end of her. "While realizing that the case was serious, he had not looked for serious consequences,"[103] wrote the *New Haven Daily Palladium*, reprovingly. Prayers were said for Jane at the Prospect Street home she and Oliver had built so lovingly, as she did not want to have a formal church service. With the minimum of ceremony, on a cold spring morning, she was buried next to her beloved at the Evergreen cemetery in New Haven. Jane's immense fortune was divided between her only surviving child, Jennie Bennett, and her black sheep of a grandson, Oliver Dye. He was to squander his riches living a dissolute life, divorcing his wife in scandalous fashion. Jennie honored her mother by building the $95,000 Jane Ellen Hope building at Yale University, which offered medical care for the poor. The dedication plaque remembered Jane Winchester as a woman "whose life was lived simply and quietly in doing the duty that lay nearest at hand with no thought of self and was filled with kindness and helpfulness to others."[104]

The staggering accumulation of wealth, which was to cascade down into the next generation, was only one of Oliver's achievements. By persevering despite earlier failures and creating the Winchester Repeating Arms Company, he had put New Haven on the map. "No other concern in New Haven has developed more enterprise or become more pre-eminent, and today their products are celebrated over the entire civilized world in a manner that would have been otherwise impossible,"[105] observed an admiring newspaperman in 1889. With acumen and boldness, despite having barely a cent at the start of his life, Oliver had turned Winchester from a bankrupt business into a boldface name. It was Oliver's dearest wish for the company to remain in the hands of his family, and he envisaged his son William Wirt Winchester as his successor. Wirt, as the family called him, was a gentle soul of a retiring nature who may not have wished to fulfill his father's dream. As it was, he never even got the chance. Tragically, Wirt fell ill shortly after his father died, and perished from consumption on March 8, 1881.

CHAPTER 3

The Wrestler

F AMILY BUSINESSES are unpredictable enterprises, and after the sudden death of William Wirt, only months after his father, the future of Winchester lay with one Thomas Gray Bennett, college wrestler, engineer, and Civil War veteran. A man of few spoken words, Tom Bennett was a tough negotiator and canny observer with supremely good judgment and an ability to make smart business decisions swiftly. It was Tom who got on a train to Utah in 1883 and signed up the legendary John Browning to make weapons for Winchester at a moment's notice, and Tom who went head to head with the Colt Manufacturing Company over market share and won. Tom's marriage to Jennie, Oliver Winchester's daughter, was to provide the company with an outstanding alternative leader from within the family's ranks. Oliver had noted Tom's considerable abilities and had groomed him for a prominent role in the business, without ever envisaging that his beloved son would be carried off by tuberculosis so swiftly after his own death.

The square-jawed, steely-grey-eyed, strapping Thomas Gray Bennett joined the Winchester Repeating Arms Company in 1870, after graduating from Yale University. In May 1872, this impressive young man married Oliver's doted upon younger daughter Hannah Jane, known as Jennie. For the next half-century, Tom proved to be a steady hand on the company tiller, and a worthy successor to Oliver Winchester. Edwin Pugsley, later Winchester's chief engineer, regarded T. G. Bennett as Oliver's "greatest strike [...] his business ability and integrity built Winchester." By the time T. G. Bennett retired for the first time in 1910, the Revised Edition of Webster's

Dictionary contained the word "Winchester" as a famous American rifle. Through Tom's efforts, Winchester became a name "well known [. . .] among the kings, queens, emperors, rulers and counselors of all countries of the globe," which would play "an important part [. . .] so far as the overthrowing of thrones and the setting up of new dynasties." [1] Clever, observant, a fine writer, and a devoted husband, Tom Bennett was as shrewd as his father-in-law when it came to finding new markets and growing the Winchester empire. He loved to sail, fish, and shoot, and built an imposing waterfront summer house at Johnson's Point in Branford, near New Haven. While the big granite house with its endless veranda is no more, a relic of the gilded age, Tom's descendants (this one included) enjoy summering at Johnson's Point to this day. Tom's love of the water led him to attach eyebolts for mooring boats to practically every rock close to the Johnson's Point shoreline – rusting, yet still in use, they are a manifestation of his legendary attention to detail.

Born in New Haven, to Joseph and Emilia Bennett, Tom Bennett was schooled at General William Huntington Russell's Military Academy, or the Collegiate and Commercial Institute as it was formally known. School was designed to be a grounding for life in the Army, as General Russell saw the Civil War on the horizon and wanted Connecticut's elite young men to be prepared for battle on the Union side. Their $500 per year education was, by all accounts, a benevolent form of tyranny:

> Discipline was the handmaiden of a proper education in the America of William Huntington Russell. The pragmatic view that the small boys endlessly and seemingly tirelessly performing their military drills in Wooster Place might in time become good soldiers, was reinforced by the Christian ethic of self-denial and dedication. And discipline there was, it emanated from the magisterial presence of the headmaster who presided over his pupils with as much authority as Moses on Mount Sinai [. . .] The inheritance of two centuries of Calvinism lay like the snows of a New England winter upon the Collegiate and Commercial Institute.[2]

Under the unflinching, beady eye of General Russell, who by the way never saw a real battle himself, Tom and the other boys endured the

Spartan conditions of their military education (it was apparently the first school in America to have a gymnasium) and upon graduation most enlisted in the Union Army. The 17-year-old Bennett was commissioned a first lieutenant in one of the North's African American regiments, Connecticut's 28th Volunteers of the Civil War, and rose to the rank of captain of the 29th. Since the Civil War was being fought over the abolition of slavery, the symbolism of this integrated regiment on the Union side was hugely important, its very existence a rebuff to the Southern States. However, the practicalities of being in charge of white and black soldiers could be extremely complicated, as Tom explained in his letters home from Fort Barnabas in Pensacola, Florida:

> Is a white officer to touch his hat to a nigger just because he is higher in rank? Two companies of white men with their officers have been put in arrest down on Ship Island because they would not acknowledge a "nigger" "Officer of the Day." You cannot imagine how exciting the topic is to Yankee troops. Massachusetts is an abolitionist place, but the idea of the best blood of Boston being placed under a nigger officer, don't seem to agree with it.[3]

As he navigated the swirling resentments of white men under the command of black officers, the teenage Tom hugely enjoyed swimming in the warm waters of Florida, eating oranges, and killing opossums, though he missed going to church on Sunday and begged his mother to send detailed letters about the family skating back in Connecticut. Still a youngster, Tom was experiencing great responsibility in this time of civil war, living a life which although austere was not without its treats. As he wrote to his mother:

> We have got a good redoubt to garrison. It mounts nine guns [...] all Parrots and Columbiads. It is very strong and lies almost entirely underground. Our officers quarters are very nice [...] If you want a piano, make out a requisition on the Quarter Master and he will furnish it upon your receipt.[4]

Fig. 8 Thomas Gray Bennett, 1st Lieutenant of the 29th Connecticut
Volunteers, 1864.

The dutiful son wrote that he intended to send his family a box of
curiosities from Pensacola when he got the chance, full of pieces of
shot and "if you so choose I can send you a (rebel) skull." There was
some action by the redoubt as rebels came across from the other side
of the bayou. This was Tom's first sight of battle. "You don't know
what a splendid piece of fireworks a bursting shell is, when you are far
enough off [. . .] there is first a short whistle, and a puff of smoke like
a balloon [. . .] they bite first and bark afterward." To Tom's
disappointment, the chance to skirmish with the rebels was lost
and he went back to watching colorful lizards cover the walls of the
redoubt, growing fat on Army cooking. "I was in the Commissary
department [. . .] and found I weighed two hundred and sixty five
pounds. You know I never weighed more than one hundred and thirty
five pounds before I left home." [5]

As his waistline expanded and his tan deepened in the Florida sunshine, Tom's much-anticipated fight finally began in the middle of one spring night. Guided by Floridian African Americans who detested the Southern rebels, Tom and his men rowed their boats in darkness and cut off a picket of soldiers posted by a bend in the bay. "Three of them were talking by the fire, two were asleep, and one was on post with his gun in his hand. None of them got away," Tom wrote with satisfaction.[6] The young soldier soon experienced the angry rebel response. "It was like putting a stick into a nest of hornets. They have been at our pickets ever since, and threaten to hang as many as we took from them, and to hang either myself or Lieut. Breckinridge for that raid." Tom avoided that fate, and earned himself a reputation as a skilled artillerist by firing upon rebel boats. His regiment moved to Louisiana, "in active service at last, I hope," Tom wrote excitedly. "General Banks is giving them thunder, I tell you." General Nathaniel Banks, commander of the Department of the Gulf for the Union side, was a politician turned soldier who had a somewhat checkered military career, and was removed from command after the failed Red River campaign of 1864. Tom's view of his leader quickly turned sour, as weary soldiers' deployments were extended:

> Banks has refused to pay any attention to the time of nine months' men, and holds several regiments here by force, whose time is fairly and honestly out. It seems to me there is little or no necessity for it now. This is the first time I have said a word against Banks (and I have thought much) for a man should always stand by his commanding officer, right or wrong, and has no right to think for himself when his superior thinks for him.[7]

The war was entering a critical phase, as Tom and his colleagues battled not only with rebels but the sticky, inhospitable Louisiana Gulf Coast climate. He wrote to his parents:

> If the yellow fever does not take me I stand a good chance of getting home. We get very used to the sight of death and disease here. Almost every day someone is carried off to the hospital, and as the

stretchers pass the men will offer bets on the probability of their occupants ever getting home.[8]

Tom's mother followed events down south with great anxiety from New Haven, where the good ladies of the Soldiers' Aid Society were holding fund-raising bazaars for the wounded troops. Mrs Bennett looked at the gaiety, the flags, and the evergreen wreaths, and was troubled by the underlying juxtaposition, "for who would guess that the hospitals full of sick, wounded and dying soldiers, could be the producing cause of this brilliant Bazaar." Scouring the newspapers for news of his regiment, Mrs Bennett had heard nothing from her son in weeks. She wrote to him:

> You don't know how we long for the capture of Vicksburg and Port Hudson. The raid of General Lee into Maryland and Pennsylvania makes matters look very threatening there [...] The newspapers keep reporting things as "progressing favorably" at Port Hudson. But how long will it take for them to come to a favorable conclusion.

As the early summer of 1863 turned into July, Mrs Bennett finally heard something about her son, though not directly from him:

> We had some news unexpectedly through a colored man who said he had been a cook and waiter in the regiment, and had just come from New Orleans where he had been in hospital. He said he knew you, and always had; that you were doing well, "fust-rate," that all the men liked you.

Her son, Mrs Bennett was told, was not a drinking man – no doubt a great relief to the upstanding New England matriarch.

By the summer of 1864, young Tom was in charge of 100 men in Virginia – where pig hunting was a favorite activity while waiting for the action. Inside his trenches, the news that Atlanta had fallen to Union forces caused great jubilation. The deep war weariness up and down America in the summer of 1864 changed overnight on September 2, when Atlanta fell. At long last, Mrs Bennett and millions of others dared to hope that the fighting was coming to an end and fractured families would finally be reunited. Tom reported:

> The Rebs are very much down in the mouth about the fall of Atlanta. They have replied to our challenge very feebly of late, and it is conjectured that they are short of ammunition [...] I begin to get very tired of this monotony and hope something may occur to break it very soon. I don't much care what it may be.

The Johnnies, as the rebels were known, were ranged across an old battlefield from Tom and his men at Petersburg, Virginia. From his trench, Tom could see the dead unburied from old battles, now skeletons whose smooth skulls shone eerily in the sunlight, guns at their sides. Tom and his men took the guns of the dead, which still worked – not Winchesters, but usable nonetheless. In the closing days of the Civil War, Tom's now 29th Connecticut regiment was engaged in a tough fight at Chapin's Farms, Virginia. Whatever difficulties and racial tensions the black and white troops faced behind the scenes, Captain Bennett's men were exemplary in battle, and Tom was proud of them. "In the midst of fire you could hear the men taunting the Reb. canoneers. 'Why don't you load your old gun?' 'You ain't killing niggers as much as you was.'" [9] Eighty-five of Tom's men were killed and wounded. "It was nothing but a skirmish, you see," was Tom's airy description to his mother. When Tom retold this story years later to Edwin Pugsley, Winchester's chief engineer, it emerged that the Union men were armed with the Spencer repeating rifle, rival to Oliver Winchester's Henry weapon. Tom's troops were able to get out of the ambush by Confederate troops at Chapin's Farms with a volley of rapid fire. "I always wondered whether this demonstration of the efficiency of the repeating rifle did not have a lasting effect on his future career," mused Edwin Pugsley. [10]

Wounded in that battle of Chapin's Farms in September 1864, Tom was honorably discharged after another year, having served out the war in Florida, Louisiana, Texas, and Virginia. Before Tom's discharge, he organized a performance of the 29th Company minstrel troupe, to an audience of colonels and field officers and Virginia newspaper reporters. Tom was pleased to be able to tell his mother that the minstrels had been "highly praised." Was the minstrel troop composed of black and white men, or only black soldiers? Tom's letters do not say. It would seem fitting if an African American regiment in a war fought to end slavery in the South saw men of different skin colors perform music together as the hostilities ended.

The experience of the Civil War was a bonding one, and as it ended, Tom wrote regretfully:

> I shall most awfully hate to leave the Army. We are all going to get homesteads after the next pay-day and have them located together. You know we can get a home-stead under the homestead law; somewhere out West for $20. I think I shall try my hand at the speculation.[11]

In the end, Tom Bennett didn't go west when the Civil War ended, though his future was to be inextricably linked to the frontier through his work at Winchester. Rather, he went back to school, graduating from Yale University's Sheffield Scientific School in 1870. On August 1, the veteran and engineer joined the Winchester Repeating Arms Company. It was an obvious choice for one of a scientific bent with experience of warfare – having fired rifles in action, Tom was interested in the technology behind guns and ammunition and its practical application.

Before too long, he had met Jennie Bennett, daughter of his boss Oliver Winchester. Quite how they first encountered one another is unrecorded. A summer party thrown by Oliver, attended by staff and family enjoying strawberries and lemonade, perhaps? However it began, theirs was an enduring love story, which can be traced through Tom's letters to Jennie over 50 years. Without fail, he addressed her as "My Dear Girl." Early in their courtship, Tom wrote sadly:

> I am not to see you for four days. What my condition will be on the fourth day is more than I can tell. I met Guy DuBois today, and told him I should have more time this week than usual as "my girl" had gone away [...] This is the first love letter that I ever wrote so you must not despair because there is not much love in it [...] Good

night deary. Come home as soon as soon as you can and I'll promise to come up real early each night.[12]

Wherever Winchester business carried him, from hotels in Philadelphia, to boarding houses in Utah, Tom wrote tenderly to Jennie every night, part of an evening ritual which included cleaning his boots. "I don't write love letters but know that I love you. Pray for me constantly," was his refrain.[13]

During Tom and Jennie's courtship, business at the Winchester company was slack – "things at the office are quite dull," as Tom reported to Jennie when she was visiting relatives.[14] Jennie and Tom were married in 1872 – and T. G. Bennett, as he was always known in the Winchester factory, rose up the company ranks to become secretary and was entrusted with sensitive work by his father-in-law.

To keep the Winchester name on the lips of every pioneer household, Oliver, the elderly father-in-law, was relentless in his demands. As we have seen, he sent Tom Bennett out on the road endlessly, far from his wife and small children. Oliver's desire for the latest and most superior weapons-making technology had Tom scouring rain-soaked England in search of the manufacturing scoop which would give Winchester the edge. In this pursuit of excellence, Tom was dispatched by ocean liner across the swelling sea to London, to "get an intimate knowledge of the process of making bullets, as here conducted."[15] He toured the Royal Arsenal at Woolwich in London, home of ammunition manufacturing and explosives research to the British Armed Forces. In the wake of the Crimean War, there had been much criticism of Britain's lack of preparation, and the sorry state of its munitions. Once known as a "museum of technical antiquity," the Arsenal at Woolwich had become the provenance of the War Office and the new, improved version was worth the attention of a visiting American arms manufacturer. Tom trekked to Woolwich in the pouring rain, to see the "bullet machines" which Winchester Repeating Arms was considering buying for the shop back in Connecticut. His travels took him as far afield as Matlock in Derbyshire, where he luxuriated in castles and mineral spas, while getting prices for machinery. Tom

greatly enjoyed his forays into what he recognized as the England of
Dickens and Thackeray – he chuckled in letters home to Jennie over
his walks down Old Threadneedle Street, and reveled in Thackeray's
satirical take on society London, to which the observant American
could now relate.

The grim landscape of industrial England came as a shock to Tom,
who had never seen anything like it. Touring Leeds, Manchester, and
Sheffield in search of machine tools for the Winchester plant, he saw:

> a country where everything was filled, covered [...] dead with the
> smoke [...] black houses, hills, trees, milk men, women, children,
> the dogs and cats even [...] The tops of the fences, hedges and
> stones get black and have a burnt look and you ride into town with
> nothing visible but the dim outlines of the [...] chimneys.[16]

This journey into the blackened heart of England included a
pilgrimage to the factory of Sir Joseph Whitworth, the famed
British industrialist who had made his fortune from machine tools.
When the Crimean War broke out in 1853, the pacifist Whitworth
nonetheless turned his skills to producing weapons – believing in the
deterrent principle of defense. The Army Ordnance Board
approached Sir Joseph Whitworth in 1854, asking him to design
and build machine tools for the mass production of their standard
issue Enfield rifle. Dissatisfied with the performance of the Enfield
rifle, he produced his own famous Whitworth rifle, which used a
smaller, more efficient hexagonal bore. *The Times* reported in 1857
on the official tests in which "The Whitworth Rifle excelled the
Enfield to a degree which hardly leaves room for comparison."
Despite its apparent superiority, in 1859 the Whitworth rifle was
rejected by the Ordnance Board because of its small bore size.[17] Just
as Oliver Winchester had trouble convincing the bureaucracy of the
US Army, so Joseph Whitworth struggled with jobsworths. The
Whitworth rifle did make its way over the Atlantic into the midst of
the US Civil War – into the hands of the Confederate side, against
which Tom had battled as a Union soldier. Confederate snipers used
the rifle, and were known as the Whitworth Sharpshooters. Tom, who
knew of the Whitworth rifle's fame from his time in the Union army,

marveled at what he saw in Whitworth's Manchester manufactory: "They were building some large steel hydraulic pressers, marine engines, propeller shafts," he reported breathlessly to Jennie, with all the admiration of the former engineering student.[18]

As a trained engineer and Army veteran, Tom was well cast to oversee the crucial area of manufacturing interchangeable parts for Winchester rifles. Whereas in the 18th century, gunmaking was considered an extremely skilled craft, and every gun was painstakingly constructed by hand, the industrial revolution shook everything up. Now machines could take over most of the manufacturing work from gunsmiths, and relatively unskilled workers could produce large numbers of weapons quickly and at a lower cost. Identical pre-manufactured parts made it easier to repair and replace worn rifles. There were many reasons why interchangeable manufacture was thought unprofitable – it required a very large initial investment in machines and tools and a long lead-time before even one gun could be produced. As Edwin Pugsley, chief engineer at Winchester, wrote; "T.G. Bennett had the nerve never to compromise, and if parts were wrong they were scrapped and interchangeability rigidly maintained. Oliver Winchester, recognizing T.G.'s ability, gave him free rein." [19]

For the Winchester Repeating Arms Company to continue its success without Oliver, it would need a talented gun designer who could develop a new and improved form of repeating action. Mass manufacturing was all very well, but it depended upon having an outstanding gun to replicate. Remington, Colt, and the Marlin Arms Company of New Haven were nipping at Winchester's heels, desperate to compete with new types of rifle. Oliver's hunt for a gunsmith in the mold of B. Tyler Henry was on. Gun and ammunition sales were profitable in the 1870s, as the Models '73 and '76 were churned out, but hunters wanted a still more powerful gun and Winchester wished to make it. None of the repeating rifles of the time would handle the heavy ammunition that shooters wanted because of its long range and effectiveness against big game. As Harold Williamson noted, "the relative merits of the single shot versus the repeating rifle were argued at great length around many a camp fire and wherever shooters gathered in frontier settlements." [20] One

Hugo Borchardt, a German immigrant who started working for Winchester in the early 1870s, seemed to have potential as the next inventor, but left the company in a huff after his designs for pistols weren't put into production. Borchardt left Winchester for the Sharps Rifle Company and eventually returned to Germany, where he produced a forerunner of the Luger pistol,[21] which was to become infamous under the Nazis.

The answer to Winchester's future lay out West, once again. In Ogden, Utah, to be precise. "A vast plain of wind and rocks completely indescribable in its unattractiveness,"[22] as Tom Bennett the urbane Easterner described the terrain, looking down his nose at it. In this unpromising setting Tom uncovered the next big thing in gun design – an unassuming young man named John Moses Browning, a Mormon, who was a firearms genius and is often called the Thomas Edison of gun design. John's father Jonathan had set up a gun-shop in Nauvoo, Illinois, but the Mormons were forced out by murderous mobs suspicious of their polygamous ways, and his family crossed the Mississippi River to Kanesville, Iowa. There Browning senior produced two repeating rifles which he advertised with a dry sense of humor in the *Frontier Guardian*:

> The Subscriber is prepared to manufacture to order, improved Fire-Arms [...] revolving rifles and pistols; also slide guns, from 5 to 25 shooters. All on an improved plan, and he thinks not equalled this far East. (Farther West they might be.) The emigrating and sporting community are invited to call and examine Browning's improved firearms before purchasing elsewhere. Shop eight miles south of Kanesville on Mosquito Creek, half a mile south of TRADING POINT.
>
> Jonathan Browning[23]

Jonathan's stay in Iowa was profitable, for his repeating rifle gave the settlers greater protection from the Native Americans than the single shot, and so his guns were in great demand. However, Brigham Young, the Mormon leader, was looking for a haven for his community outside the borders of the United States, where the

Church had faced persecution and little protection from the state or federal authorities. When the US Army sent an officer in 1846 to request companies of Mormon volunteers for the war against Mexico, Young sent 500 of his followers to fight, but also quietly began to plot the exodus west.[24] The following spring the community trekked across the high plains to the valley of Great Salt Lake. Jonathan Browning, as a renowned gunsmith, was instructed by Brigham Young to stay behind and equip the Mormon brethren for their journey westwards: "Each wagon train must be equipped [...] for survival in whatever abiding place the Lord should choose. The brethren must be provided with guns; they would need every gun which would be made or obtained and made serviceable ..."[25]

Not until 1852 was Jonathan Browning allowed to load his wagons and follow the now ingrained westward trail – he eventually settled in Ogden, Utah, 40 miles from Salt Lake City. He fathered 22 children, 11 girls and 11 boys, from three different wives – and Jonathan the younger was born in the remote and spectacular Ogden Canyon in 1855. He and his brothers carried on their father's gunmaking tradition with a shop in Ogden, near the foaming river and overlooked by the mighty Wasatch Mountains. Although Brigham Young preached feeding the Native Americans rather than fighting them, caution was the watchword of the community, and there were plenty of forts and log stockades to protect the brethren – who were well equipped with the Brownings' guns.

Quite how the Brownings of Utah crossed the horizon of the Winchester company back East is disputed – some accounts say a Winchester salesman Andrew McAusland came across one of the rifles; another has it that the Brownings were infringing an existing Winchester patent. Either way, in 1883 Tom Bennett saw a unique rifle, read Browning Bros, Ogden, Utah, USA, stamped across the barrel, and, as legend has it, leapt on a train as though the seat of his pants were on fire. Never before had Tom seen a single shot rifle of such exceptional quality. The source of this competition must be bought up before Remington or one of the other competitors got at it – and the rifle had to be utilized for the greater glory of Winchester. What's more, the failure of the Sharps Rifle Company in 1881 meant there was unused market share out there just waiting to be colonized.

After a lengthy, dusty train journey, in December 1883 Tom arrived in the railroad town of Ogden, which seemed to him to be in the middle of absolutely nowhere. Tom wrote to Jennie from Ogden's Union Depot Hotel:

> The Rockies are a sham. The weather is very cold and the air so clear that you see with great distinctness at long distances and miscalculate them greatly [...] We saw no herds of bisons and antelope as are shown in the guidebooks, only one small wolf [...] There are no houses or people for hundreds of miles.[26]

Tom did find the Browning brothers though, out on Main Street in their unassuming workshop, and after they had wiped their hands dry on an oil cloth, business began in earnest. The quietly spoken, slim, and lanky 28-year-old John Moses told the businessman from out East how in addition to the single shot gun he was also working on a new repeating rifle that could fire large cartridges. Tom was all ears. Right there and then, inside the Browning gun shop, he offered to buy rights for the exclusive manufacture of Browning's single shot gun and first refusal on the new lever action rifle for big game cartridges. All this for $8,000, a not inconsiderable sum in those days. The humble Browning, who had asked for $10,000,[27] accepted – he was delighted by Tom's interest in his work. The astute deal maker from Winchester knew this was a potential treasure trove. Tom took a wooden replica of what became the Model 86 gun back to New Haven, and so began a partnership which was to last 19 years. As Tom recalled:

> When back in New Haven I had a gun of each model made up in the finest finish and sent them to the brothers. For many years and many new models, amounting to thousands of dollars, the mutual word or a handshake was sufficient to seal a bargain between the brothers and Winchester.[28]

John Browning and his brothers Matt and Ed were unconventional gunsmiths in that they didn't work from blueprints or fancy designs. Theirs was not a factory like the Winchester smokestack out East.

The brothers worked mainly with hand tools. John Browning saw the shape of a rifle in his head and drew only basic sketches on brown butcher paper. An excellent shot, John hunted with his brothers and knew exactly how a hunting rifle should perform. He was a member of the leading trap and live-bird shooting team in Utah in the 1890s. This instinctive feel for a gun and an understanding of how it should perform underpinned his brilliance. Though Browning's name was never on the Winchester rifles he created, he sold 40-odd designs to the company, three quarters of which were never produced.[29] Whistling and singing as he worked, silent when lacking inspiration, Browning is credited with inventing the automatic pistol, rifle, and shotgun, not to mention experimenting with the development of machine guns and automatic cannon. His guns were produced by Winchester, Remington, Colt, Savage, and the Belgian gun manufacturer Fabrique Nationale de Guerre.

The single shot rifle was Browning's first contribution to the Winchester stable, followed by the lever action Models 1886, 1892, 1894, and 1895. The Winchester single shot was used as a target rifle and for killing varmints – in larger calibers it could even be used as a big game rifle, killing bears. But it was the longer range repeating rifle which was a game changer. When the Browning brothers took the prototype of the Model 1886 to show Tom Bennett in New Haven, they stopped off in New York City en route to show their precious creation to a leading gun dealer. The brothers were told their gun was "the best rifle in the world" and that they were "holding the future of the Winchester company" in their hands.[30] So it proved to be.

John Browning was very popular at the Winchester factory. When visiting with new designs for guns, he would often be in the gun shop for 18 hours at a time, operating machines just to learn how to use them. He took lessons in the engraving shop, and became a good engraver of presentation rifles, just to pass the time. As Albert Tilton of Winchester observed:

Often Mr Browning would watch a machine in operation then ask the operator if he could try it; there was probably no machine in the plant that he could not operate. Everyone at Winchester liked Mr

Browning, since he was very famous but didn't give the impression that he thought he was above working.

William Mason, master mechanic at Winchester in New Haven, was the magic link between John Browning's designs and the mass-produced rifles they became. He was one of the leading gun designers in the country in his own right, who had previously worked at Colt. Mason's mechanical modifications to Browning's designs, many of which were significant enough to be patented, meant the rifles could be manufactured in huge numbers. Later, after an acrimonious split with the Brownings, the company went so far as to claim that the Model 1886 "is more largely the invention of our own Mr Mason than it is of the Browning Bros."[31] In happier times, Browning, Mason, and Tom Bennett met a few times each year, when the gun designer made the pilgrimage from his Ogden shop to the Winchester factory in New Haven, where he would unwrap his carefully packaged guns, cutting the string with his pocketknife. It must have been like Christmas come early to this corner of New England. Browning was the bearer of gifts which were making Winchester the dominant force in the manufacture of repeating arms – not just in the United States, but around the world. Tom paid Browning $50,000 for the rights to what became the Model 1886 – a sum dwarfed by the profits made from the gun. Initially, though, John didn't seem unhappy with his financial lot.

> Bennett knows what he's doing. I sell him a gun – the 86 for instance. He pays a lot of money for it, and has a big investment in plant and materials. It would be a serious blow to him if somebody should come out with a pretty good gun of the same general type as the 86. I'm just building some protective fences for Bennett. That's what these guns are that he buys and never expects to make – fences [...] And he pays me pretty well for the fences too.[32]

Indeed, for the prototype to what became the Winchester Model 1892, Tom paid Browning $20,000 on condition the design be completed within 30 days. Just over a million Model '92s were manufactured by Winchester over the next half-century. John's

Mormon relatives in Ogden were wary, believing their man was being taken for a ride by the predatory management at Winchester. His Aunt America warned:

> John Moses, I wish you'd give up these trips back East. Do you suppose the men you meet back there want to give you all this money you bring home – thousands and thousands of dollars? No sir, John Moses! They'll poison you sooner or later – mark my word![33]

Aunt America wasn't far off the mark. It was a dispute over money which eventually broke up the long and productive partnership between Browning and Winchester. As John got to know his own worth, he not unreasonably wanted royalties from the vast sales of his guns. Browning's fame as an inventor had spread far and wide, and other companies were willing to enter into royalty agreements with him over his pistols. No longer wet behind the ears, Browning knew the potential of his new semi-automatic shotgun design. Meanwhile Winchester had received complaints about the Model 1893 shotgun, invented by Browning, and found Browning unhelpful in modifying his original design to rectify the problem. William Mason and the other engineers had created a workaround so the gun would fire properly. Relations were strained, and stage was set for a confrontation.

When Tom Bennett was away on one of his beloved fishing trips, Browning took his new automatic gun to the patent department at Winchester, who immediately set about patenting it to the hilt.[34] But Tom never committed to manufacturing the gun, to Browning's annoyance, as he felt it was revolutionary. After letters went back and forth between Ogden and New Haven, in 1902 Browning decided to ask for a share of the profits in person:

> I woke up to the fact that I was boiling mad and had been too busy for some time to notice it. Something like one of those Yellowstone geysers that take a while to get hot enough to blow. So one day I grabbed my hat and told Matt I was going to New Haven. "I want to get some action on those automatic shotguns," I said. "Those fellows down there are stalling, and we're letting the best thing I ever made die in its sleep."[35]

It was not an auspicious meeting. Having done business for almost 20 years, Browning and Bennett knew one another well, though they were not friends, being from such very different backgrounds. Browning was no longer the wide-eyed Utah gunsmith in awe of the mighty Winchester management, and demanded Tom give him a share of the royalties from the new shotgun. Tom, always loath to set a financial precedent, refused in language which Browning recalled was "certainly not diplomatic." "The word royalty was to T. G. Bennett what a red flag is to a bull," [36] observed Edwin Pugsley, Winchester's chief engineer and a great admirer of Tom. It seems Tom feared that other inventors would also start to demand royalties from sales, thus denting Winchester's profits. As John Browning told the story to his son:

> Bennett is the most conservative of men and admittedly the automatic was something of an innovation. To put it simply, he was afraid of it, and so were the few men in his confidence. They were afraid it would take ten years to develop such a gun to the point where it would be a profitable manufacturing article.[37]

Browning stomped out of the New Haven factory without even a proper goodbye to Tom Bennett – not a "dignified parting" as John admitted, and 19 years of partnership crumbled into the dust of the Winchester factory floor. Browning took his invention to Remington, but as he was waiting to see the company president word came that the proprietor Mr Hartley had died suddenly of a heart attack. Unbeknownst to Browning, Hartley and Tom Bennett had already met and agreed that neither Winchester nor Remington would pay royalties for manufacturing rights to the automatic Browning designs. Browning charged out of Remington and stepped on a boat to Belgium. There the gunmakers Fabrique Nationale snapped up his invention. Meanwhile, Remington officials, ignoring the deceased Mr Hartley's agreement with Winchester, had spent a small fortune on cabling Browning repeatedly in Belgium, begging him not to sell the American rights to his gun to a rival company. The Mormon gunmaker at long last had the control Winchester refused to give him, and he made favorable deals with both Fabrique Nationale and Remington.

Owing to Tom's uncharacteristic yet far-reaching error of judgment, Winchester ceded the semi-automatic shotgun market to Remington and Browning and bid farewell to the most influential gun designer of the age. Not that Winchester was conceding a mistake had been made. A letter to the company's salesmen from Winchester's headquarters in New Haven instructed them in the line to take with customers baffled by the high-profile split with the Brownings:

> It seemed to us at the end that they had got rather high priced, and we let them go [...] They had got to feel that they were the only people who could invent guns, that our suggestions as to what was needed by the public were of no value, and that they really were "the whole thing." [...] We shall be perfectly able to get along without the Brownings, and shall probably be better off without them than with them.[38]

A defensive statement. Surely the share of royalties from what would have been Winchester's first automatic shotgun would have been a fair price to pay for keeping Browning on board? But Tom did not have the benefit of hindsight, and may have worried that the new gun would hurt sales of one of the best performing Winchester lines at the time, the '97 shotgun. Edwin Pugsley joined Winchester in 1911, when "they were still feverishly trying to worm their way through the patent fence they had built around the (Browning) gun." The result was the Winchester M/11, New Haven's answer to the Browning semi-automatic shotgun, and "never a truly satisfactory arm."[39] T. C. Johnson wrote that the skill with which he and Winchester had created the automatic patents for Browning made it very difficult to make a gun that could compete.

During World War I, John Browning was back at the Winchester plant when the company was contracted by the US government to mass-produce Browning's Automatic Rifle. Patriotism – and the prospect of major profits for both Browning and Winchester – went some way towards healing the rift from 12 years earlier. Browning, asked about the split with Winchester, blamed Tom Bennett's decision to turn down the gunmaker's request for royalties. "Mr

Bennett would not even consider the new system, and wouldn't say
yea or nay. Just sat there with no comment and never changed his
expression at all." [40] John Browning never regretted his parting with
Winchester, and eventually died of a heart attack in 1926, at the
Fabrique Nationale d'Armes de Guerre factory in Liège, Belgium. A
plaque there reads, "while he was busily engaged at work death
overtook the greatest firearms inventor the world has even
known."[41]

Though Tom Bennett may have rued the day he parted company
with John Browning, these were still the boom years for Winchester.
Within the staff ranks in New Haven was yet another noteworthy
inventor of guns, Thomas Crossly Johnson, or Tommy, who took out
124 patents during his time with the company, and developed the
semi-automatic line.[42] After Browning's departure, Tom Bennett
himself took over the improvement of Winchester's single shot
rifles. A gifted engineer who had always tweaked rifles on the shop
floor, the loss of Browning actually gave Tom more room to
experiment.

Despite having misjudged the negotiation with John Browning,
Tom Bennett's judgment was almost always extremely shrewd when
it came to business matters. He thoroughly outmaneuvered the Colt
Patent Fire Arms Manufacturing Company, the rival Connecticut gun
manufacturing concern. In late 1882, Tom learned that Colt was
planning to muscle in on the repeating rifle market by developing a
lever action gun of its own. These developments in Hartford,
Connecticut, not far from Winchester's own New Haven factory,
were a cause for immediate concern – and retaliatory action was swift.
William Mason, he who so successfully modified the Browning rifles,
was told by Tom to start work on a single action revolver and a slide
action rifle. Through sleight of hand, Tom managed to convince the
Colt men that Winchester intended to produce both weapons, an act
of direct competition and a virtual declaration of corporate war. Colt
was intimidated by this boldness. Tom met with Major General
Franklin of Colt, and duly recorded in his diary that the two men
agreed "not to interfere in each other's Markets."[43] The Colt
company withdrew from the manufacture of lever action rifles, and
Winchester never made a pistol.

Further opportunities to eliminate competition presented them-selves in 1888, when the executors of the gunmaker Eli Whitney's estate sold the plant where the rifles had been produced and leased the patents for the guns. Winchester bought the plant and leased the patent rights, thus ridding the marketplace of a rival. The same year, Winchester acquired a 50 percent share in E. Remington and Sons of New York, another competitor. The Ilion-based company had been forced into receivership by its creditors, and Winchester, along with Remington's most important sales agent Marcellus Hartley, pur-chased the ailing firm.[44] After the sale, Remington no longer produced either ammunition or repeating rifles, clearing the way for yet more Winchester sales of both. What's more, Winchester could use Remington's sales agents in South America and Asia to flog even more guns abroad. Oliver Winchester would have been proud of such predatory behavior, which continued his own ferocious tradition of obliterating competitors.

As Tom was wheeling and dealing, either outsmarting or vacuuming up his opponents, the name of Winchester became steadily better known across the globe. This was chiefly thanks to adventures in the Ottoman Empire, and the fame of the repeating rifle led to an increase in foreign orders. Trade with China began in 1878, with an order for cartridges and muskets. The newly independent Republic of Haiti ordered $24,000's worth of guns and ammunition, and the Sultan of Morocco ordered 1,000 Model 1873 muskets and a million cartridges.[45] A delegation of Moorish gunsmiths from Morocco visited New Haven to watch the manufacture of their muskets, and learn about maintenance and repair. Their visit caused much consternation among the little-traveled citizens of New Haven, who objected to the Moroccans cooking food on open fires while wearing long flowing robes. Thomas Addis, Winchester's traveling salesman, had to convince his guests to wear conventional American clothing and persuade them that the Yankee food was clean and didn't need to be roasted in public. Visiting foreigners were given a tour of the Winchester facilities. The employees enjoyed giving names to the various areas, which must have seemed baffling to the guests. The warehouse used to store wood and steel supplies was known as the Klondike, because it was cold in winter. The heat treating and forging shops were known as Hell, while the executive office building was nicknamed the Old Folks' Home, as people sat around and talked there rather than doing real manual work.

The atmosphere inside the Winchester factory was described as being "like one big, happy family," [46] according to B. W. Claridge who joined the company as shotshell superintendent. But gunmaking could be highly dangerous work, especially when mixing explosives. The primer used for cartridges was extremely volatile when it was dry and could explode. Edwin Pugsley, later Winchester's chief engineer, noted Tom's concern for employees handling high explosives:

> In the early days of handling priming mixtures, the chemistry was little understood and all plants had accidents [...] some of which resulted fatally to the operator. Mr Bennett always investigated these incidents personally [...] as a result of his intensive study, the Company was one of the earliest to pay attention to industrial accidents and a pioneer in safety-first work. [47]

Though long-handled hoes were used by the men mixing primer components on wooden floors, a fatal accident in the late 1880s killed two men and seriously burned four others. The superintendent of the primer department, described as "a man absolutely without fear," was killed along with a new man he was teaching to mix primer material. Tom Bennett was deeply troubled by the loss of life, and thought long and hard about a safer system for mixing primers. One morning, as he was standing in his bedroom, the answer presented itself:

> It came to me that mirrors were the answer. A heavy steel plate protected the mixer, as he would be working around the steel plate using a mirror to see the mixture and what he was doing. After this system was adopted, another explosion occurred, and of the three bystanders near the mixer, none, including the mixer, were hurt. [48]

In Tom Bennett's time as president of the company, the legend of the Winchester rifle was being cemented out West. This in turn sold yet more rifles across the nation. Endless free publicity was provided by the traveling Wild West show of Buffalo Bill, which featured the

Winchester rifle front and center. Buffalo Bill, or William F. Cody, was an icon of the Frontier, in all its adventure, violence, and romance. As a teenager Bill rode for the Pony Express, galloping from the Missouri River to the Pacific Coast in ten days to deliver the mail. The Express had advertised for "skinny, expert riders willing to risk death daily," which did nothing to deter Bill. He served in the Civil War, then became a civilian scout for the Army and took part in 16 fights with Native Americans, for which he was awarded the Medal of Honor.[49] Teddy Roosevelt regarded Buffalo Bill as one who "embodied those traits of courage, strength and self-reliant hardihood which are vital to the well-being of the nation."[50] Who better to capture the pioneer spirit of the Winchester rifle than one who had used it in action?

Buffalo Bill's Wild West show began in 1883 and continued until 1916, touring as far afield as Paris. The entertainment featured Winchester rifles, buffalo, cowboys, and the famed Native American leader Sitting Bull. "A Congress of American Indians, representing [. . .] characters and peculiarities of the wily dusky warriors in scenes from actual life giving their weird war dances and picturesque style of horsemanship," trumpeted the publicity. Winchester's 1875 catalogue featured a priceless testimonial from Buffalo Bill for the Model 1873 rifle:

> I have been using and have thoroughly tested your latest improved rifle. Allow me to say that I have tried and used nearly every kind of gun made in the United States, and for general hunting, or Indian fighting, I pronounce your improved Winchester the boss. An Indian will give more for one of your guns than any other gun he can get.

Buffalo Bill went on to recount how a foolhardy bear in the Black Hills tried to attack him:

> I am certain had I not been armed with one of your repeating rifles I would now be in the happy hunting grounds. The bear was not thirty feet from me when he charged, but before he could reach me I [put] more lead [in him] than he could comfortably digest.[51]

SITTING BULL AND BUFFALO BILL.
Copyrighted 1897.

D. F. BARRY,
WEST SUPERIOR,
WIS.

Fig. 9 Sitting Bull and Buffalo Bill, 1885.

One remarkable woman made it into Buffalo Bill's Wild West show. Annie Oakley, a renowned sharpshooter wielding a Winchester, was a star attraction. This Ohio markswoman once shot the cigarette out of the mouth of Crown Prince William, later Kaiser Wilhelm, of Germany. Queen Victoria, the Kaiser's relative, saw Annie perform. Native American chief Sitting Bull was so taken with Annie's prowess that he nicknamed her "Little Sure Shot." The cowboy kid, little Johnnie Baker, joined the show too, mounted on his fiery mustang, riding, roping, and shooting to the sound of whooping from the audience. Johnnie grew up in the saddle on a buffalo ranch in Western Nebraska, where battles with the Sioux Indians were a daily occurrence. He pestered Buffalo Bill for a chance to hold his horse's reins, and then for a part in the show. The very Winchester '73 which the cowboy kid graduated to in the Wild West show is now a sought-after piece of Americana. On his gravestone, the ace shot requested a simple title, "Foster son of William F. Cody."

The most famous battle of the Old West inevitably involved both Henry Rifles and a Winchester. The fatal 1881 gunfight at the O.K. Corral in the mining town of Tombstone, Arizona was provoked by riled-up cowboys seeking to get even with the law enforcement Earp brothers for going after an audacious set of stagecoach robbers. "Stormy as were the early days of Tombstone nothing ever occurred equal to the event of yesterday [...] the claim that precedes the storm burst in all its fury yesterday," recorded the *Tombstone Daily Epitaph* weightily.[52] Ike Clanton, a vengeful cowboy, was arrested for carrying his Winchester within the town limits, twirling his rifle all the while and threatening to shoot Marshal Earp on sight. Soon afterwards, a group of armed cowboys strolled into the O.K. Corral and after being told "give up your arms or throw up your arms," a firefight ensued which left the aggressors floored, and the Earp brothers and Doc Holliday wounded but still standing. The *Tombstone Daily Epitaph* records the role of the Winchester's forerunner, as the writer finds a moral conclusion to a dramatic day:

> If the present lesson is not sufficient to teach the cow-boy element that they cannot come into the streets of Tombstone, in broad daylight, armed with six shooters and Henry Rifles to hunt down their victims, then the citizens will most assuredly take such steps to preserve the peace as will forever be a bar to such raids.

The bad guys were armed with Oliver Winchester's weapons – the good guys seem to have had Colts and Smith and Wesson revolvers.

Such was the cast of characters and battles which helped spread the fame of the Winchester and cement its place in the legend of the American West. The American genius for narrative flair was alive and well long before the days of the Hollywood studio – even before the frontier had closed, Buffalo Bill's show was celebrating and propagating the rugged pioneer account of how the West was won, with the Winchester rifle on set every night. Later, in the 20th century, cinema cemented the legend of the winning of the West, and the Winchester's leading role. John Wayne carried a Winchester in

Stagecoach, and twirled his rifle before charging the baddies as a retired lawman in *True Grit*. There was even a larger than life statue of John Wayne and his Winchester at the company factory in New Haven, as life imitated art. The rifle itself starred in *Winchester '73*, and immortalized the story about a rare variation of the Model 1873 which the company produced in 1875 to drive up sales. As the rifle barrels were tested when they came off the production line, the most accurate of each 1,000 were made into rifles and given an extra finish. The top of the barrel was engraved with "One of One Thousand" or "One of 1000." Sold for $100 each at the time, these are now priceless collector's items. In *Winchester '73*, the James Stewart law enforcement character wins a "One of 1000" rifle in a shooting match, only to have it stolen, and ultimately retrieved in a cliffhanger of a scene. The script is supposed to be based on the adventures of a real-life lawman, Henry N. Brown. The grateful citizens of Caldwell, Kansas presented Brown with an inscribed Model 1873 back in 1882, only to find that Brown turned in his badge, became an outlaw, and was caught robbing a bank. Brown wrote to his wife from jail, urging her to sell his possessions but "keep the Winchester."[53]

As Brown's story shows, the Winchester was beloved by sheriff and crook alike, and sometimes by the same person playing both roles. Then there's the role of the Winchester in the taming of the lawless Wild West. The infamous Dalton Gang, responsible for train robberies in the Indian Territory, decided to rob not one but two banks in Coffeyville, Kansas in October 1892. As the gang rode into town, hardware stores threw open their doors and encouraged people to help themselves to rifles and shotguns, including the lever action Winchester. An epic shoot-out ensued, as the late Chris Kyle vividly described in his book *American Gun*:

> Depending on the model and the caliber, the Winchesters the town was armed with fed as many as fifteen bullets through a round tube magazine into the breech. Pull down on the trigger guard, come back up with it, fire – even if most of these folks hadn't grown up around guns all their lives, they still would have no trouble learning how to fire the rifle in the heat of the battle [. . .] One by one, the Dalton boys were shot to pieces.[54]

As Kyle and his co-author William Doyle see it, the Coffeyville battle represented a climactic moment in the history of the American West:

> In deciding to stop the robbery, the citizens had drawn a big red line not in the sand, but across the West. The country was to be wild no more. Law and order would prevail. Not only were Americans taming the West, they were taming themselves.

Such episodes only heightened the fame – or notoriety – of the Winchester rifles. More than a million of the Model 1892 lever action repeater rifles were sold – everyone from Annie Oakley to Admiral Robert Peary on his trek to the North Pole had one. Admiral Peary declared:

> In facing the polar bears, in gathering a herd of musk-oxen with the least expenditure of time and priceless ammunition, and in securing the greatest number of walrus out of an infuriated herd in the least time, I desire nothing better than a Winchester Repeater.[55]

As game became more wary of human predators armed with Winchesters, the company produced a rifle which was more accurate over a longer range – the Model 1894, which became an instant classic. Over seven million were sold.[56]

The utility of the Winchester rifle out West was not lost on leaders of the African American community, who were facing a hostile climate in the aftermath of the Civil War and the abolition of slavery. The era of Reconstruction and the indignities of the Jim Crow laws was a dangerous one for blacks in the American South, who faced violence and even lynching from angry whites. African Americans could not rely on the State to guarantee their right to freedom, or their security. Ida B. Wells, the diminutive schoolteacher turned early Civil Rights activist, saw that African Americans from Florida to Kentucky were using Winchester rifles to defend themselves from lynch mobs. Wells articulated the importance of armed self-defense, declaring:

The lesson this teaches and which every Afro American should ponder well, is that the Winchester Rifle deserves a place of honor in every Black home. The more the Afro-American yields and cringes and begs, the more he is insulted, outraged and lynched.[57]

T. Thomas Fortune, who established *The Age* newspaper in New York, was a kindred spirit to Ida Wells, an activist for black civil rights who also endorsed armed self-defense. Following a new spate of lynchings, Fortune proclaimed angrily:

We have cringed and crawled long enough. I don't want anymore "good niggers." I want "bad niggers." It's the bad "nigger" with the Winchester who can defend his home and children and wife.[58]

And so we can see that the Winchester rifle was a necessity for so many – from African Americans under siege, to settlers out West and the big game trophy hunters. The most high-profile celebrity endorser Winchester ever had was undoubtedly one Theodore Roosevelt, America's youngest president, famed big game hunter, and legendary outdoorsman. Following his wife's death immediately after she gave birth, the distraught Teddy went West and found a new calling as a rancher in the badlands of Dakota territory. There he fell in love with the Winchester 1876. "It is as handy to carry, whether on foot or on horseback, and comes up to the shoulder as readily as a shotgun,"[59] Teddy pronounced. Deer, antelope, sheep, elk, and even bear were felled by Teddy's rifle. "The Winchester is by all odds the best weapon I ever had, and I now use it almost exclusively, having killed every kind of game with it, from a grizzly bear to a big-horn," he wrote happily. As if that were not enough ringing praise, he continued in the same vein:

the Winchester is the best gun for any game to be found in the United States, for it is deadly, accurate, and handy as any, stands very rough useage, and is unapproachable for the rapidity of its fire and the facility with which it is loaded.

Fig. 10 Teddy Roosevelt and his Winchester Model 1876 rifle.

Oliver Winchester could not have put it better himself. Teddy's 1885 memoir *Hunting Trips of a Ranchman* was a fine example of priceless Winchester product placement. Teddy in photos from his Western period is captured posing in a fringed suede jacket, Winchester in hand, every inch the fearless frontiersman. The Winchester was crucial in the future president's image-making – the frail child from the East had been transformed into a bagger of big game.

Teddy used his Winchester on the ranch – and to capture desperadoes in the wilderness in 1866. The Western experience helped Teddy recover from his loss, and he returned to the East, re-entering politics, leading the Rough Riders during the Spanish–American war in Cuba (with his Winchester Model 95),[60] and becoming president after the assassination of McKinley in 1901. President Roosevelt was a regular – and somewhat trying – correspondent with the Winchester Repeating Arms Company as he planned a hunting trip to Africa with his son Kermit in 1908. The pair were gathering specimens for the Smithsonian Institution, and the President seems to have spent a good portion of his last year in office considering whether to take Winchester rifles on the trip.

On June 16, 1908, the President's secretary William Loeb, Jr, wrote to the Winchester Repeating Arms Company:

> The President is going to Africa with his son a year hence. He probably has all the rifles he needs, but his son has not. Before deciding what he will buy, the President would like to see your catalog, his idea being to give his son – one a high powered small caliber rifle [...] the other a very much more powerful rifle, such as he could use for buffalo, rhinoceros and even elephant. Will you send your catalog to the President at Oyster Bay where he will arrive Saturday next?

This was the beginning of the correspondence between the White House and the Winchester company, in which Roosevelt personally dictated many of the letters. The President was not an easy pen pal: he got very upset over small details about guns and ammunition, when in fact he was frequently responsible for the confusion. Teddy's questions were also difficult to answer. Here he is, musing over whether to take his beloved .45–70 Winchester Model 86 into the wilderness:

> This is the rifle I used in Louisiana last year, and which both son Ted and Dr Lambert used on killing moose in Canada. We all of us used soft-nosed bullets, and certainly for moose and black bear it is so efficient that I am going to take it to Africa for use, altho I have been warned that the gun is not right for African game. I am rather inclined to doubt this [...] Have you any data which would show how this .45–70 would do on African buffalo and rhino, for instance [...] I do not want to use any one of our American guns for any game for which it is unsuited, because there will be a good deal of attention attracted to my trip, and I want to be sure that it comes out all right.[61]

The Winchester company doubted that Teddy's trusty Model 86 would do the trick against rhino and elephants. Instead, it was decided that Teddy would take two Model 95 rifles. The President was once again worried about how the rifles would perform.

As you know, I have always used your rifles and I am using them now instead of the English rifles which my English friends are giving to me, because it is a matter of pride with me to use an American rifle. Now I don't want to have any slip up. A friend of mine [...] has been using your .405 in Africa for elephant, rhinoceros, buffalo and lion. He found it worked well except that twice the cartridges jammed (once with a lion). Now do try these guns you are to send me for my son and myself so as to be sure that they will not jam.[62]

Winchester Bennett, Oliver's grandson, and son of T. G. Bennett, took charge of the correspondence with the difficult-to-please President. By late August 1908 the holidaying leader of the free world wanted to try out his new guns, even though they weren't ready. Temporary stocks were fitted to the rifles, and they were duly rushed to Oyster Bay, the Roosevelt summer residence on Long Island, New York. The company received a furious letter from Teddy:

I am really annoyed at the shape in which you sent out those rifles. I return them to you [...] It was entirely useless to send them out to me in such shape [...] I cannot see what excuse there was, when I had already sent you the rifles as models, for you to send me rear sights such as there are on the three guns you sent me [...] I am naturally a little unsettled by the extraordinary failure in the matter of the rear sights.[63]

Poor Winchester Bennett had to write and apologize profusely, explaining once again that the sights were only temporary since the ones Roosevelt wanted were being made to order. Late in November, after more back and forth, three new Model 95 rifles were delivered to the White House, two .405s and a '06. This time Roosevelt was delighted. "The rifles have come. They are beautiful weapons and I am confident will do well." [64]

A week later, Roosevelt had more demands:

I cannot say how much I like those two .405 rifles [...] my belief is that in Africa those will be the two rifles my son and I will habitually carry in our own hands; the rifles upon which we will most depend. As this is so, I think I should like to have you make me a third rifle [...] Could you make me a duplicate of these two rifles in time for me to take it out to Africa next March? [...] If I cabled you from Nairobi, how long would it take you to get me out extra cartridges for the rifles? Have you heard if those cartridges that you sent arrived in Mombasa yet?[65]

The demanding President knew how prestigious it was for Winchester to supply his rifles and ammunition for the Africa trip. Yet the company felt awkward about advertising its role, knowing the White House would not take kindly to being used as free publicity. However, word had spread and Winchester was being bombarded by requests for information. An agonized letter was sent from New Haven to Teddy's secretary, William Loeb, Jr:

We have been overwhelmed of late by requests from representatives of the press and individuals for descriptions of the Winchester rifles and ballistic data of the cartridges which it is understood the President is to use on his coming African trip. Not knowing whether the President would care to have his equipment exploited, we have refrained from admitting that we have made any guns especially for his [...] trip [...] Naturally we would like very much to be in a position to state frankly that the President is planning to use our product and, if agreeable to him, we would appreciate the courtesy deeply if we may be permitted [...] to state that the President will use Winchester Repeating Rifles and Winchester Ammunition on his forthcoming African Hunting and Collecting trip.[66]

Loeb replied by return, saying "the President would not want the matter used in any way as an advertisement, but there is no objection whatever to your stating in answer to queries that the President will have your guns on the trip."

Henry Brewer, superintendent of the cartridge shop, recorded how this instruction came as a blow to William Clark, Winchester's advertising manager. "It almost broke his heart not to be able to use the President's name." However, the canny Clark obeyed the letter of the instructions from the White House, while undermining the spirit, with a full-page advertisement in the monthly magazines and newspapers just as the President sailed for Africa. As Brewer described the ad, it was "a map of South Africa with a hand thrust through the map from the rear holding a Winchester rifle, the shadow of which fell directly across the central part of Africa. Beneath the picture was a caption in large letters, 'COMING EVENTS CAST THEIR SHADOWS.'" Tom Bennett was not impressed by this clear violation of the understanding with the President, and wrote apologetically to Teddy. Fortunately, "the President did not seem to be a bit annoyed – in fact loving publicity as he did, he seemed to be rather amused and tickled with the situation, and his letter to Mr Bennett was in no way critical." [67]

Teddy, his son Kermit, their Winchester rifles, and an avid group of collectors sailed from New York to what was then British East Africa on March 23, 1909. The party spent almost 11 months hunting big game, bringing back nearly 5,000 mammal specimens as well as assorted birds, fish, and other objects of interest that defied a brief description. [68]

William Clark need not have lost sleep over what he feared were squandered opportunities to capitalize on the association with the President's Africa hunting trip. Roosevelt helpfully wrote a book about his exploits called *African Game Hunting*, with numerous mentions of his Winchesters. For example, "The Winchester did admirably with lions, giraffes, elands, and smaller game." Hunting game on the Kapiti Plains, Teddy took aim at:

> the tawny, galloping form of a big, maneless lion. Crack! The Winchester spoke; and as the soft-nosed bullet ploughed forward through his flank the lion swerved so that I missed him with the second shot; but my third bullet went through the spine and forward into his chest.

Teddy vanquished more lions with his Winchester, and as Brewer noted, "his book was full of references and praises of the Winchester

Fig. 11 Winchester ammunition for Teddy Roosevelt's Roosevelt-Smithsonian Africa expedition, 1909.

rifles, so that we got a large amount of favorable free advertising from it, which of course was much more valuable to the Company than (any) paid advertisement."[69] Teddy Roosevelt used the Winchester twice in his own image-making, first to help create the legend of the brave frontiersman, and then to cement his status as a fearless hunter of big game. For the thousands of Americans who could only dream of hunting lions and rhino, Teddy's exploits inspired them to buy hunting rifles and enjoy target shooting, increasing Winchester's sales handily. The President and the Repeating Arms Company basked in one another's reflected glory, each benefiting greatly from the association with the other.

Even if the enthusiastic public couldn't emulate Teddy and Kermit Roosevelt by sailing to Africa to hunt, regular folk could attend shooting matches and tournaments across America, which were further venues for advertising the prowess of the Winchester brand.

Whereas at first Winchester only provided free ammunition for superior shooters using their rifles at these events, before long it was clearly in the company's interests to employ full-time marksmen to travel the country, competing under the Winchester name. Enter the Topperweins, a husband and wife sharpshooting team, who burnished the Winchester legend with their exploits.

Adolph Topperwein, son of a German gunsmith, grew up to become an exhibition shooter for Winchester. He found true love with one Elizabeth Servaty, then employed in the ammunition loading room at the Winchester factory in New Haven. The new Mrs Topperwein turned out to be an outstanding markswoman, even though she had never fired a weapon before meeting Adolph. Mrs Topperwein was known as Plinky, because when she was learning to shoot she'd say, "Throw up another one and I'll plink it."[70] Plinky created a world record at the 1904 World's Fair in St Louis by breaking 967 clay targets out of a possible 1,000 at trap shooting.

From then on Winchester arranged for the Topperweins to travel as a team, which they did until their retirement in 1940. Adolph, or Ad, could shoot backwards while lying down and using a mirror to see his target – while Plinky once fired for five hours solid, using a pump gun. The skin blistered and came off her hand, as the loyal Plinky advertised the name of Winchester far and wide. As a woman in a man's world, Plinky was a fine advert for Winchester, which could see the benefit of her sales pitch to the women of the frontier.

In the Winchester company house journal, Mrs Topperwein duly declared that every woman should learn to shoot:

> It gives you confidence and satisfaction to know that you can if necessary defend yourself [...] Not only should a woman learn to handle firearms for protection, but shooting is the greatest of all sports and healthful, because it takes you outdoors and close to nature. There is also a wonderful satisfaction in knowing that you can do something besides knitting, that you can play what is known as a man's game.[71]

Ad Topperwein once shot for eight hours a day, for ten days in a row, shooting at 72,000 bricks and missing only nine. But the strain of it drove him almost insane, according to a friend. "His muscles and nerves were in painful knots. At night he had horrible dreams: the blocks would be a mile away, the bullets wouldn't come out of the end of the gun."[72] Such was the cost of myth-making on behalf of the Winchester Repeating Arms Company.

For Tom Bennett, not a natural showman himself, the larger-than-life personalities of Teddy Roosevelt, the Topperweins, and others were wonderful publicity, as the Winchester Repeating Arms Company continued to grow. Rifles were flying out of the New Haven factory doors. In the first year of the 20th century, sales worth over $5 million were recorded, with profits of more than $1.1 million, or 23.39 percent of the sales.[73] By today's standards, Winchester was making a profit of some $28 million annually – a fortune whichever way you look at it.

Nothing was allowed to stand in the way of increasing profits. In August 1902 a week-long strike by the trolley car men in New Haven made it impossible for many of the Winchester factory employees to get to work. The company management promptly arranged with the train company for special trains to be run from West Haven to New Haven, packed with gun shop workers. Tom took a keen interest in all the details of the business, from the transportation of his workers to the guns they were making. Before a new gun was put on the market, he would carefully scrutinize it, take it to pieces, reassemble it, fire it, and suggest changes to reduce the cost of manufacturing or to make it a better weapon. A great deal of Tom's time was spent in the gun shop, so he could be close to his men and familiar with their work.

As the company went from strength to strength at the turn of the 20th century, domestic affairs occupied much of Tom's time. Helped by the soaring Winchester profits, he and his wife Jennie embarked upon an ambitious project: following Oliver and Jane's example, they built their own superb brick residence on Prospect Street, New Haven, complete with a dominant sun dial. The noted New York firm of architects McKim, Mead and White was engaged to design the new Bennett house, while no less a figure than Frederick Law Olmsted, landscaper of New York's Central Park, planned the gardens – including a greenhouse devoted to growing orchids, surrounded by pear trees. In fact, there were numerous greenhouses

– growing roses, carnations, and tropical plants of all kinds. The expansive planting plans Olmstead drew up for Jennie, the lady of the house, are a fascinating read for this novice gardener, who is left quite green with envy by the scale of her great-great-grandmother's private botanical gardens. Endless beds were designed with exquisite care, heaving with magnolias, rhododendrons, lily of the valley, honeysuckle, hydrangeas, and viburnums.

ARMORY of the WINCHESTER REPEATING ARMS CO.
NEW HAVEN, CONN., U.S.A.

WINCHESTER REPEATING ARMS CO., NEW HAVEN CONN., U.S.A.

Fig. 12 Engravings of the Winchester Repeating Arms Company.

Tom oversaw the construction of the mansion closely, being an engineer by training and a manufacturer by trade, and found much to complain about – from the leaking chimneys to the shoddy work on the conservatory doors and the faulty though supposedly state-of-the-art heating system. Jennie found the muck accumulated by the builders to be most distasteful, and also complained vociferously. Frederick Olmsted's plan for an elegant pergola in the garden was scaled back, as Tom and Jennie insisted they would spend no more than $12,000 on that particular project.[74] Much time was spent with the great landscape designer discussing the finer points of the pergola's lattice work, its interplay with the brick of the house, circulation of air through said pergola, and whether it would work best as a regular double colonnade. Good decisions were made by all, and the resulting mansion was widely admired by local society writers as "one of the most palatial residences in New Haven." When the Bennett family threw a wedding party for their son Winchester and his new wife Susan on April 25, 1903, it was written up with great gusto for all to read and pore over the fine details. The event

> was characterized by a quiet refinement that made it one of the most enjoyable functions of the season. The spacious rooms were decorated with palms, asparagus ferns and bouquets of cut flowers [...] So perfectly planned is the Bennett mansion for social festivities that the hundreds of guests who came and went during the evening hardly realized how immediate was the throng that offered their congratulations to the bride and bridegroom.[75]

At that crowded wedding party, watching her brother marry, was Tom's daughter Anne Hope Bennett, who also lived graciously in an architecturally distinguished home on Prospect Street. Anne never married, and devoted her energies to prominently supporting the Church and the arts. Given her wealth, it's hard to imagine that Anne lacked suitors. Perhaps domesticity was not for her, and she preferred the independent life enabled by her money and standing? Like her sister-in-law Susan, Win's wife, Anne was painted elegantly by the society portraitist Cecilia Beaux. She frequently organized dinners, brunches, and receptions at her home for musicians, artists,

Fig. 13 Thomas Gray Bennett's home in Prospect St, New Haven, *c.*1905.

and friends in the clergy. Sacred art and music were very dear to Anne, and her chief philanthropic cause was attempting to cure sickness in New Haven. Inspired by the generous example of her grandfather Oliver, who was a member of New Haven's Board of Associated Charities from 1878, Anne was prone to giving the "ostentatiously dramatic gift if it could inspire donors to give as well."[76] She gave generously to New Haven's Christ Church, Center Church, the Church of the Redeemer, St. John's Episcopal Church, and the Berkeley Divinity School at Yale University.

In March 1910 the paterfamilias Tom Bennett reached his 65th birthday, and was about to celebrate the milestone of 40 years with Winchester. He wished to retire from his position as company president, in order to enjoy time with Jennie and their children at both their gracious new home on Prospect Street and at Islewood on Johnson's Point, where Tom was looking forward to sailing and fishing peacefully. His health was failing – he suffered from high blood pressure and heart problems, and had been spending time at a hotel spa in Germany receiving treatment from an eminent doctor. The cost of bottled water there – two marks – infuriated the frugal industrialist, who fulminated about the expense in letters home. Being unwell gave Tom time to reflect upon his priorities.

The minutiae of life, the great man decided, were becoming tiresome. What he wanted more than anything was to spend his remaining time with his great love Jennie Bennett, in whose honor he named the Bennett family pleasure boat *ENAJ* (Jane spelt backwards). As Tom wrote to Jennie when she was on one of her many trips to Europe, seeing the cultural sights of the Old World:

> When you get back let's sink the housekeeping and the flowers, coupons, bank deposits, and LIVE instead of wading around in a morass of perplexities and accounts. When I stop to consider the short time that is left me, I'm impressed with the foolishness of our little lives. How shall we mend them for things worth having.[77]

Jennie's love was most certainly worth having and cherishing. Whilst recuperating, Tom was thrown by a letter he received from his wife, questioning whether she had been good enough to her nearest and dearest over the years.

> I don't like you to write of your not having been good to your mother and to me, certainly not to me. You have probably helped me to all I am, and to my record, which should have been a more distinguished and better one, the aid being what it was. No one could have been better to me, or more necessary [...] It makes me feel how lacking I must have undoubtedly been in outward recognition of all my life debt to you.[78]

Tom was determined to pursue a quieter life, and reluctantly, the board of Winchester agreed he should step down, provided he retain a more important position than merely a director of the firm. A new role of consultant director was created, to which Tom was duly elected. The board took the opportunity to express "its deep appreciation of the inestimable value of his services to the Company, whose business during the period of his incumbency has more than quadrupled."[79] Tom's son Winchester Bennett was elevated to the position of first vice-president and George E.

Fig. 14 Thomas Gray Bennett, great-great grandfather of the author.

Hodson became president. However, Winchester Bennett, grandson of the company's founder, closely advised by his father, was undoubtedly the most influential figure.

Despite such meticulous forward planning, turbulent world events and a weaker third generation of family leadership collided to undermine the foundations of the company built so carefully by Oliver Winchester and Tom Bennett. At the time of his promotion to first vice-president, Winchester Bennett was in his early 30s. A diligent, intelligent, but highly strung individual, he had never thrived as a child and was frequently ill as an adult. His parents Tom and Hannah Jane were in a state of constant anxiety about their heir, as was his watchful wife Susan. Winchester was steeped in the family tradition, but he suffered from recurring illnesses and what was euphemistically called nervous anxiety throughout his life, making him ill suited to assume a key role in the company just as World War I was looming. While one might reasonably assume that the war would only have increased the profits of an arms manufacturer, it was not quite so straightforward as that. The bloody conflict which engulfed

Europe and dragged in the United States irrevocably damaged the Winchester Repeating Arms Company.

Here, though, we will take a detour from the drumbeat of the approaching war, and begin to consider the strange case of Sarah Winchester, daughter-in-law of Oliver Winchester and sister-in-law of Tom Bennett. The finances of the Winchester Repeating Arms Company were kept firmly in the control of the family, with the Winchesters and the Bennetts owning the majority of the stock. Of the 10,000 shares of common stock, Oliver Winchester at the time of his death in 1880 had left 4,000 shares in trust for his wife, who already had 475 shares of her own. After the death of Mrs Oliver Winchester, her trust was divided between her daughter Jennie (Mrs Thomas Gray Bennett) and her daughter-in-law Sarah Winchester, widow of Oliver's son William Wirt Winchester. As of 1904, Mrs T. G. Bennett owned 2,875 shares, Mrs William Wirt Winchester 2,777 shares, T. G. Bennett 32 shares, and Winchester Bennett 6 shares – so the family owned 5,690 shares out of a total of 10,000.[80]

To ward off predatory buyers, a Winchester Purchasing Company was formed in 1905 to ensure that no outsider could gain control of the Winchester Repeating Arms Company via secret purchases of stock. Family members and minority shareholders deposited 5,025 shares of stock with the Winchester Purchasing Company and Tom Bennett voted on behalf of the new entity at stockholder meetings. Healthy dividends on the stock were paid annually, and the women of the family were wealthy beyond measure. Sarah Winchester, grieving for her dead husband and child, left New Haven for California where she, her history, and her money became the subject of fascination, rumor, and intrigue.

CHAPTER 4

Lady of Mystery

T HE MOST UNOBSERVANT of visitors to the sunny Santa Clara Valley in California cannot fail to miss the billboards, enticingly inviting the unwary to visit the Winchester Mystery House. The casual driver will pass by endless shopping malls, gas stations, and Starbucks, a vista enlivened by the occasional palm tree, before ending up in a vast parking lot outside the peculiar red-roofed mansion built by Sarah Winchester, widow of Oliver Winchester's son William Wirt, and heiress to a substantial fortune. A bronze plaque at the entrance to this 160-room curiosity proclaims:

> Mrs Winchester was convinced by an occultist that the lives of her husband and daughter had been taken by the spirits of those killed by 'The Gun That Won The West' and that she too would share their fate unless she would begin building a mansion for the spirits on which work could never stop, nor be completed. She was promised life for as long as she kept building. So with $1000 a day with royalties from the Winchester Rifle Fortune, the sounds of the carpenters' tools could be heard 24 hours a day for almost 38 years as the diminutive lady built to live.

Therein lies the legend of Sarah Winchester, kept alive by our own obsession with the unknown. Sarah was a rather more nuanced character than her Mystery House caricature suggests. Fact and fiction have become entwined over the decades, as the truth recedes into the distant past, and the handful of people who knew the real Sarah have vanished like ghosts at cockcrow. Those who defend the myth of Sarah say that if the stories aren't true, it seems odd that none of her relatives or former employees ever came forward to contradict the wild tales told about her. As we'll see, those who knew Sarah did try to correct the record once her memory was being traduced. But their timid voices were too muted to be heard, and were drowned out by the cacophonous row of rumors and half-truths.

Sarah Winchester was fabulously rich, of that there is no doubt. She was born Sarah Pardee in September 1839, one of four sisters and one son in a wealthy New Haven family. This well-born child grew up to marry the catch of the city, William Wirt Winchester. Sarah's older sister Mary married William Converse, who worked for the Pardee family, and eventually became president of the Winchester Repeating Arms Company, in sad circumstances. Sarah was clever, thoughtful, and accomplished in music and languages. Daughter of a carriage manufacturer, Leonard Pardee, Sarah had the means to enter New England society, and was known as the "Belle of New Haven." A photographic portrait from her youth shows her posing in a long gown engulfing her slight figure, her brown hair framing a delicate, intelligent, slightly pensive face. Sarah's expression is enigmatic – is she shy or withholding, subtly engaging us or withdrawing? Later in life, she withdrew from the public gaze almost entirely – but in 19th-century New England, a well-connected young lady was expected to pose for the camera lens, so posterity could record her status, and young Sarah obliged.

It is easy to see why William was charmed by Sarah – and why her parents would be so pleased with their daughter's choice of husband. William was the only surviving son of Oliver Winchester, the successful shirtmaker who was just beginning to invest in manu-facturing rifles when William and Sarah married in 1862, in New Haven. Sarah's father, Leonard, was one of the investors in Oliver Winchester's new concern. William managed operations at the shirt factory before moving into the rifle business. The young couple initially lived with Oliver and his wife Jane in their series of ever more spacious abodes, Oliver's living quarters reflecting his rise up the ladder. Sarah was thrilled to become a mother to her baby daughter Annie Pardee Winchester in 1866, but the infant failed to thrive and died of malnutrition after only a few weeks. Sarah sunk into a deep

Fig. 15 Sarah Winchester as a young woman.

and damaging depression, and was inconsolable after Annie's death. She and William had no more children. Life's upward trajectory had stalled, and the sensitive Sarah took refuge in her sadness. William was a great comfort to his wife – also a gentle soul, he shared her overwhelming grief and understood her need for solace.

Oliver Winchester died in 1880, believing the Winchester Repeating Arms Company would be inherited and run by his son William, now vice-president of the family concern. Oliver left a hefty fortune to his heirs – $500,000 to be divided up between his son and daughter upon the death of his widow. Oliver's best-laid plans were never realized, for William became ill almost as soon as his father died – doctors believed he had gastric trouble, and failed to diagnose the consumption eating away at his lungs. Once it became clear that he had pulmonary consumption, or tuberculosis, an exhausted and debilitated William moved to New York for treatment, taking up rooms at the Windsor Hotel. Sarah was horrified. Not only had her daughter perished, but now her young husband was dying too. The *New York Times* reported of William's final journey: "On Saturday last he returned to New Haven, remarking to the conductor of the train, in passing the usual compliments of old acquaintanceship, that he was taking his last trip. He lingered until Monday evening. He was 44 years of age."[1]

For the second time in 15 years, Sarah was smothered by grief's suffocating rituals. William's funeral was held at Oliver's splendid home on Prospect Street, up the hill above the Winchester factory. His remains lay in a cedar casket covered with cloth and velvet, with a collection of orchids from Oliver's magnificent conservatory mounted on top, next to a cross. Sarah stood in her black mourning clothes, staring at the floral tributes from friends and the large pillow embroidered with "peace," sent by Mr and Mrs Davies, the next door neighbors and close family friends from Oliver's days in the shirt business. New Haven's prominent citizens had turned out in force to pay their respects, only months after mourning Oliver. All the orchids and violets in the world could not make up for the loss of Sarah's comforter in chief. She could only listen tearfully as the Reverend Mr Samson praised William's fine character at the Calvary Baptist church service. Newspaper obituaries echoed the eulogy:

> He was in the true sense of the term a gentleman, tender of the feelings of others, generous to a fault, with a nice sense of humor [...] He was of a retiring nature and averse to filling public office or position, which he might easily have obtained had he desired it. He was highly esteemed in all the relations of life. A wife mourns a tender, loving husband.[2]

A wife mourns a husband, and a baby daughter. New Haven represented death to Sarah – and grieving. Misery had brought her money: Sarah inherited 777 shares of Winchester stock from William, which paid her an annual income of $43,335. William also left her shares in the New Haven water company, the New York, New Haven and Hartford Railroad Company, and the West Shore and Whitney Avenue Railroads too. Sarah stood to inherit another 2,777 Winchester shares when her mother-in-law Jane died – riches beyond measure, which newspapers regularly tried to quantify, reporting that Sarah was worth $20 million. Yet the cash was no compensation for her devastating loss. Sarah's distress at her double bereavement made her easy prey for the myth-makers. "It is said, she ultimately sought help from a spiritualist," reads the guidebook sold at the Winchester Mystery House, without specific attribution:

> According to some sources, the Boston medium consulted by Mrs Winchester explained that her family and her fortune were being haunted by spirits – in fact by the spirits of American Indians, Civil War soldiers, and others killed by Winchester rifles. Supposedly, the untimely deaths of her daughter and husband were caused by these spirits, and it was implied that Mrs Winchester might be the next victim. However, the medium also claimed there was an alternative. Mrs Winchester was instructed to move West and appease the spirits by building a great house for them. As long as construction of the house never ceased, Mrs Winchester could rest assured that her life was not in danger.[3]

Guides to Sarah's labyrinthine house play up her unbearable grief over the deaths of her husband and daughter, suggesting that this drove her to consult a Boston psychic, who informed her she was being punished for her association with "The Gun That Won The West." Yet evidence of Sarah having consulted a medium in Boston is thin on the ground. Ralph Rambo was the nephew of Edward Rambo, the West Coast agent for the Winchester Repeating Arms Company and a financial advisor to Sarah who frequently visited her in the unwieldy California mansion. Thus, although his information is second hand, Ralph Rambo is one of the better sources on Sarah's demeanor and activities. Of her supposed visit to a spiritualist and subsequent move West, Rambo writes: "Doctors and friends urged her to leave the East, seek a milder climate and search for some all consuming hobby. One physician did suggest that she 'build a house and don't employ an architect.'"[4] Rambo notes that Sara was visited by Mary Baker Eddy:[5] significance unknown, as he puts it. Mary Baker Eddy was a Christian Scientist and founder of the Church of Christ, Scientist. She was said to have been a spiritualist and medium in Boston before becoming a Christian Scientist,[6] which is the one tenuous link between Sarah and the occult, and could at least explain why Sarah is thought to have visited Boston.

Raised an Episcopalian, with a husband buried by a Baptist minister, Sarah had no obvious spiritualist pedigree – and her devoted companion of many years, Miss Henrietta Severs, always firmly denied the rumors about Sarah's spiritualist leanings. Yet now it is seemingly accepted as fact that Sarah visited the Boston medium Adam Coons. Take this "description" of the encounter by Susy Smith, author of *E.S.P. for the Millions*, *World of the Strange*, and similar titles:

> "Your husband is here," the medium said, and gave a description of William Wirt Winchester that was startling in its exactness. "He is standing right beside you, can't you see him?" "Oh, if only I could," Sarah moaned. She had gone to this medium anonymously. How could he know she had just lost her husband and what he looked like?[7]

How indeed?

Poor Sarah. Her grief, her solitude, and her gun millions amounted to an irresistible license for gossips down the ages to invent the most lurid of stories, now passed on as the unvarnished truth. An effective demolition of the many and varied tales of Sarah's life was written by a San Jose student in the early 1950s, who had grown up with the myth and decided to write a probing doctoral thesis on the topic. Bruce Spoon concluded:

> legend moves through the element, time, much as the party game where some sentence is whispered around a circle of guests only to appear completely changed. In the case of Sarah Winchester it is carried either involuntarily and unconsciously by those individuals who pass it on verbally and change it so as to make themselves more important with the sensationalism of the exaggeration; or purposely by groups who stand to gain from the propagation of the legend.[8]

More than 60 years after that masterly summation, it is hard to improve upon it.

What we do know is that Sarah left New Haven and moved to the sunlit Pacific coast, arriving in the Santa Clara Valley in the mid-1880s. Sarah's sister Mary had died of cancer in October 1884, grief piling up upon unbearable grief. So Sarah's move was practical and therapeutic: she was leaving both the harsh New England winters and New Haven with its constant, searing memories of William and baby Annie firmly behind her. The widow of Sarah's coachman, who accompanied her from New Haven, told a reporter how Mrs Winchester grieved so much after her husband's death that her health was affected.[9] The sun-soaked Pacific coast was going to help her recover, far better than New Haven's climate. What's more, Sarah's sister Nettie had already moved to California with her husband Homer Sprague, a professor at a college in Oakland. As Mary Jo Ignoffo explains in her biography of Sarah, her other sisters Belle and Estelle headed for the West Coast too. The young widow would have family companionship in her new life, and her affairs in New Haven would be well looked after. Sarah's brother-in-law William Converse, grieving husband of her deceased sister Mary, had succeeded Sarah's dear William as president of the Winchester Repeating Arms Company. He and Sarah's other brother-in-law Tom Bennett would watch her stock in the Winchester company carefully.

According to the more extravagant stories about Sarah, in the years between William's death in 1881 and her move West, she toured Europe and the Orient seeking to immerse herself in learning more about the mysteries of the occult. Mediums in London, Paris, Berlin, and Rome supposedly became her friends, and in India she visited masters of Yogi. Once again, there is no evidence to support the melodramatic stories. Sarah did go to Europe after William's death, but of any travels further afield there is no trace. Sarah is also supposed to have received the news of both William and baby Annie's deaths during a New England thunderstorm – the storms apparently represented the ghosts of all the victims of the Winchester rifles seeking revenge. Sarah was told by the many and varied mediums she allegedly met on her purported travels that thunder and lightning would again visit her, and would succeed to take her too, unless she built for the spirits a final resting place.

Sarah's entry to the American West caused quite a stir, as seen through the eyes of Ralph Rambo, then a child:

> Our Valley was thrilled by this dramatic entrance of a millionairess; by those freight cars sidetracked in Santa Clara, unloading rich imported furnishings; by building activity that mushroomed an eight-room house into a 26 room mansion, in the first six months. Here was fair game for all! WE TALKED ABOUT MRS WINCHESTER! Gossip would be a more fitting word, gossip no-one claimed to like – but everyone enjoyed. Talk begat rumor and as the years passed and new towers and gables rose behind the six-foot hedge of Llanda Villa, the rumors grew to established legend.[10]

The wealthy widow moved into what was known as the Caldwell property, a modest house which she called Villa Llanda, on 6 acres of ground, some 4 miles from San Jose, then the county seat. Sarah had brought with her from New Haven a favorite servant, who was devoted to her and enjoyed carpentry as a hobby. One morning soon after Sarah's arrival, a crew of workmen arrived at the house. Here legend and fact almost cross over. The myth has it that the workmen never left, and worked around the clock building a sprawling mansion for the next 36 years, until Sarah's death in 1922. Actually, Sarah did briefly interrupt the building work – after the earthquake of 1906, and during a year-long trip she took when the rumors about her intentions became particularly hard to bear. But it is undoubtedly true that Sarah built, and built, and carried on building. Daughter of a carriage-maker and master carpenter, she had grown up surrounded by construction, and had lived in Oliver Winchester's flamboyant creation in New Haven. She was no stranger to large-scale building projects, and money was no barrier to her ambitions. It is almost as if Villa Llanda were her own life-size doll's house, which kept growing and growing.

Wagons rolled along the dusty roads from San Jose in the days before cars, carrying all manner of building materials. Freight cars from the East carried precious cargo of silks, linens, bric-a-brac, and furniture. Sarah's construction naturally caused great interest in what was then a rural area. Curious farmers came to watch what was going on – and the intensely private Sarah immediately ordered her gardeners to plant hedges and trees to shield her house from the road. That only set the tongues wagging further. A delegation of inquisitive neighborhood women, determined to make the first social call on their wealthy new addition, were given a sharp refusal, according to Ralph Rambo. The San Jose Chamber of Commerce asked permission to show off the almighty house to President Theodore Roosevelt, who was in the area, but they too were given the cold shoulder. Ralph Rambo recalls seeing the President drive right past Sarah's grand creation.[11] Sarah realized the outside world thought her a freak. As her mechanic Fred Larsen recalled, "She wasn't crazy [. . .] She was a plenty smart woman, and she had all these people pegged as plain busybodies."[12]

Before the carping chatterboxes cowed Sarah, she did entertain the young folk of the Santa Clara Valley in her beautiful haven. Ralph Rambo reported in 1967:

> Living today are senior citizens who still tell of parties in those incomparable gardens lush with acres of blooming flower-beds bordered with rare dwarf boxwood and shaded by imported ornamental trees and shrubs. They speak of the great mound called Strawberry Hill where maids served "French ice cream made from real cream."[13]

As one who had lost a daughter in infancy, Sarah was particularly fond of little girls, and allowed them to "romp through her gardens or, short legs dangling, to thump her rosewood grand piano in the Great Ball Room while their little audience of one sat and beamed."[14]

Before too long the neighborhood busybodies had a lot to talk about. Sarah's eight-story house soared into the sky, with cupolas atop turrets, looking like nothing anyone had ever seen before. The style was Italianate, in the broadest sense of the term. "Weird and eerie, strange as a dream and fantastic as a fairy tale [. . .] bristling with turrets, gables and roofs [. . .] the queerest house, surely, that was ever built," was the verdict of Frank P. Faltersack, who wrote for a popular men's magazine.[15] "A pathetic five million dollar witness to a deranged mind" was another comment,[16] and "A mysterious combination of Paleozoic palace and Coney Island fun house" was one of the kinder descriptions.[17] "The house is like a problem in mathematics with faulty figures cropping up again and again confusing you until you can't be sure whether two and two are four or five. Inaccuracy abounds in this house. As architecture, it is untrue, improper and illogical,"[18] wrote a bemused journalist who toured the property soon after Sarah's death. Sarah never explained to her neighbors why she was building this ungainly colossus on their doorstep – and so they tried to come up with explanations of their own. It's really not surprising that the reclusive widow with the fortune made by the Winchester rifle, which had killed so many out West, was assumed to be building this weird structure because she was haunted by ghosts, guilt, and guns.

In 1895, reports Sarah's sympathetic biographer Mary Jo Ignoffo, the very first article linking the never-ending construction to Sarah's supposed superstitious beliefs appeared. "The belief exists when work of construction ends disaster will result, and it is rumored among the neighbors that this superstition has resulted in the construction of domes, turrets, cupolas and towers covering territory enough for a castle."[19] After that, practically every newspaper feature writer who made the pilgrimage to Sarah's folly repeated this assertion as fact. In the absence of any denial from Sarah herself, the myth was born and rapidly grew out of control.

The mansion is extraordinary even by today's standards of flamboyant ostentation – so just imagine what the neighbors must have thought back in the 19th century. No wonder they scratched their heads and tried to imagine what Sarah was up to, and what her motivation could possibly be. My favorite characterization comes from 1923, when a local newspaper writer described Llanda Villa as looking "a good deal like a half size Vendome hotel gone Cubist."[20] At Sarah's death, the sprawling mansion contained 160 rooms, 2,000 doors, 10,000 windows, 47 stairways, 47 fireplaces, 13 bathrooms, and 6 kitchens. There are skylights aplenty, a bell tower, and exquisite Louis Comfort Tiffany stained glass windows. The daisy is frequently featured in the stained glass panels – it appears to have been Sarah's favorite flower, and her dearest niece to whom she left a considerable amount of money was named Daisy.

Sarah was a woman of considerable style, who one can just imagine having her magnificent home featured in *Architectural Digest* today. Her fireplaces were decorated with Swedish tile and brass, the sinks were Italian porcelain with elegant inlay, silver chandeliers were from Germany, the walls and parquet floor in the Grand Ballroom were made of not one but six different hardwoods – mahogany, teak, maple, rosewood, oak, and white ash. Ornate, embossed Lincrusta wallpaper in more than two dozen different patterns was imported from England at what must have been considerable cost. Cargo ships sailed across the Atlantic laden with Sarah's fine household furnishings from Europe. When she died, a storeroom containing exquisite unused materials imported from Europe was valued at $25,000 – just looking at the rolls and rolls of Lincrusta wallpaper, crystal light fittings, elegant stained glass panels, and fireplace mantels, one can only marvel at the millions of dollars' worth of fine craftsmanship on display today. Sarah loved luxury: towards the end of her life, she was chauffeured around in a Pierce-Arrow motor car, upholstered in lavender and gold.

Observing this largesse, the obvious question is why did a single woman find it necessary to build such a luxurious, gigantic home for herself? There's no good answer, which partly explains why speculation has filled the void. It seems Sarah entertained hopes of her sisters and their families moving in with her, and so she planned separate quarters for them, though they never lived in them as she'd envisioned. More importantly, the project kept her busy and occupied. Sarah enjoyed design, and found it diverting to draw up the plans, which she did herself, despite her lack of architectural training. Her library was full of architectural textbooks and technical works, to assist this amateur builder with her works.

Choosing tiles, fabric, flooring, and so on gave Sarah a creative and artistic outlet, and diverted her from thoughts of William and baby Annie. The building clearly gave her a purpose and a focus, but she sometimes found it overwhelming, given her poor health. Sarah wrote to family in New Haven:

I hope some day to get so situated that I shall feel that it would not be an imposition on my friends to invite them to visit me [. . .] The house is very rambling, and to keep it properly warmed is a problem but I hope it will be solved before next winter. If I did not get so easily tired out, I should hurry things up more than I do, but I think it is better to "go slow" than to use myself up. Just having the furnace man here and going over all the details with him used me up completely for a day or so. But sometime, Jennie, I hope to get all straightened out so that I can say with confidence, I want you all to come and make me a long visit.[21]

One psychiatrist who visited the house back in the 1940s suggested Sarah's ceaseless construction was based on known behavior patterns:

Mrs Winchester suffered a great shock with the loss of her husband and child, so this house became the instinctive and symbolic expression of an unfulfilled desire, wherein every room represented the creation and presence of a child. Building is for a woman a maternal expression.[22]

Certainly, Sarah was still preoccupied by loss years after both her husband William and baby Annie had died. The death of her deeply loved mother-in-law Jane Winchester in 1898 caused Sarah great sadness, and seemed to revive memories of her earlier losses. As Jane's estate was divided up, Sarah wrote tentatively to her sister-in law Jennie Bennett, trying to get possession of portraits of her deceased parents-in-law Oliver and Jane:

When William presented his father with Mother's portrait and Mother with Father's, it was with the explicitly recognized under-standing that they should revert to him, so in this light, Mother's portrait has really been mine for a long time [. . .] I thought possibly Mother had forgotten it and I never felt like referring to it. I do not know whether it was ever mentioned to you, so thought, in case it had not been, or in case it had been and you had forgotten it, I would mention it, though the changes which give occasion for referring to these things are so unutterably sad that it pains me to do so.[23]

Thoughtful, precise, and kind even when melancholy, Sarah wrote after Jane Winchester's death to ask if silver items she had lovingly sent to her mother-in-law as Christmas and birthday presents could now become gifts to Jennie's children, Winchester, Ann, and Eugene:

> There is one thing which could be done in connection with the silver articles which would gratify me. I do not know if I recollect all the things but there was at least as follows: a crumb tray and scraper, a candlestick, a berry or bon-bon dish, a bread tray and vase [...] Now if sometime you would have some inscription placed on the articles, nothing would please me better than to know that thus inscribed they would be "heirlooms" for your children.

Feeling the loss of William's mother, her last link to her beloved husband, Sarah asks mournfully: "If not too painful for you, I wish you could sometime tell me how Mother was robed for burial and if her appearance was life-like."[24]

Despite this touching attachment to the Winchester family in New Haven, Sarah was strangely reclusive and unavailable to the relatives she spent so much time corresponding with. Although she thoughtfully gave engraved silverware to her nephew Winchester Bennett, when he and his new bride Susan tried to visit Sarah on their honeymoon trip to California, she refused to receive the young couple. Perhaps Sarah was overwhelmed by the prospect of seeing her dear husband's nephew. Or did she not want Winchester and Susan to see how she lived, fearing they would gossip about her back in Connecticut?

Burdened by sadness and frailty, with means and time at her disposal, Sarah continued to build and build. No expense was spared in the construction of Villa Llanda. Sarah bought the most expensive lumber, and would discard it if she found a knot in the wood. One of her carpenters told a reporter how Sarah would have the woodwork rubbed to a piano finish, and then if she decided it didn't fit her decorative scheme, out it came. As Sarah made mistakes, which she inevitably did given her amateur architect status, she simply demolished the rooms that didn't work, hid them with drapes, built over them, or left them undisguised. She provided plentiful work for the craftsmen of the Santa Clara Valley. Carpenters, plumbers, painters, tile-setters, and other workmen were employed as needed, some for years and years. One newspaper article described Sarah in pointed terms as "the Spirit Saver of the Carpenter's Union,"[25] since she employed so many carpenters. In letters to family back East, Sarah explained:

> For one reason and another since I started in to make alterations in my house I have not been able to get anything like settled [...] In the first place it is infinitely more difficult to get the work done than it would be in New Haven. I am constantly trying to make an upheaval for some reason.[26]

The centerpiece of Villa Llanda is the Grand Ballroom, where two art glass windows frame a brick fireplace, each decorated with a quote from William Shakespeare's plays. The quotes have been pored over by those seeking to discern Sarah's motivation in building her monumental home. One quote, "Wide unclasp the table of their thoughts," is from *Troilus and Cressida*. The other, "And these same thoughts people this little world," is from *Richard II*. The quotations have been used to suggest that Sarah was alluding to the spirits that were giving her building instructions! "By having seances every night, she may have felt she was opening the door to the thoughts and ideas of the spirits, and that in these thoughts, they took shape in the form of the rooms she built."[27] More likely, surely, is that Sarah, an educated, thoughtful woman who had been raised in New Haven reading Shakespeare and going to see the Bard's plays performed, was simply reflecting her love of literature. "Wide unclasp the table of their thoughts" in context is spoken by the sage Ulysses as part of a description of Cressida, after she's met leaders of the Greek Army. Though it sounds like an invitation to open one's mind to creativity, Ulysses means it as a put down to Cressida, whom he sees as intelligent and sluttish. As for Richard II and "these same thoughts people this little world," it's from Richard's soliloquy in prison, when he is approaching death, and is playing with the notion of thoughts contented and tormenting – a condition familiar to Sarah, who lived with loss and longing thoughts about her former happiness.

Plays were important to Sarah, and she invited local theater groups to perform in the Grand Ballroom, beneath those Shakespeare quotes. Sarah's French maid attended productions in San Jose on her night off, and reported back to her mistress on worthwhile performances. According to Leo Sullivan, an orchestra leader in San Jose, the players were invited to perform excerpts from the play in the Grand Ballroom setting after midnight, for which they were generously rewarded by their grateful hostess.[28]

A patron of the arts, and a lover of fine furniture and paintings, Sarah also put much effort into creating manicured gardens, in which she loved to sit peacefully. She had a team of skillful gardeners. Tommy, her Japanese head gardener, was so devoted to Sarah because of the kindness she showed him that he died soon after her death, grieved by her departure. Once again, Sarah imported plants, flowers, trees, and shrubs from countries around the world – some of her original rose bushes, which are more than 100 years old, are still flourishing today, as well as her distinctive feather and fan date palms. Sarah's favorite daisy flowers throughout the grounds, and she planted working orchards too. The entrepreneurial New Englander grew plums, apricots, and walnuts, employing ten men to look after her farm year round. The fruit was dried in another ingenious Sarah innovation, her special dehydrator, which had a coal furnace and could dry half a ton of fruit in 30 hours. The fruit was sold at market, bringing in a tidy income.

Sarah's practical farming know-how and artistic temperament are not what lure tourists to visit her mansion today, however. Far more compelling is the notion of her conducting seances with the spirits of dead American Indians, and it's that which is central to the appeal of the Winchester Mystery House. As the house guidebook states, somewhat baldly, Sarah supposedly made a nightly pilgrimage to the Blue Room, or Seance Room

to commune with the spirits. This room consisted of a cabinet, a table with a pen and paper, a closet, and a planchette board – similar to a Ouija board – used for transmitting messages from the beyond. Legend has it that she would wear one of the 13 special colored robes and receive guidance from various spirits for her construction plans.[29]

Sarah is meant to have meekly received the spirits' designs for her home, living in fear of her own life being taken if she didn't appease the tortured souls of those slaughtered by the Winchester rifle, which had made her so many millions of dollars.

The miles of hallways in Sarah's house have given rise to speculation that she used the many twists and turns to confuse ghosts who might be following her. The official Winchester Mystery House guidebook does describe what comes next as a "wild and fanciful" version of Sarah's nightly journey to the Seance Room.[30] Six years after Sarah's death, the following appeared in *The American Weekly*:

> When Mrs Winchester set out for her Séance Room, it might well have discouraged the ghost of the Indian or even of a bloodhound, to follow her. After traversing an interminable labyrinth of rooms and hallways, suddenly she would push a button, a panel would fly back, and she would step quickly from one apartment into another, and unless the pursuing ghost was watchful and quick, he would lose her. Then she opened a window in that apartment and climbed out, not into the open air, but onto the top of a flight of steps that took her down one story only to meet another flight that brought her right back up to the same level again, all inside the house. This was supposed to be very discomforting to evil spirits who are said to be naturally suspicious of traps.[31]

Susy Smith, author of *American Ghosts*, also suggests that Sarah's curious building techniques were designed to keep the ghosts from harming her:

> After all, some of the victims of her guns had been "badmen" of the West, or malicious criminals of the city slums. They certainly had not reformed just because they had passed into spirit life. And so she had to watch out for them at all times.[32]

Tales of the spooky sights and sounds from the Seance Room abound. Passers-by were said to have heard ghostly music, as the bell in the belfry tolled at midnight to summon the spirits. Ralph Rambo points out that the sacred blue so-called Seance Room, far from being locked to all but Sarah, was actually used as a bedroom by her foreman, the chauffeur, and the head Japanese gardener and his wife.[33] As for the creepy tunes late at night – they came from one of the mansion's reed organs. Sarah was an excellent musician, and when sleepless, she exercised her "talent and her arthritic fingers."[34]

Poor Sarah never slept well, consumed as she was by grief and melancholy, so neighbors would have heard music in the dead of night frequently. As Sarah wrote to her sister-in-law Jennie Bennett back East:

> For years I have been more or less troubled with insomnia but for two or three weeks I have been so sleepy all of the time that I find it very difficult to summon energy enough to do anything. At the same time I am very tired and listless. I don't know to what to attribute this somnolent condition, unless it is the result of having left off drinking coffee. In some respects I think I am better for the abstinence but it is horrible to be so dull and good for nothing.[35]

A statue of a Native American, Chief Little Fawn, stands in the grounds of Sarah's home, complete with bow and arrows, as if making his gallant last stand against the rapid fire of the Winchester. Tour guides present this as Sarah's atonement for the slaughter of Indians by the Winchester repeating rifle, her "tribute" to the dead. Ralph Rambo punctures this myth, informing us that the heart-rending figure of Chief Little Fawn was a common cast-iron statue of the day. "If our gossipers had taken a sharper look they would have seen him more practically engaged in stalking his companion piece, a cast-iron deer in the nearby shrubbery."[36]

Much is made of Sarah's strange deference to the number 13, the number considered unlucky by the superstitious. The main staircase has 13 steps. There are 13 cupolas in the greenhouse and 13 fan palms lining the driveway, 13 hangers in a closet, 13 wall panels, 13 lights in the chandeliers, 13 windows in a room, and some placed in an inside wall if necessary to make up that number. Since 13 was supposedly Sarah's favorite number, this is used as further evidence that she was a worshipper of all things strange and spooky. "The

Fig. 16 Postcard of Sarah Winchester's house before the 1906 San Francisco earthquake.

number 13 is predominant everywhere, because Sarah was convinced that it had an uncanny potency to hold in check the bad spirits she also had to contend with,"[37] writes Susy Smith. However, as Mary Jo Ignoffo discovered through her extensive research, a carpenter who worked on the house for years, James Perkins, said these 13th pieces were all additions. "The number 13 in chandeliers, the number of bathrooms, windows, ceiling panels and other things were certainly put in after Mrs Winchester died." Perkins's verdict is clear: "The more irregular features which have made the house a world famed oddity were built after Mrs Winchester's death."[38]

There is absolutely no evidence in Sarah's letters of her alleged guilt over the deaths of so many Native Americans from the Winchester rifle. In her writings, her main topics are family, finances, building work, and her health. Sarah often reflects upon her rheumatism and the ways it has constrained her life. "You ask me if I sew," Sarah writes to Jennie Bennett:

> I wish I could say yes, but for years it has only been at long intervals that I have been able to do more than sew on a button without suffering [. . .] the first thing I do after dinner is to go to bed. Just think how stupid I am, to go to my night's rest before dark! That is

what I have been doing lately. I sincerely hope I shall soon feel more wide awake and develop more energy and enterprise.[39]

That Sarah seemed peculiar and reclusive to the outside world, there's no doubt. But her servants and workmen knew her as friendly, intelligent, cultured, kindly, and extremely studious. She read omnivorously in four languages, including French and Turkish, and had one of the most complete French libraries on the Pacific Coast.[40] Fred Larsen, Sarah's chauffeur for many years, told a reporter the only time he ever thought his boss peculiar was when she ordered her wine cellar smashed at the beginning of Prohibition.[41]

A newspaper delivery boy who brought Sarah copies of the *San Jose Mercury Herald* recalled how she never seemed either strange or secretive to him, indeed quite the reverse. When Elmer Jensen asked if he might shoot robins in her garden with his air gun, Sarah said no, but:

> I will always remember her giving me the complete story of the life of a robin and how they were hunger driven from the snow and ice clad slopes of the Sierras down to the warm valleys along the coast. It made such an impression upon me that never again did I ever shoot at any song bird.[42]

Dr Clyde Wayland, Sarah's doctor, never found his patient eccentric in any way, and said her mind was perfectly clear to the very end.[43] Death was omnipresent in Sarah's thoughts, but it wasn't the ghosts of those killed by the Winchester rifle. She was obsessed by her own losses, of William and baby Annie, both buried in the Evergreen Cemetery in New Haven, where Sarah eventually planned to join them. As she wrote to her sister-in-law Jennie, when inquiring about family and the disposal of her dead mother-in-law's possessions,

> There is so much sadness inseparable from thoughts of all these things that I try not to allow myself to dwell on them long. I often feel concerned about my cemetery lot. I write occasionally to both Mr Phillips and the Cemetery Association but yet can not always feel sure that everything is properly attended to.[44]

Shy, retiring, and in later years a semi-invalid, Sarah only retreated further when the newspapers began to print the neighbors' fanciful theories about her reasons for building the sprawling mansion. By hiding behind her construction, she set the already over-active tongues wagging even more speedily. It was said that the floor of her Seance Room undulated like the sea, and ghostly nocturnal music was heard nightly before the lady of mystery emerged with new architectural blueprints from out of the blue. At first Sarah laughed about these ridiculous reports, but Fred Marriott, her nephew by marriage, said the unpleasant persistence of the stories caused her to shut herself away from curious, unsympathetic eyes.[45]

There are explanations for the unorthodox appearance of Sarah's villa. The epic San Francisco earthquake of 1906 damaged her creation greatly – much of the house was damaged, including the seven-story tower, and ceilings and walls crumbled. Sarah talked of wrecking what was left of the place, remarking that it looked "as though it had been built by a crazy person."[46] Instead, Sarah decided to have the unsafe sections pulled off or boarded up. Hence the outside door on the third floor, pointed to as evidence of her unbalanced mental state. As for the exterior second-story water faucets, they probably had window boxes under them. The floor with a skylight may have been a roof before Sarah built yet another layer of mansion. The bar-protected inside windows were almost certainly on the outside of the house until even more construction enclosed them. The room full of trapdoors was an upper-floor conservatory with an ingenious double floor for drainage purposes – one of Sarah's many practical ideas. As for the strange-looking stairways with 3-inch steps and 18-inch treads – remember Sarah was stricken with arthritis and neuritis which made climbing the stairs very painful, so she created these small steps specially. The clear glass doors in certain bathrooms, variously presented as evidence that Sarah was "immodest," were innocent enough – the maids could watch their aged employer lest she fall while bathing.

Learning on the job as she was, Sarah the self-taught architect nevertheless came up with many practical and ingenious schemes. Brass corner plates were installed on the stairways to make it easier for the servants to clean the many steps, by preventing dust pockets.

Sarah improvised a window catch patterned after the Winchester rifle trigger. An early type of intercom called the annunciator allowed her to summon the servants from anywhere in the house, and a card would drop showing the servant which room she was in – an innovation years ahead of its time. Carbide gas lamps in the house were fed by the estate's own gas manufacturing plant, which used a new process. The gas-lights were operated by pushing an electric button. Sarah's 47 fireplaces had the first hinged iron drops for ashes and concealed wood boxes.

What's more, Sarah pioneered the use of and may even have invented household laundry tubs with built-in washboards. In the early 1940s, an American manufacturing firm was sued by an obscure inventor who claimed that the company had stolen his idea for a tub with built-in washboards. The company's lawyers swiftly produced photographs of Sarah's laundry tubs with their ingenious feature, showing that these labor-saving gadgets had been in use for more than 50 years.[47] Sarah was a practical problem solver, who also developed an inside crank to open and close outside shutters.[48] Window drip pans and a zinc subfloor were installed in the North Conservatory so when the plants were watered, the runoff would be captured and directed onto the gardens below.[49] And on and on it goes. This smart woman used her considerable intellectual energy to make the deeply impractical house easier for the servants to keep clean, and was streets ahead of her time in trying to conserve water and energy. For example, Villa Llanda was one of the first residences to use wool for insulation.

Letters to family back in New Haven reveal Sarah's devotion to every detail of the never-ending program of work on her expanding home. She was meticulous, with high standards, and construction on Villa Llanda took up her available time and energy. Confiding in her sister-in-law Jennie Bennett, she wrote:

> I have had such dreadful luck with plaster. I have tried different plasterers, having, after my first experience, the work done by the day, but not with much better results. They excuse the defects in all sorts of ways, an occasional earthquake serving them well. I had so much trouble with ordinary plaster, that I thought I would try

adamant and had two rooms done with it. It seemed all right for a time but now in the room I had used for a guest room, it has loosened so as to be unsafe and as soon as I can feel equal to this disagreeable task, I shall have it all removed from the walls and re-plastered, and this is about the way I progress.[50]

Any homeowner can empathize with Sarah's tendency to worry about her property – it's just that most of us don't have 160 rooms to concern ourselves with! She spent many long and frequently inconclusive hours with contractors, fretting about aspects of her heating and plumbing. "Day before yesterday I spent a good part of the morning in the cellar with a heater man, trying to study out how we can introduce the pipes for steam heat, it is quite a problem and it is not yet solved," Sarah explained to Jennie Bennett in a lengthy letter:

I have also been looking into the matter of sanitary plumbing and find that my system has serious defects. I have from time to time rectified some glaring deficiencies, but have decided that nothing but a radical change can make my plumbing beyond reproach. I do not think it is so bad as to be actually dangerous and don't know whether I can summon up the courage to make the required changes.[51]

When not puzzling over plumbing problems, Sarah pursued other California properties and dealt with family matters. She purchased a ranch in San Jose, a houseboat (nicknamed The Ark, for its resemblance to Noah's Ark) on Burlingame land, another ranch in what's now Los Altos for her sister Belle, and bought land in Atherton upon which she built a beautiful, modern home in the Mission Revival style. Frank Leib, Sarah's attorney and friend, wrote to her saying the Atherton residence "struck me as being a very beautiful home." Sarah's acquisition of real estate was partly a hobby, and partly a service to her family members. Of Sarah's four sisters, Mary had died when Sarah was still in New Haven, Estelle died young out in California, Nette moved from California to New York, and Belle lived in a ranch close to her sister purchased by Sarah. Belle's daughter Daisy came to live with Sarah, and Sarah was most generous to her niece, who must, in some way, have been a substitute for her daughter Annie in her affections.

Sarah's sister Belle Merriman was a quirky character, who only fueled the rumors about Sarah. Belle had somewhere along the way befriended a Bahai leader named Abdul Baha Abbas, and was dubbed "the prophet of Abdul" by a local newspaper.[52] Belle and Sarah were furious when the Southern Pacific Railroad wanted the land Belle's ranch sat atop. Sarah was given $30,000 in compensation for the loss of the ranch she'd bought her sister, but wrote miserably to Frank Leib, "I will sorrowfully accept it, claim no more 'damages' and consider one more distressing episode added to the list of harrowing experiences which I have met with since coming to California."[53]

As Sarah became more solitary, shrinking from the caricature of her as a spirit-obsessed crank, corresponding with family in Connecticut became an ever more important link to the world outside. At least in New Haven she wasn't considered eccentric. Sarah followed news of her dissolute nephew Oliver Winchester Dye, son of William's deceased sister Ann, with keen interest. Oliver had inherited a considerable amount of money after his grandfather Oliver Winchester died, and he came into yet more funds with the death of his grandmother, Jane Winchester. Oliver Junior was the classic black sheep of the family, who never had a proper job, spent money like water, womanized, and had an expensive, high-profile divorce which the newspapers covered in exhaustive detail. "Heir To Millions Whose Wife Says She Was Left With Eight Cents," read one disapproving headline.[54] "Turned into the streets by her husband, while he is worth thousands and one of two heirs to the $3,000,000 of his grandmother, is the sad plaint of Mrs Oliver Winchester Dye," went the affecting story of the abandoned Mrs Winchester:

> Another woman, Mrs Dye asserts, has alienated the affections of the man to whom she has been married ten years and caused him to demand that she get a divorce [...] This remarkable story has been whispered about in the clubs and exclusive circles [...] It involves some of the best known and oldest families in the country.

This was a serious scandal, by the standards of the day, which caused Sarah to shake her head reprovingly in letters back East. "Is Ollie

really making a failure of his life, or has he redeeming qualities?"
Sarah asked her sister-in-law Jennie Bennett. "From such knowledge
as I have, I should judge that money in trust would serve his interests
far better than actual possession of it."[55] Oliver's spending sprees
clearly influenced Sarah when it came to drawing up her own will. She
left her nieces and nephews tightly controlled trust funds, which
generated an annual income, but prevented them from getting their
hands on the principal money. Legend has it that when the feckless
Oliver turned up at Villa Llanda one fine day to ask his aunt for
money, Sarah refused to see him, but ordered the butler to present
her nephew with a check, carried out on a silver tray.

Vilified by newspapers for being a batty old lady obsessed by the
spirits, Sarah retreated further, stricken by rheumatism. As we have
seen, the San Francisco earthquake in 1906 devastated the house she
had spent 20 years building. Sarah moved into her eccentric-looking
houseboat while essential repairs were carried out. Sarah chose not
to rebuild after the earthquake, opting instead to make the Villa
Llanda safe. Sarah's sadness multiplied – now she had the destroyed
sections of her home, with all their glorious craftsmanship, to mourn
too. Nostalgia from her lost past with William and Annie persisted.
Hearing about New Haven's attempts to establish a tuberculosis
hospital, Sarah made an initial anonymous donation of $300,000,
according to her lawyer Frank Leib. This gift gave her great
satisfaction, for it was tuberculosis that had taken William from her
when he was only in his 40s, and now she could contribute to
research into this deadly disease. Sarah continued to give money to
the fund, and eventually waived her anonymity. It pleased her greatly
to have the new hospital dedicated to her husband, and named after
him. A bronze plaque announced that the hospital was erected and
endowed by the wife of William Wirt Winchester. This immensely
practical woman was putting her fortune to good use, in memory of
her beloved. Sarah gave more than $1,325,000 to this cause just to get
the facility built.[56] The William Wirt Winchester Hospital, to be used
for the care of patients suffering from tuberculosis, opened in 1918.
Tom Bennett attended the opening ceremony, and wrote to Sarah
that it was:

appropriate, graceful and dignified. There was good attendance – all the hospital board and all those you named [...] we saw all the appointments and conveniences said by the commandant and the architect to be the best in the world. In my time soldiers were not so well taken care of. To see the elevators, electric lighting, heating, venting, sterilization, cooking, washing and ironing machinery was in itself a liberal education. I regret you could not have seen it yourself.[57]

A memorial gateway to the hospital honored William Wirt Winchester, built with an additional $25,000 donated by the ever thoughtful Sarah.[58]

Sarah could not be in New Haven to see the hospital dedicated in William's name, since her health was failing her still further. As she became less and less mobile, in constant pain because of her arthritis, her mourning for William only seemed to intensify. Perhaps as the end of her own life neared, she felt closer to the person who had defined her happiest times. In letters to New Haven, she asked wistfully for William's shirt buttons, so she might have another memento of his. As Sarah entered her final years, she carefully drew up her will, in which she generously endowed the William Wirt Memorial Hospital for Tuberculosis in New Haven. The TB hospital was discontinued in 1940, as the incidence of the disease known as the white plague declined. Sarah's fund is now used by Yale–New Haven hospital to help patients with TB and respiratory diseases, as I like to remind family members who indignantly ask where her millions went!

The extent of Sarah's generosity and charity was never widely known, which is how she wanted it. Yet Ralph Rambo clearly recalls her kindness:

There were the little but visible acts that we nearby dwellers particularly noticed, those daily carriage trips with soup and hot food for a newly arrived settler on Stevens Creek Road, a man dying from tuberculosis; those annual, unheralded trips to old Cupertino Church from where my mother and other women of the Ladies Aid Society collected used clothing for the local poors' children. I remember a small boy's thrill as he watched her liveried coachman alight from the polished Victoria [carriage] and stagger up the church steps with a huge hamper of clothes, not used clothes but dozens of newly purchased garments! This was the Mrs Winchester the writer and many another contemporary remember. We never knew her intimately but how we now wish we had![59]

Some years before Sarah died, a fair-minded article by Merle H. Gray attempted to explain how the widow was not a fruitcake but "an unusually talented woman." Gray accurately referred to Sarah's colossal mansion as "The Workshop of a Woman Architect."[60] Sympathetically, Gray observed:

> Perhaps not more than a dozen people in California know that Mrs Winchester is a musician with a genius for composition, that she is a remarkable businesswoman, that she is a French scholar, that her philanthropies alone would make her a national figure if they were known, that she is a full-fledged architect familiar with the building peculiarities of all countries, that her famous house of mystery at Campbell is merely a workshop and the structure itself is merely a collection of notes taken by a woman of great wealth while educating herself in the architecture of several countries.

Sadly, Merle's insightful analysis of Sarah's obsessive building was overlooked. The myth of Sarah was already well established, in pieces in *Coronet*, *Holiday*, *Reader's Digest*, and others – the truth was so much more boring than the ghost story.

Sarah Winchester died in 1922, having made it into her ninth decade despite so much ill health. Meticulous to the last, she had made precise arrangements to be buried in New Haven's Evergreen Cemetery, next to William and baby Annie. Her funeral invoice details the cost of shipping her embalmed body from San Jose to New Haven, where at long last she was reunited with the family she had mourned for so many lonely years.

Once Sarah had died, news of her will was eagerly anticipated by the gossips of the Santa Clara Valley. There was general surprise in the parlors of San Francisco over the total value of Sarah's estate. It was worth about $3 million, not the $20 million figure which had been casually tossed around over the years. She had given away or spent much of the money during her lifetime. Sarah left money to five of her servants (in the range of $800 to $3,000), lump sums to some nieces, and investment funds for a whole variety of nieces and nephews. Sarah's doted-upon niece Daisy, daughter of sister Belle, received property, pictures, jewelry, and a $200,000 trust. Yet the most generous bequest was to the William Wirt Winchester Hospital in New Haven. She also instructed that the principal money of the trusts she established for her nieces and nephews would revert to the TB hospital when the individuals died. In this ingenious way, Sarah's endowment in memory of her husband William would keep growing, continuing to provide funds to treat patients suffering from tuberculosis.

Today, Sarah's thoughtfulness is in daily evidence at Yale–New Haven hospital's Winchester Chest Clinic, which provides state-of-the-art, world-class treatment to patients with asthma, pulmonary disease, lung cancer, cystic fibrosis, respiratory problems, and tuberculosis. Over the years, the clinic has grown tremendously, and now serves as the regional referral center for pulmonary diseases of all types. Patients have access to clinical trials of new treatments for advanced lung diseases, which would please Sarah greatly. The mission of TB treatment and research continues at the clinic, as Sarah had intended it should. William Winchester's portrait is on display at the clinic, a reminder of the generous legacy that has benefited countless numbers of patients. The director of the Winchester Chest Clinic, Dr Lynn Tanoue, says: "I sometimes look at William's portrait and wish that Sarah Winchester could know of the immense and immeasurable good she has rendered our patients with lung disease by her bequest, which will endure into future generations."[61]

Upon Sarah's death, her attorney and friend Frank Leib told a local newspaper, "Mrs Winchester was all that a woman should be, and nothing that a good woman should not be [. . .] If there is a heaven, there she surely must be."[62] Leib's attempt to underscore Sarah's kindness and good works was followed up by others. The *Evening News* of San Jose soon published a piece by Edith Daley, which promised to tell the life story of Sarah Winchester, "one of the most interesting persons who ever lived in the valley," for the first time. This whimsical article, which relied on an anonymous source, painted a portrait of a sorrowful woman who had a room in one of her towers with walls, carpet, and ceiling of white satin, which no one entered but herself. However, Ms Daley did highlight Sarah's philanthropy, with her sweeping purple prose:

> I have had much interesting information, each detail being kindly given, offered to refuse less friendly criticism of the woman with the grieving mother-heart whose years of lonely widowhood were marked by more than ordinarily generous giving to all charitable institutions considered worthy. Beautiful giving – because it sought no publicity.[63]

Yet the beautiful giving was soon obscured as the bandwagon of the grieving, guilty widow haunted by guns rolled on with fresh impetus. Sarah's lawyer Roy Leib sold the house and grounds to a group of investors on behalf of her estate – the contents of Villa Llanda were left to Sarah's niece, Daisy. In 1923, the investors leased Sarah's mysterious home to John Brown, who had a background in rollercoasters and amusement parks, and an eye for a marketable tale. He and his wife Mayme opened the house to the public that same year, and created advance publicity by inviting journalists for a sneak preview. After years of rumor and gossip, at last there was a chance to see inside the crazy lady's mansion. The Browns must have been thrilled to bits to read Ruth Amet's piece for the *San Jose Mercury Herald*, which announced: "There is something of the awful 'House of Usher' about it [...] I, for one, would tremendously like to give a Hallowe'en party in this old home. First, each guest would be given a lighted candle." Amet pronounced the walls of the house to be "teeming with atmosphere for those who would a-ghosting go."[64]

Sarah's former employees looked on with mounting disbelief as her house became a prominent tourist attraction, and the myth of her nightly sessions with ghosts became accepted as fact. In 1924, the Browns invited Harry Houdini, the magician and escape artist, to visit their haunted house. Houdini had been critical of spiritualism, and was supposed to be a debunker of myths rather than a willing accomplice in their creation. Instead, Houdini went to the house at midnight on Halloween and claimed he saw that "Mrs Winchester has a vast wardrobe of variously colored robes, and she uses a different robe for each spirit."[65] Houdini's sighting of Sarah's ghost surrounded by spirits cemented the legend of the Winchester Mystery House.

Henrietta Sivera, Sarah's companion in her final years, wrote to another of Sarah's former employees, saying her husband was upset by the misrepresentation of Sarah. "What disturbs Dr Noe is that the Browns are making money out there by telling a lot of falsehoods, and that is obtaining money under false pretenses, which is against the law." Mary Jo Ignoffo reports that Sivera wrote to Minnie Yeager Hall, who lived across from the Winchester house as a child, telling her: "It just made my heart sing to know you understand all that is going on at dear Mrs Winchester's home which is not the truth."[66]

Other employees were also shocked by the speed at which the fantasies about their former boss were being repeated as the incontrovertible truth. As Ralph Rambo wrote, "Recorded opinions of her few associates are interesting and also revealing. 'Utterly false that she was eccentric or mentally unbalanced' [...] 'She was preyed on by people' [...] 'She was a sweet person and not at all crazy.'"[67] These and other testimonies to Sarah's sanity came from such acquaintances as John Hansen, foreman of her estate, Elmer Jensen, W. T. Creffield, and Roy F. Leib, her attorney for many years and executor of her estate.[68] These voices of reason were far and few between, since her servants were extremely shy about speaking out, and anyway, no one was interested in the less magnetic tale of Sarah the studious, saddened, architecture buff. So the Winchester Mystery House bandwagon was transformed into an unstoppable juggernaut.

Since 1923, thousands of teeming tourists have swarmed through the house every year. More than 90 years after Sarah's death, she and her house have an enduring appeal. San Jose cab drivers will tell you that one in every five of their passengers is heading to the Mystery House. The visitor to California will stumble across the strange story of the guilt-ridden Winchester heiress Sarah Winchester, who spoke to the spirits of those killed by the Winchester rifle, and be drawn to visit her house. Tourists can pose with Winchester Rifles before embarking on the deluxe house tour, and buy as many cowboy hats and as much Winchester paraphernalia as they like. Tour guides have a script, peppered with "it is believed that [...] legend has it [...] it is thought that" and other generic disclaimers. The official guide to the Winchester Mystery House concludes:

> Nobody has adequately answered the final questions: Why did Mrs Winchester spend so much time, money, and energy to live the way she did? And why did she build what is arguably one of the world's oddest houses? Was she obsessed by the ghosts of those killed by the Winchester rifle? [...] No-one will ever know, but this bizarre and beautiful mansion has, we think, allowed Mrs Sarah L. Winchester, Lady of Mystery, to achieve a unique kind of eternal life.

It is certainly true that a version of Sarah's life lives on. At the time of writing, a supernatural thriller movie based on Sarah's gun guilt and spooky séances was due to be filmed at the Winchester Mystery House, directed by the Spierig brothers. "We can't wait to see what the Spierig brothers unearth as they delve in to the mysteries of Sarah Winchester and her infamous haunted house," Tobin Armbrust of Hammer Films told *Variety*.[69]

So resonant is the image of the widowed Sarah haunted by grief and ghosts of dead Winchester rifle victims, that there's a website dedicated to her – the truth about Sarah Winchester. The outer recesses of the Internet reveal bloggers who believe Sarah strongly identified with Francis Bacon, and was herself a Rosicrucian and a Freemason whose architecture embodies the idea of a fourth, spatial dimension. There's even a lengthy eponymous novel based on the theme of ghosts and gun guilt. The author returns frequently – and enthusiastically – to Sarah's supposed sessions with the spirits:

> She entered the room carrying her candelabrum and placed it onto the table draped with black cloth [...] Then she donned a robe, pulled her armchair to the table, extinguished flames leaving two of six lit, and sat down [...] In short time, her eyes began fluttering, and then they closed. Her hand with the pen began to move, slowly, then

more rapidly. Again, she felt the presence of a small misty figure above her arm over the paper. It guided her hand, drawing lines in all the available space on both sides of the paper.[70]

And so the inflated legend of Sarah and the mansion designed by spirits lives on, and on.

Sarah's true legacy lies not in California but in New Haven, at the Winchester Chest Clinic. "The ironic twist we find here," observed Bruce Spoon, the perceptive student who wrote his thesis on Sarah, "is that the community in which she chose to live and spend her life reveres her memory with ridicule and laughter, whereas the community she left behind has nothing but praise for her."[71] In New Haven, Sarah's abiding love for William endures. Her devotion to William's memory coupled with her astute financial foresight enables patient after patient to be treated for diseases of the chest, now and in the future. Never mind the bizarre Mystery House, which fuels our understandable fascination with guns, ghosts, and guilt – the Chest Clinic is a far more fitting memorial to Sarah's thoughtful life and work.

CHAPTER 5

Decline and Fall

A S SARAH WINCHESTER was becoming notorious out West, the Winchester Repeating Arms Company that had made her so wealthy was in serious trouble. The most prominent family member in the telling of this story is Sarah's nephew, Winchester Bennett. Through his life and times, we can trace the downfall of a storied family name. Thanks to the runaway success of the gun he was named for, Winchester Bennett was born into privilege and luxury, an upbringing that was the polar opposite of his grandfather Oliver Winchester's. While Oliver grew up in a humble farmhouse, Winchester (known as Win) had a majestic childhood home in New Haven and, in later life, a summer mansion in nearby Branford too. Win's father Tom had spent his late teenage years as a soldier in the Civil War, whereas Win's adolescent life was a social whirl of dances, shooting parties, and sailing. Wanting for nothing materially, Win was a very different character to his grandfather and father, and lacked their unrelenting drive. In addition, unfortunately he suffered from many different ailments throughout his life. For years, the Winchester Repeating Arms Company had been fortunate in that costs and prices had been stable, and it had coasted along generating expansive profits. World War I shattered all the old assumptions about how to do business, and Winchester Bennett was suddenly at the helm attempting to lead the company through the hurricane force winds it encountered.

Born in New Haven on August 22, 1877, Win was doted upon by his mother Jennie and his father Tom. Early photographs show a handsome child in a sailor suit posing in the approved Victorian style,

Fig. 17 Winchester Bennett, the author's great-grandfather, photographed as a child, *c.*1884.

the backdrop signaling his lofty status. Win had an older sister, Anne Hope Bennett, who became a patron of sacred music and arts in New Haven, and a younger brother, Eugene. All three children were drilled in the social skills deemed necessary for their elevated station in life. Win attended Professor Loomis's dancing classes in New Haven, where he learned to waltz and polka, and bow with hand on heart before inviting a lady to dance. Tom could be a stern father, who scolded Win for being repeatedly late to breakfast and failing to tend to the fires. He oversaw the children's education meticulously, instructing Jennie to get their offspring tutors in French and German. Yet Tom was also a fun-loving parent. During the great New England blizzard of 1888, one of the sevcrest ever recorded in the history of the United States, when snowfall of 60 inches was recorded in one week, Tom took the boys out for snowball fights and delighted in their general merriment.

Win followed in his father's footsteps, attending Yale Sheffield Scientific School, and dutifully entering into the employment of the

Fig. 18 Winchester Bennett, *c.*1906.

family firm in 1899. Win spent the next few years in Winchester's gun shops learning about the production side of the business. In 1905 he was elevated to the position of director of the Winchester Repeating Arms Company, and appointed to the newly created role of second vice-president. Company photographs show Win to have been a physically imposing man with the broad-shouldered stature of his father. Edwin Pugsley, later Winchester's chief engineer and Win's brother-in-law, wrote that the heir to the company was a "very hard worker, with the result that he became obsessed with the mechanical side of the business." [1]

As a young adult Win enjoyed fly fishing, golf, sailing, and other pursuits of the gilded age. At the dawn of the 20th century, Win met the beautiful and bright Susan Silliman Wright, a well-born young Connecticut lady, great-granddaughter of Benjamin Silliman, the noted chemist, and one of the first science professors at Yale

University. Susan was a descendant of Jonathan Trumbull, Revolutionary War governor of Connecticut, and her father Arthur Williams Wright received the first science Ph.D. ever awarded in the United States, after studying at Yale University.[2] One Yale college was named after Trumbull and a second after Benjamin Silliman – Susan's intellectual pedigree was impeccable, and now she was being hotly pursued by a scion of the Winchester family.

The course of true love never did run smooth, and so it was in Susan and Win's courtship, blissful as it may sound. The pair went for all day sails off Connecticut's Thimble Islands, swam in the moonlight, played ping pong, traded dance cards, went eel fishing, shooting, and ate oysters. Win attempted to woo Susan by giving her a darling seven-week-old bull terrier puppy, Sidar Junior, white and fluffy with a brown patch on his eye. But after a formal dance, Susan confided to her diary that she found Win overbearing:

> He made me awfully mad, the way he hung around for dances and insisted on having them [...] bored me to death in fact [...] Win was horrid and I hate him [...] I nearly cried with rage and gave him an awful scolding.[3]

Susan's parents wanted her to marry Win, no doubt seeing the social advantages this would bring both families, as the scholars could marry into money and vice versa, each dynasty conferring prestige upon the other. Susan, though, had another suitor, one Henry Brewer, later a vice-president of the Winchester company.

> Win insisted he was coming for me tomorrow night to take me out, but I will NOT go with him. There is terrible discord in the family as Dad is for Win, and I am for Henry. The latter telephoned just after Win to say he'd be up in ten minutes, and he came at 9.30pm just after Win had left [...] I cried myself to sleep.[4]

Susan, who was training to be a nurse, had clearly not yet committed herself to Win. She found him to be very impatient, which could make simple social situations such as finishing dinner rather stressful. Meanwhile, his parents were watching the situation carefully, hoping

Win's sometimes erratic behavior would not put off his prospective bride. "Win seems in good spirits," Tom wrote to his wife Jane. "So far he has not seemed impatient or nervous." [5] As the romance progressed, Tom wrote to Jane:

> Now don't read this aloud. Win went to New York on Sunday just as I wrote Eugene. Called on Susy Wright [Susan] Saturday evening and took her out in an automobile Sunday afternoon. She is on night duty [...] He imparted the above information without being "squozen" [squeezed]. Just leaked it naturally as though it was pressing to get out. [6]

By the end of 1902, after Win courted Susan with flowers, American Beauties candy, baskets of grapes, driving trips in Central Park, and long walks, she accepted his second proposal of marriage. "We are engaged, and I am the happiest girl in the world," Susan wrote in her diary. "Father was delighted." [7] Susan had weighed up the relative merits of Henry Brewer and Winchester Bennett, and perhaps influenced by her father's enthusiasm for Win, had settled for the gun magnate's son. Although Brewer was to become a prominent official at Winchester, he lacked the enviable prospects of Oliver Winchester's grandson. The Bennetts were also extremely pleased with the match, and relieved that Win had settled down. His tendency towards nervous irritability concerned Tom and Jennie, and they saw Susan as a calming influence on their son's unpredictable temperament.

As befitted Yankee newly-weds from prominent families, Sue and Win honeymooned in St Augustine, Florida, the nation's oldest city (settled by the Spanish), at a resort community complete with hotels and a railway thanks to Standard Oil's co-founder Henry Flagler. The Winchester Bennetts settled into life in their New Haven home on Cold Spring Street, next door to the Spock family, parents of the noted pediatrician Dr Benjamin Spock, the eldest of the Spocks' six children. His entry into the world in 1903 was lovingly chronicled by Susan in her diary. "Mil [Mildred Spock] had a dear little baby this spring and he is a sweetheart." Win and Susan's marriage coincided with Tom Bennett's completion of another prominent house-building

Fig. 19 Susan Silliman Bennett on her wedding day, 1903.

project, this time a waterfront property on Johnson's Point, in Branford, Connecticut, named Islewood. It had commanding views of Long Island Sound, and the Bennetts expected to enjoy the company of their close family during summers at the shore. Susan worried about living at such close quarters with her magisterial, dominant in-laws.

> Win is looking forward to it very much. I am not so enthusiastic as I have my doubts about how the combined families will get on. It's one thing to meet two or three times a week and exist in peace, but it's quite another to live in the same house for two or three months. However, I shall do my darndest, and hope for the best.[8]

Susan's greatest trial in life was not to be her in-laws, but rather her husband's ill health. Early on in their marriage, Win became seriously unwell, suffering from fever, digestive complaints, and stabbing back pains. His ailments were to be a recurring theme throughout their marriage.

As Win and Susan were building their life together, the Winchester Repeating Arms Company was a dominant concern in New Haven, its fortunes inexorably entwined with those of the city itself. As the newspaperman Frank Lynne wrote in 1903:

> The fact that its work is continuous and steady means in itself a great deal to the business and industrial interests of the city. Employing, as it does, so many, it has become, although a private concern, in many respects a public one.[9]

Prominent in this private yet public concern was Winchester Bennett, who among other duties was responsible for VIP relations at the company. He entertained Henry Ford, creator of the Model T Ford car, who wanted to visit the factory to find out how all the components of the firearm were made absolutely interchangeable. The same principle would be used by Ford in his mass production of the automobile. Mixing business with pleasure, Ford purchased rifles for himself – he later added the deluxe special order Model 1894 rifle to his collection, which he was photographed firing at his hunting camp in Maine.[10]

As we have seen, corresponding with Teddy Roosevelt over his forthcoming hunting trip to Africa took up a lot of Win's time, and all the while the profits from sales of sporting rifles kept on rising. Win kept up the aggressive patent fence Winchester had built around its guns, applying for quite a few of his own. In 1907, Win filed a patent for his invention of a cartridge deflector for top ejection guns, followed by one for his tubular magazine firearm. When Win was elected first vice-president of the company in 1911, Winchester old timers like George Hodson and Arthur Earle were not surprised. As Earle predicted, "The big bear [Tom Bennett] was going to install his cub in the top position."[11] Tom drove Win hard, which may have been a factor in the son's nervous difficulties. Earle frequently saw Tom summon his eldest to the management office. "The big bear was often harder on the boy than anyone else, and expected more of him than was reasonable; Winchester Bennett was one of the hardest workers and knew the business as well as anyone in the plant." [12]

As Win tried to rise to his father's unrealistically high expectations, his wife became a leading light of New Haven society. Susan was an enthusiastic founding member of a women's cultural society, the Thursday Club, where she and her companions would research, write, and present papers over lunch on such important topics of the day as "Feminism" and "The Servant Problem." A member of the New Haven Country Club and the New Haven Lawn Club, she was an avid gardener who loved to exchange tips on roses with her friends. As those with a distinguished New England pedigree were wont to do, she became president of the Connecticut Society of the Colonial Dames of America. Win, for his part, was a member of a supper and debate club called The Inquisitors. Susan, who managed six children, two large households, and a small army of staff, often envied Win his evenings with The Inquisitors, which sounded considerably more fun than her fireside nights spent doing the household accounts. Occasionally the good ladies at the Thursday Club would have awkward and argumentative sessions, usually when the time came to choose the secretary for the following year – a greatly sought-after position. The genteel world of New Haven could be rather prickly, as well-born, wealthy, intelligent, and competitive young women jostled for their position in the social hierarchy. Interested in civic work, Susan, who had trained as a nurse, became president of the New Haven Visiting Nurse Association, a cause to which she devoted a good deal of time and thought.

Susan's place in the firmament was assured when she had her portrait painted by the society artist Cecilia Beaux, a contemporary of Mary Cassat's. Sitting for the portrait, which was of Susan and baby number two Dorothy, my great-aunt, became an exercise in logistics that took two months to complete. Baby Dorothy posed for Cecilia the portraitist for an hour at a time, on her mother's lap, but more than that could not be expected of the wriggly infant. Dorothy's doll, called Flaky Rice, substituted for her impatient owner frequently, sitting immobile on Susan's lap during sittings. Susan had to manage relations between the sometimes temperamental Miss Beaux and the rest of the Bennett family, who were keen to see the celebrity at work:

Fig. 20 Portrait of Susan Silliman Bennett and her daughter Dorothy, painted
by Cecilia Beaux, 1909.

We got started at 10 am and Mother came along at twelve to hurry us
through. Miss Beaux hates awfully to have anyone come in at the end
of the hour, and asked us to speak to Mother about it. Not a
particularly pleasant talk but I did it![13]

Cecilia Beaux was most particular about painting in a peaceful
environment, and Win was next to be reprimanded. "Miss Beaux was
in a terrible hurry and the arrival [. . .] of Win (unexpectedly) [. . .]
did not help matters any. In fact she was so rude to poor Win that he
left in a rage." [14] Cecilia wrote in her diary that it was "a tearing day
[. . .] people beginning to come at 11.30 am and sent away." [15] The
effort was worthwhile, and Cecilia's portrait of Susan and her
daughter Dorothy is charming, showing a reflective Susan in an
elegant blue silk gown with chiffon sleeves, with Dorothy sitting

effortlessly in repose on her mother's lap. The social standing of both parent and child is telegraphed by their fine clothes and gracious surroundings, in the manner of John Singer Sargent's work. Yet the painting is also a moving image of mother and child in harmony.

Work and life were closely intertwined for Susan and Win. Susan's sister Dorothy married Win's colleague Edwin Pugsley, a gentle giant of a man, with a genius for tinkering with firearms. Pugsley, much like Tom Bennett a generation earlier, married into the family and assumed a leadership role in the company, becoming the chief engineer and later director of research. The Bennetts and the Pugsleys lived parallel lives, wintering in New Haven and summering on the Connecticut shoreline. Their children grew up together, roaming through the eccentric and fascinating households of their parents and aunts and uncles. The attic of the Pugsleys' 76 Everitt Street home in New Haven, sold to them by Susan and Win, was full of treasures – extraordinary collections of clocks, watches, chronometers, antique navigation instruments, music boxes, cylinder phonographs, and player pianos. Stuffed animal heads adorned the walls of the Everitt Street house, which had a gigantic third-floor playroom. The whole area became known as Offspring Street, as children raced in and out of various households. In the idyllic summers, sailboats ferried Susan and her children and grandchildren from Johnson's Point to Leetes Island in Connecticut, where her sister Dorothy spent the warm months, and reverse trips were made for picnics on high days and holidays in Branford.

Edwin Pugsley designed sundials as a hobby and amassed a leading collection of firearms. His friend and fellow arms collector Charles Addams, the New Yorker cartoonist, is said to have modeled the character of Pugsley in the macabre Addams Family cartoons after Edwin.[16] The fictional Pugsley is the overweight child of Morticia and Gomez Addams, a jovial and inventive engineer, given to playing with dangerous toys such as guillotines. The humor, creativity, and physical stature of the Addams Family's Pugsley were traits apparently copied from the real life Edwin Pugsley; though Charles Addams's biographer maintains the Pugsley character was named after a stream in the Bronx.[17] Relatives remember Uncle Ed as an inventor par excellence, who had an amphibious military vehicle with a crane that he used to construct a seawall. Uncle Ed also owned a giant telescope, an unparalleled collection of gadgets, and an organ in the attic of his house, which he lovingly repaired. Uncle Ed built paths and walkways all over his Leetes Island summer residence, with a swing that went into the water and a school bus that he fixed up as a playhouse for his grandchildren. He once drove his delighted grandson into the water in his amphibious car, retreating when he realized there were too many rust holes in its metal bottom.

Engineering and guns were Edwin Pugsley's heritage. His father had been a civil engineer who built the railroads, and in later years purchased a small plantation in north-western Florida. Edwin grew up in a rural part of the state, where life

> still smacked quite largely of the frontier. The average white man was generally armed with a revolver and shooting scrapes were very common [...] Almost every Saturday night there would be some shooting or cutting episode [...] In my very early boyhood one of the most popular sheriffs the town ever had was shot and killed.[18]

Edwin's passion for collecting firearms began as a small boy, when his houseboy gave him an elderly Colt pistol to assemble. By prep school in Philadelphia the young Pugsley had added rusty Civil War carbines to his collection, which expanded still further when he studied at Massachusetts Institute of Technology (MIT) in Boston – there the enthusiast purchased an entire Civil War collection of 600 guns and a few pistols from a Boston dentist. Pugsley's collecting activities were cramped when he started his training at Winchester in 1911 – he was working 59 hours a week and initially had no car. But before too long he had saved up for a Model T Ford and was on the road again, off to Woodbury, New York in search of a French Gras rifle complete with bayonet. Such was the thrill of the chase for Pugsley, who had grown up in a gun culture in which he had heard tales of men who fought to the death with dueling pistols, settling disputes once and for all.

As Ed Pugsley joined Winchester, times were changing, and the gun business which had ticked along profitably for so long was

Fig. 21 Edwin Pugsley and colleagues at the Winchester Repeating Arms
Company. Pugsley is second from left.

experiencing a slowdown. At the end of 1912 and the start of 1913, a
prewar depression set in and Winchester began to run out of orders,
an unheard-of state of affairs. Winchester's Model 90 and Model 94
guns had for years been produced at the rate of 400 rifles a day, per
model – but production of these standard guns began to slow, and
workers were left twiddling their thumbs, anxious and unnerved by
this unfamiliar scenario. Ed Pugsley saw there were some US
government orders being advertised, and asked Tom Bennett if
Winchester shouldn't consider putting in a bid, given how slow
business was. The big man was emphatic in response. "He shook his
head and said that he did not want U.S. Government business as it
was a sure way to lose money. He refused to bid in spite of the
decreasing demand for his product."[19]

As Tom Bennett was turning down US government business, and
the Winchester shop floor fell uncharacteristically silent, Germany's
actions thousands of miles away were causing consternation in

European capitals – and in Washington DC. Germany under Kaiser Wilhelm II had moved from maintaining the status quo to a more aggressive posture. A treaty with Russia was not renewed, as the Kaiser opted for an alliance with Austria instead. Germany's neighbors France and Russia signed an alliance in 1894. Germany had started to build up its navy in 1898. By the summer of 1914, the Germans were prepared to risk starting a war. After the 1914 assassination of Archduke Franz Ferdinand, heir to the Austro-Hungarian empire, Serbia was blamed for the attack in Sarajevo. The fading empire declared war on Serbia, having received assurances from Germany's government of full support, and within days Russia, Belgium, France, Great Britain, and Serbia had lined up against the Austro-Hungarians and Germany, and World War I had begun. The United States under President Woodrow Wilson initially distanced itself from entanglement with Europe's conflict, which was seen as having no immediate impact on America. Wilson announced that the United States must be neutral and impartial. This meant that, in theory, the Winchester Repeating Arms Company could sell guns to any of the combatants.

However, Winchester Bennett was not inclined towards neutrality. He was not a New Englander for nothing – ties with the land of his ancestors were strong. On September 14, 1914, Win wrote that he found it "difficult to maintain in person the neutrality which our national position demands and one is inclined to feel from all one sees and hears, that the neutrality is of the nation and the federal government only, for certainly much sympathy [for Great Britain] is evident."[20] By the time those words were written, Winchester the company had already received its first order from Britain. The British government ordered 60,000,000 rounds of .303 ammunition on August 4, 1914, the day Britain declared war on Germany.[21] In Whitehall, London, the mandarins of government were moving quickly to secure war supplies. The speed at which events were moving was rapid, and should the war last beyond the autumn of 1914 more guns and ammunition would have to be found, and fast.

The London Armoury cabled New Haven just a few weeks later, knowing Britain's War Office needed more rifles than it could possibly produce in the time available. Winchester received a cable

on September 9, 1914, asking for "considerable quantities of rifles
[. . .] Cable could you supply and what date delivery." [22] Winchester
officials suggested it would be much simpler if the British sent their
own man to New Haven with the power "to treat and settle all details
that might arise." After some back and forth, London cabled again.
"An officer and chief draftsman from Government factory leaving for
States on Saturday next, taking with him samples English latest
pattern Mauser rifle with complete drawings. Very simple arm to
manufacture. Prepare to make contracts. Early deliveries essential.
Not only seeing you but others."

The steamship *Lusitania*, the sinking of which by the Germans later
in the war helped propel America into the fight, carried one Captain
Bernard Cecil Smyth-Pigott to America without incident, docking in
New York on October 31, 1914. The Captain was not a gun expert, and
so he followed the specifications laid down by the Royal Armoury back
at home very seriously indeed. Winchester Bennett tried to interest
Smyth-Pigott in the company's bolt action musket, but the Captain
swiftly pulled out a sample Enfield Model 1914 and said that was what
the British wanted manufactured. "It was with some surprise,"
recorded Winchester Bennett, "that we learned this arm was designed
for the .276 cartridge, a cartridge recently developed by the English
military authorities which we had never seen but which we learned
from Captain Smyth-Pigott was a rimless cartridge."

Not wanting to alienate a customer planning to place a large order,
the Winchester engineers nonetheless had to tell Smyth-Pigott that
modifying the Enfield so it would fire a rimless cartridge was going to
require compromise, and "compromises were seldom satisfactory."
The good Captain assured the assembled company that "his country
was at war and in need of arms, and that the matter would be treated
tolerantly," as Winchester Bennett recalled. Even though Smyth-
Pigott had the authority to make changes on behalf of the British
government, by his own admission "he was none too conversant with
the details of gun manufacture and design." The fiddly business of
modifying the Enfields so they would work and fire the Brits' rimmed
cartridge became a fraught negotiation with Smyth-Pigott and his
subordinate Mr Reavill, who did know a thing or two about making
guns. Despite the doubts aired by all, the British ordered an initial

200,000 Enfield rifles in November 1914 and the Winchester factory went into hyperdrive. A second order was placed for another 400,000 rifles.

The assorted war orders received by the Winchester Repeating Arms Company added up to a hefty $16.7 million by the end of November 1914 – of which about $5 million was profit. Five thousand people worked on the day shift at the Winchester factories, with another 2,500 doing the night shift.[23] War was big business. Winchester's stock price soared $500 a share,[24] and it was breathlessly reported that the company had been guaranteed $52 million of profits in wartime contracts.

However, the war exposed the company's weaknesses, as it confronted an unfamiliar landscape. As Edwin Pugsley, brother-in-law of Winchester Bennett and later Winchester's chief engineer, put it:

> The beginning of the First World War found the Winchester Repeating Arms Company completely unprepared for the role it was destined to play. It had drifted along a phenomenally profitable course producing the most popular and world famous line of sporting arms, and through the genius of T. G. Bennett [...] had attained an almost impregnable position in the American jobbing trade. Its gun line was protected by a strong patent position, ably and ruthlessly enforced.[25]

Now, with a string of orders, the complacency of the company was shaken. It had to find a way to rapidly mass-produce ammunition and guns for the Allies. Matters were not helped by the changes Winchester Bennett had introduced to the long-standing way of making guns at the factory. He was rightly trying to modernize the antiquated working practices, but the men were resistant to changing their ways.

For many years, contractors had reigned supreme in the Winchester company's way of doing business. The management would select an outstanding man, who would be set up as a contractor in his department. The company would charge him with the cost of components, and there would be a profit left over at the end for the contractor. "This system concentrated the manufacturing know-how in the hands and heads of the contractors, and they regarded this as their personal property, jealously guarding it from the Management,"[26] wrote Edwin Pugsley. Contractors had become all-powerful, figures of great influence in their own neighborhoods, with the power to hire and fire. When a contractor died, his knowledge and patronage went with him, leaving the company in a bad way. One by one, Winchester Bennett terminated the contracts and the super-intendent's office took over the operation of the gun shop. Win had also decided to divorce the maintenance shops from the gun factory and form a non-production department. This too caused resentment and confusion – a collision between workforce and management just as World War I began.

The gun shop was completely unprepared for production of the Enfield rifle: 2,000 were to be churned out per day, at a fixed price which included the bayonet. As seen through Edwin Pugsley's eyes,

> this meant more than doubling the output of the gun plant and called for new buildings to house the necessary new machinery [...] a tremendous load in building and buying new machinery was dumped overnight on an inadequate and unprepared organization. The result was utter confusion and it took a year to produce the first Enfield rifle.

Discussions about whether to expand the plant or lease buildings were heated within the company's management. There were obvious arguments in favor of new buildings – they would be easier to heat and light, and the older buildings could be abandoned after the war. But such was the rush to meet wartime demand, that decisions were made in a hurry and the new buildings were built within the old, which created immense problems when the war was over and the additional space was surplus to requirements.

As Winchester's top brass went back and forth over what to do about new facilities, newspapers caught wind of the unfamiliar whiff of disorganization from behind the company's gates. The *Hartford Courant* wrote:

> It's rumored in New Haven that the British Government is furnishing some of the funds for the erection of buildings in order that its

supplies of rifles, shrapnel, machine guns and ammunition may be greater than could be possible under the former facilities of the company. Winchester Bennett, vice-president of the company, when asked if this were true, expostulated "tommy rot." [27]

Captain Smyth-Pigott would only say tantalizingly that his lips were sealed.

The Brits weren't investing in the new factories directly, unfortunately for the company – Winchester's postwar fate might have been very different if the burdensome cost of new facilities had been met by others. Instead, the whole cost was on Winchester's balance sheet. Under the beady eye of Smyth-Pigott, laborers were imported from cities up and down the East Coast to meet wartime demand. "A hundred of them marched through the streets of New Haven in the early morning hours on their way to the dock of the steamboat coming to the Winchester factory and got immediately to work," [28] went a typical newspaper report. As the Winchester plants operated night and day, with workers hidden behind screened windows, Smyth-Pigott had become "socially prominent" in New Haven. The handsome young man was described as being "well built [. . .] of military bearing, about 35 years old and the perfect expression of the perfect English gentleman." [29] Hailing from Brockley Hall in Somerset, Smyth-Pigott's brother was an ace pilot and wing commander in the Royal Air Force, which no doubt added to the glamor.

While New Haven may have fawned over the dashing English captain from the crack infantry regiment, at the Winchester factory Bernard Smyth-Pigott clashed with the management frequently. Though Winchester Bennett personally demonstrated to the Englishman how it was going to be difficult to close the gun because of the size of the Brit's beloved rimless cartridge, the Captain was having none of it, and would not allow the engineers to deviate from the blueprint he'd hand carried from Britain. "We were instructed to proceed as per his directions," wrote Win gloomily. Poor Smyth-Pigott did not live to see the results of his orders – he died following complications after an operation for appendicitis, and is buried in New Haven.[30]

In the wartime propaganda battle between Germany and the Allies, Winchester became a pawn. Germany's Ambassador to the United States, Count Von Bernstorff, dramatically presented evidence to the US State Department of what he claimed was Britain violating the rules of international law. "The British Government has ordered from the Winchester Repeating Arms Company 20,000 riot guns, with 50,000,000 of 'buckshot cartridges.' The 'buckshot cartridge' contains nine bullets. The use of these weapons and this ammunition has hitherto been unknown in civilized warfare," thundered Germany's ambassador, highlighting what may seem like an antiquated concept of war played by gentlemen's rules. Still, the company's attempts to sell its riot gun and buckshot cartridges to "executives responsible for millions invested in buildings and machinery" caused consternation in some sections of the left-wing press, which questioned whether employees were really going to riot. A circular from Winchester read:

> the best insurance against trouble is preparedness. Usually the sight of efficient guns in the hands of resolute men will stop a riot. You do not want to use force, but if you must, you want a gun that has maximum defensive and stopping power.[31]

American newspapers eagerly lapped up what appeared to be propaganda from Washington – "German Agents Plot Strikes in Great American Plants to Hold Up Supplies for Allies,"[32] read one banner headline, sourced to "reliable quarters." The article outlined plans by German sympathizers to start labor agitation in the big plants, including the Winchester Repeating Arms Company, to stop war supplies making it over the Atlantic. This leak may well have come from Win himself. Winchester Bennett was extremely concerned about German spies in his gun shop, going so far as to write to the Secretary of War. "It seems likely that her [Germany's] secret agents have been at work in this country collecting information as to the places to strike and devising the most effective means for striking swiftly." In the spirit of preparedness, Win urged the government to deploy secret agents to protect factories like Winchester's and to "lend the Administration's moral influence to discourage, check and quell such labor disturbance wherever it may reveal itself."[33] Newton Baker wrote back, explaining "the War Department has no secret agents," adding for good measure that if war with Germany was declared, "with the limited resources in troops that we would have at the outset, it might not be possible to afford military protection to the plants at the beginning, in other words when protection might be most necessary."[34] Private guards were suggested as the best line of defense for Winchester's factories.

Win Bennett, always in rather frail health, was struggling with the added burden of dealing with the complex British order and overseeing wartime production. As Harold Williamson described the situation,

> by that time the problems connected with tooling up and scheduling the war work were serious enough to demand the responsibility of a strong hand. Winchester Bennett, who had assumed this responsibility, was already feeling the strain and he began looking for someone who could take over this burden.[35]

This was a defining moment in the firm's history. From Oliver Winchester through Thomas Gray Bennett to Winchester Bennett, the Winchester Repeating Arms Company had been family run since its incorporation in 1866. Now the influence of the family was being diluted. Win knew himself to be struggling with the task at hand, and he hired John Edward Otterson as general superintendent on July 1, 1915. Otterson rapidly became the power behind the throne and he was formally put in charge 18 months later. With the loss of family control came the slow descent into chaos, debt, and ultimately insolvency. But there was nothing to be done – Win was a competent production executive, a dedicated member of the team, yet he was dogged by persistent illness and felt unable to run the business, much to the disappointment of his father Tom.

John Otterson was a young and handsome Naval architect, who was somewhat randomly recommended to Winchester Bennett by the Aberthaw Construction Company, the contractor for the new buildings at the gun shop in New Haven. A student at MIT, where he had studied naval architecture, Otterson was greatly interested in the theories of scientific management that were in vogue at the time, because of the works of Frederick W. Taylor. These theories involved making the workforce more efficient through the use of time and motion studies, to boost productivity. Otterson had attempted to put these principles into practice in the Brooklyn and Charlestown Navy yards, where he'd met with a resounding thumbs down from the workforce, and had resigned from the Navy in 1915, just before accepting the position with Winchester.

The superintendents of the various departments resented the newbie Otterson being appointed general superintendent over their heads and acted mutinously. What does he know about guns seemed to be the general sentiment. Otterson had to exert his authority and fire the head of the cartridge shop for flagrant insubordination, just as orders for millions of Allied shells were piling up. Edwin Pugsley, then second assistant superintendent of the gun department, found that Otterson did in fact know a lot about heavy machinery and eagerly sought information about Winchester's manufacturing processes. However, in Pugsley's words,

> at the height of the confusion when Otterson needed the backing of the vice-president, Winchester Bennett, the latter was stricken with typhoid fever, which turned into pneumonia, and he nearly died. Just as he was recuperating and thought almost out of danger, he had an emergency appendectomy. When he came home from hospital several of his children came down with whooping cough. Fearing that he might get it and open his appendix wound, he was ordered to go south to escape the possibility. This he did, practically throwing Otterson to the wolves.[36]

Winchester Bennett's wife Susan, usually such a reliable chronicler of family life and Win's ups and downs, seems to have abandoned her diary entries during this torrid time – or perhaps she preferred not to donate a record of that difficult period to the Connecticut Historical Society, where the Bennett family papers are archived. The years between 1911 and 1922 are a blank – her last entry, after a blowy "bully" sail at Johnson's Point, reads: "Win came out feeling very miserable and I am quite worried about him."[37] Thomas Gray Bennett reluctantly came out of retirement to act as temporary president and treasurer. Writing to his sister-in-law Sarah Winchester in California, Tom explained:

> Poor Win was so used up by the anxiety and the burden of uncertainties as to be near a breakdown. He resigned and I took his place temporarily [...] He went to bed at once and after a month's illness was operated on for abscess of the liver. We had a week of great anxiety [...] the doctors say he should not work for months.[38]

Edwin Pugsley and his wife Dorothy, Susan's sister, were asked to move into Win and Susan's house and "ride herd on his children and operate his household during his absence, which we did." [39] What the extremely competent Pugsley thought about the simultaneous demise of his brother-in-law's health and the company's fortunes we can only guess, since the prolific memoir writer did not commit his innermost thoughts on this topic to paper. Family loyalty no doubt played a role in his tactful silence.

In Win's absence, Tom Bennett relied heavily upon John Otterson to run the gun shop – and the old stager consequently found himself at the center of Winchester's internal strife. The company, which had run so smoothly in Tom's day, was now a nest of vipers, as men jockeyed for position. The atmosphere was unrecognizable, and no doubt upsetting to Tom who had dedicated his working life to Winchester. Edwin Pugsley observed a company vice-president by the name of Harrie S. Leonard trying to take advantage of the limbo caused by Win's departure in an Iago-like fashion:

> He [Leonard] began to work on T.G. Bennett, telling him it was too bad his son had been so ill, and that his mind was undoubtedly injured by his illness; hence the possibility of his successfully resuming the presidency was very remote; that under these circumstances he [Leonard] was the logical choice for president due to he being younger.[40]

Leonard didn't get very far with his bid, since Otterson got wind of the plot via Edwin Pugsley. There was too much work to be done to waste time on positioning and poisonous politicking. For starters, the

Enfield Rifle Winchester made for the British troops was initially a disaster, just as the gun shop engineers had warned it would be. It was seen by the soldiers as a big, clumsy weapon, and they didn't like it one bit. The British Ordnance Office tightened up the inspection regime in New Haven until it was hard to get a gun passed. Guns were rejected for having telescope sights that rocked, for being hard to load, and for "lazy ejection" of cartridges. "These faults, which result in bad functioning of the rifle, are the result of careless assembling, and it ought to be possible to have this stopped. I fully understand the difficulties you have in keeping your assemblers up to the mark, but it is somewhat disheartening to find such obvious faults continuing to come through day after day," wrote the irate official from the British Inspection Department in New Haven.[41]

Edwin Pugsley and Bill Thiel, the gun office foreman, spent ten hours a day proof shooting the Enfields, and found they could easily be improved. There were also problems with the bayonet inspection. As Pugsley recalls, the British government "had imported a very large and powerful Englishman who requisitioned an oak log thirty inches in diameter and he would bang these blades against the log with all his strength. If he could detect any curve in the bayonet the lot was rejected." Pugsley discovered the English giant only rejected bayonets in the morning when he was fresh, and invariably passed lots submitted in the afternoon.

Win briefly returned to the Winchester Repeating Arms Company, after recuperating in Florida over the winter of 1915. Much had changed in his absence, as the production effort had been revolutionized for wartime and he no longer recognized the environment. In 1916 he was thrust into the midst of acrimonious contract negotiations with the British. The British wanted to cancel part of their order for the Enfield, since it was taking so long to make the rifles, whereas the company insisted on being compensated for the losses they had incurred. Win Bennett's negotiating stance was that the British had made so many changes to the Enfield gun, it had affected production and delivery dates. Eventually, the British reduced the number of rifles on order and agreed to compensate Winchester (and also Remington and Eddystone, other gunmakers in the same situation) for the manufacturing costs.

Even though the British canceled their original contract, orders from France and Russia flooded in, and the Winchester plant in New Haven had to expand to meet demand. Efficiency was increased, thanks to Otterson's scientific theories of management. A time study was introduced – and the men in the gun shop realized that by dropping some of their bad practices (such as including stages in the making of a new gun which they had no intention of doing) they could earn more money by beating the time study. Five hundred Model 95 arms were being produced daily for the Russians, modified to handle the Russian service cartridge – and there were problems with the Russian arms inspectors too, who were complaining about the weapons in what seemed to those at Winchester to be a blatant attempt to get bribes in return for a satisfactory inspection. The management refused, and Stetinus, the purchasing agent for the Russian government, straightened out the inspectors, according to Ed Pugsley. Staff stretched themselves to the limit to meet the orders of the Allied Powers. A total of 535,517 rifles, 273,483,500 rounds of ammunition, and 1,965,000 British shell casings, plus 7,604,600 primers for the shell cases had been manufactured by the Winchester Repeating Arms Company by April 6, 1917.[42] Countries as far afield as Norway and Serbia ordered Winchester's explosive primer. In 1916, the Winchester plant used a colossal amount of raw materials – 75,000 tons of coal, a million gallons of fuel oil, 1.1 billion cubic feet of water, 10,000 tons of steel, 13,500 tons of lead, 4,500 tons of copper, and 1,600 tons of zinc were swallowed up to make the rifles and ammunition on order.,[43]

The financing of the wartime expansion was problematic. The only money available to fund the huge investment in buildings and machinery required for the Allied contracts was the 25 percent deposit on the contract price – which wasn't enough. By November 1915, the company had to turn to the big banks, a humiliating and wholly unfamiliar experience for an enterprise which had been financially sound since the 1880s. Turning over sensitive financial information in return for aid was "repugnant" to the thrifty New England management,[44] but it was inescapable in the circumstances. By December 1915 $8.25 million had been borrowed from J. P. Morgan. Yet that wasn't enough. As Harold Williamson meticulously detailed, by February 1916, only $12.7 million of the $47.5 million contracts had been delivered, leaving $35 million's worth of unfilled orders, while working capital was $20 million. Because of the difficulty in meeting production schedules, more ready cash was needed.[45] The contracts with the Allies were fixed price, but the costs involved in making the guns and ammunition – labor and raw materials – kept rising, which made the true price of making the weaponry higher than anticipated. It was time to borrow yet more money.

Holding its nose, on February 17, 1916 the company directors voted to take out a second loan of $16 million with Kidder, Peabody and Company, a Boston bank. Half of that was used to pay off J. P. Morgan. In return, Charles Sargent of Kidder, Peabody came on the Winchester board.[46] Credit was easily available given the demands of wartime – and the Winchester company took full advantage. In public documents, Kidder, Peabody boasted to its investors about what a good bet the gunmaker was:

> The Company [...] is engaged in the manufacture of rifles, ammunition and machine guns for the United States government, and is actually manufacturing the Browning Machine Gun. The large business on hand, the ample assets and earnings, together with an excellent management, make [...] a most attractive investment.[47]

Such was the positive spin from the bankers.

At the time of the second loan, Tom Bennett was greatly upset by his son's illness and the state of the world, and uncharacteristically had no clear sense of the best way ahead for the company. Such was Tom's disenchantment and lack of confidence that he was even willing to turn Winchester over to outside interests. He offered Kidder, Peabody an option to purchase the majority of stock held by the family.[48] The Bennett family staggered on as majority stock holders, though George Madis writes that Kidder, Peabody had insisted on this right to an option to purchase a controlling interest in Winchester, and attempted to sell their interest in the company to Du Pont.[49]

Winchester Bennett had resumed the office of president and treasurer when he returned to work in 1916, but he held the positions in name only until 1917. Winchester's anguished father Tom could not at first decide whether Harrie Leonard or John Otterson should become the active head of the company. His loyalties were with the Old Guard represented by Leonard, but he knew the challenges of wartime were daunting, and required new thinking. After being racked by indecision, Tom finally opted for what he could see were Otterson's problem-solving skills. And so John Otterson was elected first vice-president in January 1917, in belated recognition of his role as the de facto head of the company. Though the Winchesters and the Bennetts still had financial control of the business and Tom Bennett retained an important role, the family's role was diminishing. George Hodson resigned as president in December 1916, after his attempt to change lenders and get out of the clutches of Kidder, Peabody and Company failed.[50] Hodson wanted new financiers who would interfere less in management decisions, but the bankers were now embedded in the company.

Despite new management and colossal loans, the financial position in 1917 was not promising. "The year 1917 was a terrible one. We were all the time facing large debts and handling what for us were enormous sums which came and went leaving little for us," as Tom Bennett summarized the situation in a letter to Sarah Winchester. According to Harold Williamson, high priest of Winchester historians, the war contracts with the Allies were supposed to total $47.5 million and yield a manufacturing profit of $15.5 million. Instead the contracts produced $30.7 million with a profit of $5.47 million. The extraordinary rise in costs resulting from the increase in labor rates and the rising price of raw materials, coupled with the fixed price contracts negotiated with the Allies, and not to mention the cancelled contracts – all this led Henry Brewer, the top Winchester official and former suitor of Susan Bennett, to say later: "Out of all the foreign contracts taken we made practically little or nothing."[51]

The US entry into the war provided a temporary reprieve for the New Haven management and workers. The commander-in-chief of the American Expeditionary Force, General John Pershing, had nearly 1.5 million men in Europe by 1918, all needing guns.

Winchester was poised to supply them with rifles, making first a modified version of the Enfield rifle and then the Browning Automatic Rifle, brainchild of John Moses Browning, the former Winchester creative force.

American public opinion had been swayed in favor of entering World War I as unannounced attacks by German submarines on American merchant ships in the Atlantic increased. The sinking of the British passenger ships *Lusitania* and *Arabic* in 1915 had killed 131 US passengers, and caused uproar in America. The Bennett family cruising boat, the *ENAJ*, had been pressed into service patrolling the coastal waters of Connecticut looking for German U-boats. President Woodrow Wilson severed diplomatic relations with Germany, and once it became clear that the Germans were also attempting to cause mayhem in Mexico, America declared war on April 6, 1917. It was not a moment too soon for the dwindling finances of the Winchester Repeating Arms Company. As Edwin Pugsley explained:

> At the end of 1916 and the early months of 1917 we had either completed or had cancelled practically all the work we had for foreign governments [. . .] so that the first part of 1917 found us with a plant entirely equipped for making small arms and ammunition and an organization completely trained and nothing to do. Great portions [of the plant] were idle.[52]

Not for long.

America entered World War I with the Army woefully ill-equipped. Woodrow Wilson had won the presidential election of 1916 on the platform "He Kept Us Out of War." The millions of Americans who could trace their heritage back to Germany had no wish to go to war against the old country, and there had been little domestic pressure to arm the United States for battle. Thus there was a shortage of that most basic of requirements for a soldier, an individual weapon. "It is the men with rifles who hold the front line trenches, who go "over the top" and who will bullet and bayonet, (that) settle the final issue of every battle. What is Uncle Sam's situation today with regard to this most vital branch of equipment?"[53] So asked the newspapers, concerned about the fate of the "doughboys," as the US infantry men were known, being sent "Over There," to the battlefields of France. Winchester was ready to equip America's soldiers. Winchester's sales manager offered this opinion of how the draft of young men into the Army would affect business:

> Ninety-eight per cent of the wage and salary earners will be fully employed at the HIGHEST WAGES THEY HAVE EVER RECEIVED. Women will now rapidly enter gainful occupations formerly occupied by men, and will help to fill the gaps in the customers' ranks. Government expenditures are growing to enormous proportions and will continue to increase. Everything points to an UNUSUALLY HEAVY VOLUME of gross business this fall.[54]

The company became virtually an outpost of government once America entered the War. "We do not bargain for contracts," Tom Bennett wrote to Sarah Winchester, sadly. "They are as it were orders to do so and so. To decline would probably mean taking over our property." The newspapers were brim-full of articles about Woodrow Wilson's government dealing blows to excessive war profits. "One Manufacturer Directed to Furnish Large Order of Supplies at Prices Far Lower Than He Submitted," read a banner headline in the *New York Sun*.[55] Winchester's management sent telegrams to the War Office offering to place the company's facilities at their disposal, and John Otterson was invited onto the board of the specially created Munitions Standards Board. As the urgent search for a service rifle got underway, Otterson suggested the Ordnance Department adopt a modified version of the Enfield rifle that Winchester had manufactured for the British. Government tests showed this to be a good option under the straitened circumstances, and the company was in business. On June 1, 1917 the Secretary of War ordered 225,000 of the modified Enfields. Such was Otterson's confidence that he had already started manufacturing the rifles, knowing he could sell them elsewhere in the unlikely event of the War Office passing.

The Winchester Repeating Arms Company's war effort on behalf of America dominated New Haven. As the *New Haven Register* put it,

Where ever a New Havener may travel, in this country or abroad, the sign of the big red "W" recalls to his mind a plan situated in the northern part of Elm City, with massive buildings stretching a half mile in either direction, covering many acres of ground and with innumerable chimneys reaching far into the sky.[56]

Nearly 20,000 people worked beneath those smokestacks at the height of production, and Winchester Avenue was jammed for the entire length of the factory when shifts changed. Girls as young as 14 worked at the plant. There were constant worries about fuel rationing, and John Otterson had to cable the Ordnance Department in Washington demanding that Winchester be put on the fuel priority list or else production would shut down. The factory was gobbling up 120,000 gallons of oil per month to manufacture not only Browning rifles, but also an order of 50,000 Colt pistols from the US government. This latter order caused Edwin Pugsley great astonishment. "I asked him (Otterson) where he thought he could fit these new requirements into our already bulging plant. He said he thought we could farm the component manufacturing out to local plants [...] I was told to see what could be done along these lines."[57] To Pugsley's surprise, "I was amazed at the eagerness with which the management of the best plants in town grasped the opportunity to enter war work." Patriotism and pride were riding high – equipping American soldiers for battle with the Germans in the far off fields of northern France was seen as necessary, noble work. As Winchester, Remington and others manufactured 10,000 army rifles every day, there was relief that "the charge American forces are compelled to use broomsticks for lack of rifles no longer holds."[58]

Tom Bennett, in his 70s when America entered the conflict, also threw himself into Winchester's war effort with his trademark enthusiasm. Tom visited the Secretary of War Newton Baker in Washington DC, and offered to go to France himself with a team from Winchester to show the troops how the guns should be fired. Baker replied, thanking Bennett for his "generous offer," and suggesting he would instead take some of Tom's expert employees to France under the auspices of the War Department's demonstration team.[59] It was typical of Tom's attention to detail and his devotion to country that he would be eager to travel across the Atlantic Ocean to show American troops how the guns built by Winchester fired, and what their quirks were. As a soldier in the Civil War, he knew first hand the importance of having trust in one's weapon.

The bruising experience with the British and the Enfield Rifle contract earlier in the war had taught the company a valuable lesson. Fixed price contracts did not protect the firm against rocketing costs and subsequent indebtedness. So in dealing with the US government, Winchester's management "made it clear to the Chief of Ordnance of the Army that it would, in effect, have to be guaranteed against losses on Government work. It was agreed in principle that a payment of cost-plus-ten-per-cent would be a fair basis for participation in the 'partnership.'" [60] Though Otterson pushed hard during negotiations to get the cost of the gigantic expansion of the Winchester plant undertaken before the United States entered the war included in the costs plus 10 percent equation, this was never fully signed off by the War Department. Therein lay the postwar problem of what to do with the surplus capacity. However, in Congress, suspicion was rife that Winchester was making out like a bandit. Newspaper leader writers reported on the animus in the nation's capitol directed at Winchester:

> They are guaranteed a ten per cent profit under the contract. The contract is now under fire at Washington, members of Congress objecting that the rate is too high though army men say it is a good bargain. Because the government has nine million dollars worth of machinery in the plants, the claim is made that the contract gives the concerns as high as fifty per cent increment on the capital involved. [61]

Not only was Winchester facing antagonism from within Congress, but closer to home, there was friction between Winchester and the US War Department's small arms division. Winchester's old-timers sighed, for this was a re-run of the tension with the British and their factory inspector earlier in the war. While John Otterson liked Major Armstrong, assigned by the War Department to check on Winchester's progress in manufacturing the modified Enfield rifle, the Major's military colleagues considered him an ignoramus. "He has been very energetic and very effective," protested Otterson when the War Department suggested moving Major Armstrong from New Haven back to base as an instructor in the musketry school.[62] Tom Bennett argued that any change in executive control should be avoided at such a pivotal moment in the US war effort. But one Major Woodbury, an associate of Armstrong's at the Winchester factory in New Haven, stated that Armstrong "was not a technical man, he had no knowledge of manufacturing, and [...] he was dependent upon others for decisions on technical matters." Major Woodbury had in mind for the post a certain Major Smith, a pal from the Springfield Arsenal. Winchester Bennett, Tom Bennett, and John Otterson were furious, whereupon Major Woodbury "was quite impatient in our desire to retain Major Armstrong and ultimately said there must be something behind our actions in the matter. He evidently thought we had some ulterior motive."[63] The Army presumably suspected Winchester of trying to hoodwink the not-so-technical Major Armstrong with sub-standard rifles. Major Smith also had his problems with insubordinate fellow officers. Poor R. C. Swanton, Winchester's industrial engineer in charge of costs, wrote despairingly to Otterson:

> I understand that Major Moore does not recognize Major Smith's authority, and that plans are being made by the Machine Gun section to duplicate the offices of Property Officer, Shipping etc that are established for the Government by Major Smith. This procedure will cause the Company to spend more money and will also be more expensive for the Government. Can we not have some arrangements whereby Major Smith will be recognized by all Army people [...] ?[64]

The obduracy of the Army bureaucracy and its obsession with hierarchy had the practical gunmakers of Winchester tearing their hair out. As war raged across the Atlantic, in New Haven the focus was on smoothing over difficulties and supplying the doughboys with rifles – including John Browning's automatic rifle, affectionately known as the BAR. This rifle was commissioned by the US Army in an attempt to break the stalemate of trench warfare in the battlefields of France and Belgium – it fired over 300 rounds a minute, and became a fearsome weapon. In a historical irony, a variant of the rifle Tom Bennett had rejected at the turn of the century, leading to a parting of the ways with Browning, was now to be mass-produced by Winchester. And Browning himself would return to the factory at New Haven to check on production of his rifle, years after storming out over a row over royalties. War made strange bedfellows indeed.

The Colt factory in Hartford had the only working model of Browning's gun, which was borrowed by Winchester on a Saturday afternoon. Sketches were made rapidly and measurements were taken in double quick time, and the BAR was returned immediately. On December 29, 1917, three months after the model was borrowed from Colt, Winchester had assembled their first complete Browning Automatic Rifle. By December 1918, over 27,000 of them had been produced.[65] The War Department's contracts were cancelled after the Armistice was signed, but Browning's rifle arrived on the battlefields in time to make an impact for the young American soldiers in France. It was an instant favorite with the troops, who found it light, accurate, and robustly engineered. Browning's son, Lieutenant Val Allen Browning, was one of those who fired the rifle against the enemy. Once again, Browning's superior design showed its worth. Though introduced very late in the war, the BAR was used during the Battle of the Argonne Forest, part of the final Allied offensive in September 1918 that stretched along the entire Western Front. General John Pershing's men fired Browning's rifle at the German Second Army, and ultimately forced the demoralized enemy to retreat.

As the war drew to a close, Otterson's energy and focus on time management had paid off, and during 1918 the company delivered over $50 million's worth of orders to the government. Those like Ed Pugsley, who had worked so hard to meet the demands of the US and Allied contracts, felt Winchester had come through World War I "with flying colors." [66] Otterson was praised as:

> probably the most efficient factory manager that ever came into New England [...] Those who are in the position to know the "inside story" of Winchester's feel they cannot give enough credit to John E. Otterson, the young naval mechanical man who came here in the face of probably the greatest sacrifice a man could make in these modern

days, fought against incredible odds a battle that is amazing, and finally re-made the concern that induced him to give up the place of superintendent of construction at the Brooklyn navy yard and come to New Haven.[67]

There was much back-slapping in New Haven as General Pershing's men came home from the mud-bath and the nightmarish conditions in the trenches of France. The job of both soldier and arms manufacturer had been successfully completed under trying circumstances. But as Winchester celebrated, the postwar landscape was perilous. According to Henry Brewer, vice-president of Winchester during the war,

> Otterson remarked to me that when the war was over, our problems would be entirely changed. At the present moment our problem was one of production – we could sell everything that we could manufacture. However, as soon as the war was over, our problems would become one of sales and distribution, that we could produce more than we had distribution channels to get proof. Although Otterson foresaw this change in conditions long before others in the company, nothing was done seriously in the way of preparing for this change until the war was practically at its close.

In addition, there was still the matter of the millions the company had borrowed from the bank of Kidder, Peabody and Company. President Woodrow Wilson was contemplating a War Profits bill, which would bring in revenue by taxing those seen to have profited most from the bloodshed. Congress was on the offensive against what were portrayed as the outrageously high profits guaranteed to the arms manufacturers by the Department of War. One of the government's representatives at the Winchester factory, one Lieutenant Jackson, went so far as to accuse the company of deliberately trying to defraud Uncle Sam through fake wartime accounting.[68] Suspicion that Winchester and other firms had been engaged in rampant profiteering was rife. Yet the true picture was bleaker than anyone could have imagined. Tom Bennett was losing sleep over the underlying state of the finances, as he explained in a letter to his sister-in-law Sarah Winchester:

> The matters of Winchester have progressed favorably so far as our U.S. Government contracts are concerned. This year we shall probably make eight million dollars and this sum would, with our present cash assets, put us nearly out of debt.
>
> Unfortunately new tax laws are being devised and which instead of taking 48% of our earnings will take 80% of our excess profits over 8%, which will leave us quite poor, our indebtedness being considered.
>
> It seems to me dangerous for the family to keep control longer. Win is, at a vital time, unable to do much. I am 73 years old. The problem is a large matter and I could not advise you or Jane [Tom Bennett's wife] [...] to put more money into it. I fear it will be difficult to borrow next March when our notes come due.[69]

The newspapers picked up on Winchester's impending crisis. "'Starving in the midst of plenty' is a term peculiarly fitted to the stockholders of the Winchester Repeating Arms Company," observed the *Wall Street Journal* in 1917, when the company failed to pay a dividend on its stock yet again and the share price plunged. "Strange to say that in 1915, when war orders began to pour in and fabulous profits were expected, dividends of $25 a share paid in 1916 were the smallest of any year (1904–15)." The *Journal* saw this as "a bitter pill for holders of the Winchester stock, which has long been regarded as an exclusive possession." However, the *Journal* was spot on in its analysis of why Winchester, like other manufacturers who had taken on large war orders, was in a tight financial corner. "Profits on these contracts were pared off to a fine point by mounting costs of raw materials, working capital requirements to finance new buildings [...] stringent requirements of foreign governments on rifles and high labor costs."[70]

The company tried vainly to get the American government to contribute towards the cost of the expensive expansion of the Winchester plant – but the Winchester claim was turned down by the War Department, on the grounds that this had nothing to do with the United States. Winchester's management had built the new factories for the British and Russian contracts, before the United States even entered the war. An exchange at the War Department Claims Board reveals the threadbare state of Winchester's accounts. Asked by a US representative what the financial result of Winchester's foreign contracts was, a Winchester official named Mr Anderson replied: "It left us with a big plant, and that is about all. It brought about a cessation of dividends." [71]

John Otterson knew the constraints better than anyone, and was extremely anxious about the company's exposed position. Surveying the array of new buildings built for Winchester's wartime production, which unhelpfully sat in amongst the old factories in New Haven and could only be leased separately with great difficulty, he tried to come up with a postwar plan for this excess real estate. If all the different plants were in use, Otterson saw they could produce "more sporting arms in a month than could be sold in the entire world over a year; therefore it became necessary to increase the outlets to keep pace with the increased production." [72] Otterson was an excellent manager who could meet massive orders under trying circumstances, but he was not confident in his abilities as a salesman. And anyway, what was the Winchester Repeating Arms Company going to use all this spare production capacity to make?

For answers, Otterson turned to a golfing pal and salesman extraordinaire, Louis Liggett, founder of the phenomenally success-ful Rexall drugstore chain. Rexall was a Latin word play, meaning King of All. Otterson and Liggett were friends from Boston days, and since Rexall stores were making more money per square foot than any other retail outlet in the country, Liggett seemed like the logical savior of the Winchester sales dilemma. Liggett, a larger-than-life character who had persuaded independent drug stores to invest in a retailer's cooperative selling products under the Rexall name, agreed to serve three months on the Winchester board and see if he could make a difference. Edwin Pugsley always felt that Otterson's decision to invite Liggett onto the board was "his first and possibly greatest mistake." [73]

Hailing from Detroit, Louis K. Liggett was a whizz kid with charm, street smarts and the gift of the gab. Rexall druggists across the nation were independent store owners who sold the products of the

United-Rexall Drug Company – they carried the lines of gripe water, baby cough syrup, and such like exclusively, and did not compete against other Rexall stores since only one was permitted in each town. This network of drug store owners received regular letters from Liggett, famously addressed in a folksy style to "Dear Pardner." As Liggett's childhood friend and biographer Samuel Merwin describes it, this contact with Liggett made the owners feel sprinkled by his fairy dust:

> The American druggist had left far behind his dingy little shop with the big bottles of colored water in an otherwise meaningless window. He was a considerable merchant now [. . .] L.K. was the man who had evoked the miracle. L.K. had seemed to walk right into his personal life, stir it to the roots, pour the ichor of the Gods of big business into his arteries and make him an integral part of the Great American Spirit of Success. L.K. had the magic touch; he simply had it. L.K. wrote him letters – long letters – that bristled with unconquerable vigor, that bubbled with humor, that glowed with humanity.[74]

Charismatic and imbued with a Messianic sense of certitude, Louis K. Liggett persuaded Otterson and Tom Bennett that replicating the Rexall model of dealerships while selling hardware and sporting goods manufactured in the myriad Winchester factories was the way for the company to thrive. Liggett even persuaded Winchester to invest in annual conventions, expensive get-togethers which had proved an important bonding event for the druggists. The fact that Liggett's druggists didn't make anything, they only sold pharmaceuticals, and that the drugstore and gun businesses were hardly comparable didn't strike anyone as a problem. Ed Pugsley, Winchester's chief engineer, watched with grim fascination, as Otterson brought Liggett onto the board to rejuvenate the company; but, as he ruefully wrote in his memoir, "What Otterson did not know was that Liggett was a wild man who had to be closely controlled by his own organization."[75]

Thanks to Liggett's persuasive powers, the rifle manufacturers were about to go into the hardware business, using the Winchester brand to sell razors, ice-skates, washing machines, and all manner of metal household goods as well as the famous guns. This was Liggett's bold vision. Winchester was a household name, emblematic of excellence, so why not use that prestigious brand to sell goods for the home? Tom Bennett, once the wise counsel, was now feeling his age and didn't have a better idea. Doing business with the US government had been ruinous for Winchester, he felt, and now it was imperative to have a rapid clean-up operation. This seemed as good a concept as any, and it was being promoted by Liggett, who had an impressive track record in retail.

With a sense of great urgency, Tom Bennett, John Otterson, Louis Liggett, and Charles Sargent (the banker on the company board) worked out the details of the postwar foray into retail. Diversification was the buzz word of the time, and Winchester was going to embrace that, making and selling garden tools, saws, scissors, roller-skates, cutlery, screwdrivers, flashlights, and fishing reels – all "as good as the gun," [76] as the slogan went. On August 7, 1918, before the war was even officially over, the board of directors approved the outline of this plan for the refinancing of the company. On October 26, 1918 a confounding letter was posted to Winchester stockholders, who had hitherto happily assumed that their investment was at long last making millions from the business of war. Choking over their cornflakes and coffee, the investors across the country learned the true state of Winchester's finances. Tom Bennett, the grand old man of rifle-making, was a signatory to the letter – which must surely have been read by stockholders with a mounting sense of disbelief.

In the early days of the European War the company entered into large contracts for arms and ammunition with certain foreign governments, notably the British Government, and greatly expanded its plant facilities for the purpose of these contracts. It became necessary to obtain loans upon the Company's notes to the extent of some $16 million [...] At present the Company has outstanding notes payable of about $8 million. In addition the Company has other current liabilities aggregating over $9 million, of which $4 million is an advance from the United States Government against Government contracts.

The Company's earnings prior to the war may be taken as an indication of the earning power of its commercial business. There seems little likelihood that the Company's normal commercial business can be materially increased after the war. The Company will, therefore, find itself with a large investment in plant facilities subject to taxation, insurance, depreciation, and interest [...] without existing business sufficient to carry these charges, and at the same time pay adequate dividends to stockholders.

It becomes necessary, therefore, to divert the plant facilities in substantial degree to the manufacture of articles other than those previously manufactured, involving the rearrangement of the existing machinery, and the purchase and installation of machinery suited to the new purposes.[77]

This was breaking news to the stockholders, who had gone without dividends since 1915 because of the war, but at their last annual meeting earlier in 1918 had been assured matters were improving. First, they had to absorb the shocking headline about Winchester's near insolvency, and the plan to diversify into unspecified products that weren't guns and ammunition. Then, shareholders were told that financial control of the organization was being turned over to Kidder, Peabody and Company at a rate of $750 per share in new preferred stock for each share of old stock – in return for investment of additional capital of $3.5 million.[78] Oh, and Otterson and Liggett would take over the management, for good measure. The investors could either accept this fait accompli, or refuse, and face deferred dividends and the need to raise more money. A considerable number of minority stockholders protested about what they saw as a wretched deal, imposed by fiat. But since the majority of stock was family held, they were outvoted.

This crossroads brings us to the beginning of the end of direct family involvement in the management of the Winchester Repeating Arms Company. The reorganization plan required the consent of the two principal stockholders – Mrs T. G. Bennett, aka Tom's wife Jennie, and Sarah Winchester, the widow of Oliver Winchester's son William. The ladies dutifully followed the advice of Tom, to whom they deferred in financial matters. Tom did not want to see the family at incur, and Liggett had ny to enter the hardware pocket knives to washing s lawyer, Tom compared g, unused buildings to a

n ditch, with deep banks le the water runs and the ut as soon as the water and embankments and and is a target only to the

in, a new corporation, the l 16, 1919. Edwin Pugsley er launched what became idea was that in return for being appointed Winchester Dealer for your territory, the appointed salesperson for the household goods, you could buy stock in the company and get a good price on Winchester guns and ammunition. This infuriated Winchester's existing network of gun salesmen, called jobbers, and they cut Winchester off their lists and began to push rival lines such as Remington and Savage – thus damaging the core business of Winchester, selling rifles. Meanwhile, the new sales teams were feted, as per Louis Liggett's instructions on team building. Just as the Rexall druggists enjoyed annual conventions, so the Winchester salesmen were to be launched in style, in a massively expensive operation. In New Haven, a week of training for the retail staff was topped off by a theater party at the Schubert, followed by an extravagant banquet at the Garde. "The banquet will be a Winchester family gathering where the Winchester spirit and good fellowship will prevail. A vaudeville set, performed by the Yale Glee club quartet and other features are being planned for this occasion,"[79] reported the local newspaper excitedly. The sales staff did indeed enjoy a gala event – they sang "I'm forever blowing bubbles" en masse, and applauded as a banner was unfurled in front of the orchestra bearing the legend "We Put the Win in Winchester." Tom Bennett, loyal company man that he was, delivered a speech on "Winchester, the Old and the New." Unfortunately, the company coffers were being drained faster than you could say Winchester repeating rifle. The New England values of frugality and honest, hard work were smothered by this ill-advised rush to embrace retail.

Ed Pugsley looked on morosely as the arms manufacturer launched itself headlong into the real estate market, buying shops in prime locations nationwide. Ironically, 1919 was the biggest year in company history for gun sales. Pent-up demand after the war had led to sales of over 300,000 rifles.[80] Yet the company was losing focus on what it did best, and was instead searching for fancy shop fronts. The Winfield building, with its signature grandiose arched windows on the busy corner of 5th Avenue and 40th Street in Manhattan, was to be the venue for the marquee Winchester Sportsmen's Headquarters in New York City. A second Manhattan store was planned for Madison and 42nd Street. "During the early period all sorts of irregularities developed in this new Winchester organization," Pugsley observed. "Buyers went on wild buying sprees. The real estate crew began bribing owners to sign exorbitant leases, to mention only a few." [81] Pugsley reported his concerns to Otterson, who promptly fired the head of real estate. Pugsley, the chief engineer on the gun side, was suddenly appointed head of retail sales. Pugsley told Otterson that as an engineer he had no experience of sales, and clearly wasn't the man for the job. Otterson was adamant. "If I would take the job he could sleep nights. And so I [Edwin Pugsley] changed from Chief Engineer of the Company to Manager of the Retail Stores Department."[82]

There were 11 stores in operation when Pugsley was suddenly put in charge of them – so naturally enough, he went to visit his new empire. He was appalled by the stores and the crucial missing ingredient:

> They had cost a mint of money and there wasn't a customer in any of them. At the end of the week I was back and recommended to Otterson that we close them. This was a shocker to Otterson and he said he couldn't do that; that he had built me up to Liggett as the

savior of the Stores and that I would have to run them [...] I found that the plan was to open 52 stores per year at the rate of one store per week. I pointed out the amount of capital this would require and got permission to cut the stores to be opened to those too far along to stop.

Horrified by the waste, Pugsley tried to prevent the costs of the empty shops from spinning completely out of control. He managed to contain the wildly optimistic expansion plans, so in the end there were only 13 Winchester retail stores – two in New York, three in Boston, and one each in Providence, Worcester, Springfield, Fall River, Lawrence, Troy, New Haven, and Pawtucket, Rhode Island.

The Providence hardware store in Rhode Island was the first to open to the general public, amid much fanfare. "Some four thousand persons passed through the doors on a tour of inspection," reported the newspapers, leaving out no detail. "The store front is of gray with the name 'Winchester' set out in vivid red [...] Everything from sneakers to snow shoes will be sold, and the carpenter, the plumber, the athlete, and the housewife will all be taken care of." There was an elegant ladies' reception room, where the women could read the latest magazines and enjoy the tasteful wicker furniture while taking a break from shopping. There were even female sales assistants on the shop floors, a rarity for hardware stores of the day, as the company made a push for women's business as well as men's. The Winchester house journal underscored this attempt to appeal to the head of the household:

> Due to its [the Providence store's] arrangement, displays and general attractiveness it is so unlike the average hardware store that the difference will make a deep impression upon the mind of the woman buyer, so deep in fact that when she thinks of home needs she will think of the Winchester Store.[83]

The layout and content of the stores were seen as enticing to male shoppers too. "Every hardware man will agree that the Winchester store of Boston is a 'Tiffany' of hardware stores," gushed the *Hardware Review*, after an exclusive preview tour.[84]

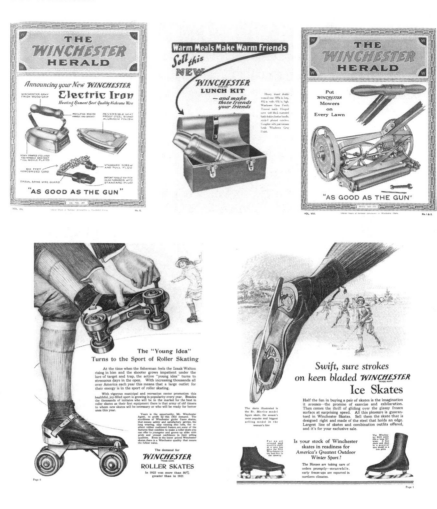

Fig. 22 Advertisements for Winchester household goods.

Once inside these temples to Winchester, there was a bewildering array of items to choose from – axes, saws, pocket knives, fishing rods and reels, athletic supplies such as jerseys, bats, baseballs, helmets, and footballs, as well as arms and ammunition. Dealers were instructed by the company literature to underline the superiority of Winchester products, making implicit parallels with the famous guns. "When they come in for a Wood Saw, sell them the Winchester – order Winchester Saws for their high grade steel blades, teeth that are sharp and stay sharp longer." [85]

Manufacturing these new products caused numerous difficulties, since Winchester either didn't have the requisite expertise or ran into the thicket of patents around successful designs. Just as Winchester had adeptly protected its guns with aggressively enforced patents, so others were ring-fencing their money spinners. As Henry Brewer recalled:

> We had hoped that we could stamp our knife blades of chrome-vanadium steel and use the automatic grinders acquired when we purchased one of the knife machines. We soon found that only forged blades would take the high polish required by dealers and buyers. We also had difficulty in making flashlight switches, since all good designs were covered by existing patents [...] Clay target equipment patents turned out to be impractical and we had to design and patent entirely new designs, after the time and money of trying to use the old styles, which we purchased.[86]

Just as the empire her father Oliver Winchester had founded began to crumble and fade, weakened by this disastrous foray into flashlights and clay pigeon targets, Tom Bennett's wife Jennie died. Virtually her final act was to sign away family control of the Winchester Repeating Arms Company to Louis Liggett and the bankers. This stalwart of the family and doyenne of New Haven was widely mourned. "She spent all her life in New Haven and by her generous giving and wise advice had a strong influence on its important philanthropic activities, serving on many boards governing the charitable and religious work of the city," reported the *New Haven Times*.[87] The beloved Jennie to whom Tom Bennett was so devoted was mourned at a simple funeral in the family home on Prospect Street, the spectacular mansion the couple had lovingly planned together. Tom had hoped their final years could be spent enjoying the life they had worked so hard to build – instead it was dominated by one crisis after another, as their son Win became seriously ill and the family concern lurched towards insolvency, forcing Tom to come out of retirement. Theirs had been a long and contented marriage – 48 years of quiet encouragement and unquestioning support for one another. Tom was left to face the

Fig. 23 Thomas Gray Bennett, Winchester Bennett, and baby Thomas Gray
Bennett, *c.*1907.

turbulent end of Winchester's days without the wise counsel of his
lifelong companion.

Jennie died shortly before Tom's 50th anniversary with
Winchester, which was marked by the declaration of Bennett Day
at the company. A band played a concert at the plant, and in the
evening Winchester luminaries gathered at the Hotel Garde in New
Haven to honor the man himself. The company's current plight was
lost on no one, but this was a moment to celebrate Tom's service.
John Otterson toasted the quietly spoken, stoical Tom, saying:

> Governor Oliver F. Winchester gave the Company its name and Mr
> Bennett gave it its character. Someone has said that an organization
> is the lengthened shadow of an individual. If this is true, then
> Winchester is the handiwork of Thomas G. Bennett. I can say nothing
> more to you.[88]

Tom accepted an engraved silver loving cup, and with characteristic
modesty concluded:

Fifty years is a good long time. I have always tried to do the best I could, to be as kindly as possible in the management, to meet you all on equal terms, and I am glad to know that I have come so near to it.

As Tom reflected on his half-century with the firm, John Otterson, the new president, was embarking on a fateful shopping expedition. Between 1919 and 1921, Winchester bought the Eagle Pocket Knife Company, the Mack Axe Company, the Napanoch Knife Company, the Walden Knife Company, and the roller-skate makers Barney and Berry Incorporated, to name just a few. This expansion was justified in the name of providing enough goods to sell in the stores – volume was the mantra, with little regard for the cost. Louis Liggett, architect of this retail strategy, could not be relied upon for advice during this critical period – he was in England, busy buying up Boots the chemist. The haphazard acquisition of many and varied companies was a further drain on Winchester's still rocky finances.

At the end of 1921, Edwin Pugsley, in his unfamiliar role as head of retail, told Winchester officials that the stores had a lack of working capital and had been forced to go to the banks to finance their spring and Christmas business. Pugsley estimated that the stores had to generate $2.5 million's worth of sales to break even in 1922. Winchester's basic problem remained – the high cost of manufacturing the new goods to be sold in the stores was not being covered by sales. Not even close. Worse, the depression of 1921 was keeping shoppers at home. At the end of 1921, there were nearly 4,000 privately owned Winchester stores nationwide and 11 highly expensive flagship retail locations owned by the company. In a sign of the lop-sided nature of the retail experiment, there were 250 people in New Haven managing Winchester's owned stores while 228 folk actually worked on the shop floors.[89]

Watching the financial plight closely was Sarah Winchester, daughter-in-law of Oliver Winchester and grieving widow of Oliver's son William Wirt. Thanks to her inheritance, Sarah was the largest single shareholder in the new Winchester Company. As we have seen, she had moved out West after the twin tragedies of losing her child and husband to illnesses, and busied herself building the colossus now known as the Winchester Mystery House. Sarah's devoted legal and financial adviser Samuel Franklin Leib found a Winchester official on his doorstep in San Jose early in 1921, begging Sarah to allow the company to issue $10 million's worth of bonds to take care of its debts. Leib could not see another way of covering the debt, but he objected strongly to Sarah being asked to consent to the Winchester Company (owner of shares in the Winchester Repeating Arms Company as per the 1918/19 reorganization) guaranteeing payment of the bonds in the event that the Winchester Repeating Arms Company couldn't pay when the debt became due. "The creation of this indebtedness was of itself rather a shock to me, and doubtless to you also," Frank Leib wrote to Sarah. "I had to take, and did take, a very decided stand against allowing you to sign any consent that the Winchester company sign any guaranty of the kind." [90]

As the account books went further into the red, in 1922 Winchester merged with the Associated Simmons Hardware Companies of St Louis, Missouri. Simmons had been ferocious opponents of Winchester's dalliance with retail stores and dealers – and here they were going into business together. This was a head-scratcher, indeed. "Otterson, like a drowning man, seized upon every straw to no avail," [91] was the judgment of Edwin Pugsley. George Simmons, elder statesman of the St Louis-based hardware chain, explained his new-found interest in Winchester:

> it has been proved that while these gentlemen did not know from experience some of the things which our experience has taught us, still their ideas and ours are entirely in harmony as to the proper methods of distributing hardware [...] we have not found any other manufacturing concern big enough for us to tie up with because no other has the capacity for a broad variety of production that the Winchester Company has.[92]

For their part, Winchester hoped to reduce their distribution costs, push up profits, and get their hands on badly needed capital. Tom Bennett himself, in his final attempt to salvage the firm, visited the venerable Simmons in St Louis and negotiated the last ditch joint venture. Notably, Winchester acquired the Roanoke Spoke and Handle Company of Roanoke, Virginia in the merger. They were makers of the Louisville Slugger line of baseball bats, and this acquisition was thought to dovetail well with Winchester's production of baseball bats and tool handles – however, the Roanoke plant operated at a loss until 1925 when it burnt to the ground.[93]

Despite merging with Simmons and developing 1,000 new products in a year, matters went from merely dreadful to deplorable. Winchester made an operating loss of $1.267 million in 1923. Liabilities totaled $9.4 million and available cash and receivables amounted to only $4.1 million.[94] Though sales in the stores were increasing somewhat, they never approached the volume necessary to cover the colossal costs. Flashlights, batteries, fishing bait, wrenches, hammers, and chisels were making a modest profit – but most everything else was breaking even or being made at a loss. Cutlery was the worst offender – expensive to make, and not selling well enough. Ed Pugsley had scoffed at those who asked what Winchester knew about cutlery, and now he had to defend the anemic outlook. Kidder, Peabody and Company, the bank which was keeping Winchester on life support, demanded that Louis Liggett do something, since the retail experiment had been his bright idea. Liggett had sold his investment in Winchester at a profit,[95] when facing financial difficulties of his own.

Liggett's idea of drastic action was to send two of his henchmen to New Haven early in 1924, to put the management of Winchester under the microscope. Edwin Pugsley sardonically observed the duo at work:

> The Liggett organization, through wide experience, had developed a mop-up crew who took over whenever Mr Liggett broke loose and made an unfortunate deal. It consisted of two men, a Mr McCallum, who had been raised as a newsboy on the streets of New York, and W. A. Tobler.[96]

After six months, the pair had completed their investigation, and Tobler, a native of Switzerland, coolly told Liggett that Otterson could not manage the company properly. The financial outlook was so bad that Tobler recommended immediate receivership as the best course of action. Receivership was too drastic for the bank, but Tobler's intervention meant the end of the road for John Otterson. Ed Pugsley dolefully closed the last of the retail stores in New Haven, spread out the forlorn and unwanted cutlery and roller-skates on large tables, and steeled himself to look for a new job the next day. In the morning, Pugsley and other stalwarts were summoned into the directors' room at Winchester, and Otterson's resignation was announced. Frank Drew was promoted to president. To his surprise, Ed Pugsley found he had been named factory manager – back to the gun shop once again, after a brief and disastrous flirtation with baseball bats, paints, hammers, brushes, batteries, and bread knives. The storied name of Winchester was teetering on the edge of insolvency, after an embarrassing experiment went publicly awry.

Tom Bennett could take it no more, and in August 1924, he resigned as chairman of the Winchester Repeating Arms Company – to be replaced by Louis K. Liggett, still a favorite of the bankers Kidder, Peabody and Company despite the complete and utter failure of his retail idea. Tom was now 80 years old, and had completely lost all faith in both Liggett and Wall Street. Steadfast and upstanding to a fault, Tom could not bear to see the $200,000 spent on conventions for salesmen or the endless loans which were bleeding Winchester dry. He had become ever more caustic about the bankers and their motives in his private correspondence:

> The financiers were pretty well in control of Winchester, and they were arrogant. It was not their money that was used to gain control of Winchester, but these people assumed that because they controlled the money, they could control, not only Winchester, but the customers of the company [...] Every loss to Winchester was their gain. Each loan was secured by real property, and they made their money before the company got the money. Some of the investments they insisted on profited them privately. It was a bad situation, and they were like carrion eaters, advising on subjects so as to cause Winchester to expire.[97]

The carrion eaters, as Tom rancorously described the bankers, allowed Liggett to double down on his original flawed plan. Though the retail stores closed, the Winchester dealers carried on selling farm and garden tools alongside rifles. There was an ill-fated investment in refrigerators, which were growing in popularity in the 1920s. Despite ads proclaiming that superior Winchester fridges could be built to meet the demands "of any size home and every pocketbook," the models needed much more development before they could be sold successfully. The company wrote off that loss, and introduced yet another new product – a washing machine, called the Whirldry, which Ed Pugsley suggested. It proved popular in apartments, but once again, it was difficult for the gunmaker to compete credibly with established manufacturers. Pugsley, by now general superintendent of the plant, cut back on the absurd production costs associated with so many varied goods, and by 1927 even cutlery was making a small profit. Yet it was not even close to being lucrative enough to make a difference to the company's pallid finances. There was yet another emergency reorganization in 1929. This time Liggett's dealer plan was ditched, and Winchester decided to sell all its goods on the open market. Shareholders still weren't seeing a return on their investment, and nor would they – whatever modest hopes the company had of making it into the black were dashed by the stock market crash and the depression of 1929. Sales slumped as Americans panicked.

Susan and Win Bennett, relieved of their managerial association with the family firm, celebrated their silver wedding anniversary against the backdrop of this raging contagion. Twenty-six friends came to a celebratory dinner and the house was filled with flowers as Susan gave Win his Patek Philippe watch before breakfast. Win was still extremely poorly – he suffered from chronic rheumatism, and had spent time in Coconut Grove, Florida trying to recover. Susan stuck firmly to household matters in her diaries of this period, though one cannot help but wonder what the couple made of the company's move into household goods of every shape and size. Susan's sister Dorothy and her husband Edwin Pugsley dined with the Winchester Bennetts several times a week – but perhaps the topic of the company's downfall was simply too painful to discuss, with Win ailing and absent from the family firm and Ed Pugsley still on the front line.

Susan, who had trained as a nurse, needed all her medical background to deal with Win. He continued to suffer from excruciating back pain and digestive troubles, perhaps caused by kidney stones which had gone undetected earlier in his life. Susan's diaries detail Win catching flu frequently, feeling "seedy," being in pain, sitting on the veranda at Johnson's Point all day, having a temperature, and needing to take long naps. Win's was a difficult existence, which must have been tremendously hard for Susan to manage. She would get away when she could, to her own summer hideaway in Maine.

Despite the pain Win endured, his grandchildren remember him as a kindly figure with an enticing workshop in his New Haven home. There, Win would show his descendants how to melt down the pure lead foil that was used to wrap candy in those days, and pour the molten lead into molds to make toy soldiers. The grandchildren would make and etch copper trays in Win's workshop, and watch him set quartzes from what was known as Jewel Beach at Johnson's Point, where amethysts could be found after a storm. A little cart and runway which operated as a mini-rollercoaster in the playroom were a source of great delight to Win's tiny relatives, who enjoyed taking tea, complete with a three-tiered cake stand holding cakes and other goodies, with their grandparents. Whether at home in New Haven or at Johnson's Point, Win and Susan adored their growing family and made every effort to entertain them. Astrid, the maid who made the butterballs, Mr Coopie, the chauffeur, and his wife, who said she was a proud Seminole Indian, are fondly remembered characters from what was known as the Big House at Johnson's Point. Independence Day, July the Fourth, was always a special time at the Big House. Susan would provide kites and hats for everyone, and serve the children with a special drink made from ginger ale and grape soda. Peas and salmon served at room temperature were for dinner. Buckets and sand buildings at the beach would be blown up with cherry bombs and other explosives, in true Winchester style. Occasionally, the odd mailbox would meet with the same fate during the festivities.

Win's health never really recovered from his illness during World War I. He had a series of strokes, and after years of indisposition, in

1946 he checked into the Silver Hill hospital in New Canaan, Connecticut. Silver Hill was at the time a pioneering psychiatric hospital that provided treatment for addiction. His doctor was Franklin Du Bois, a famed neurologist and psychiatrist, whom Susan found "so nice and he handled the case so well." [98] Susan never mentioned specifically why Win went to Silver Hill, but given it was a psychiatric facility it seems reasonable to conclude there was a mental health or addiction component to the many ailments which had dogged him over the years. Perhaps Win had become addicted to painkillers or alcohol, to mask the pain he had endured for so many decades.

Win's brilliant, distinguished, demanding father Tom Bennett died in August 1930 at the age of 86, six years after quitting the firm he had served for half a century. "Ex-President of Winchester Arms Company and Civil War Veteran Dies in New Haven," [99] read the banner headlines. The old soldier went to his deathbed fulminating against the reckless bankers whom he held responsible for ruining everything. Winchester should have "stuck with guns and ammunition, which had made the company."[100] Though Tom did not live to see the ignominious end, he knew full well what was on the horizon. Less than six months after his death, the inevitable came to pass.

By the end of 1930 Kidder, Peabody and Company wouldn't keep Winchester afloat any longer and refused to extend yet another loan to the drowning company. On January 22, 1931 the famous name of Winchester, which had "meant defense to those in peril, succor to those in need, vengeance to the wronged, health and sustenance to those far from civilization, pleasure and happiness to the sportsman, creative joy to those who, generation after generation, have devoted themselves to designing and making epoch-making firearms" [101] went quietly and humiliatingly into receivership. At the end of 1931 the Western Cartridge Company, a one-time competitor sent packing by Tom Bennett four decades earlier, bought the tattered remnants of the Winchester Repeating Arms Company for a song: $3 million cash and $4.8 million in preferred Western Cartridge stock plus a few other expenses was all this once proud name was worth – $8.1 million for Oliver Winchester's colossus of the gunmaking world.

Another family concern, the Olin Corporation managed by F. W. Olin and his two sons, would now be in charge of Winchester's destiny. With strong leadership and smart decision-making, the Olins were able to get Winchester "back on track and on the way to a profit," in the words of John Olin.[102] But the glory days in which the founding family ran the eponymous Winchester firm were gone forever. All that was left were the legends. Win died quietly in his Florida home at Boynton Beach in 1953, of a kidney ailment known as Bright's disease. Win was nursed by his stalwart wife Susan until the very end.

CHAPTER 6

Aftermath

ONCE THE WINCHESTER Repeating Rifle Company was sold to the Olin Corporation in 1931, the Winchester and Bennett family association with the firm founded by Oliver Winchester was virtually over. Ed Pugsley, who was related to the Winchesters by marriage, since his wife Dorothy was the sister of Winchester Bennett's wife Susan, continued working for Winchester. Pugsley was a shining star in the firmament. But the bloodline was gone, though another gritty family with a nose for business, the Olins, returned Winchester to something approaching its former glories, for a time.

When the Winchester Repeating Arms Company went ignominiously into receivership in 1931, there was an unseemly race to go through the fallen giant's books. Franklin Olin's Western Cartridge Company initially vied with Du Pont, also makers of gunpowder. Du Pont had long considered whether to buy a stake in Winchester, and had backed out before. This time, Olin believed Du Pont was prepared to finance a merger of Winchester and another rifle manufacturer, Remington, with the idea of getting a guaranteed market for their explosives. Remington, like Winchester, had been trapped between the rising costs of doing business in wartime and fixed price contracts for guns. However, Du Pont backed away from buying Remington after examining their waning business. Franklin Olin and his sons John and Spencer had to think long and hard before buying Winchester. The country was in the depths of a recession, financing was hard to come by, and Western wasn't much bigger than Winchester. The Olins decided to hold off for a bit, and play hardball.

While Winchester twisted in the wind of receivership, Western picked up the sick company's ammunition business customer by customer, bringing down the purchase price by making Winchester a smaller concern.

This aggressive strategy worked, and on December 22, 1931 the Olins marched into the New Haven courthouse and paid $8.1 million for Winchester. The Olins had financed their purchase through smoke and mirrors, and a series of 90-day loans from the First National Bank of St Louis. "Believe me, I didn't think we had any Christmas present," John Olin told *Fortune* magazine 20 years later. From their vantage point in Wilmington, Du Pont watched delightedly, believing the Olins had overpaid for a huge headache of a company. Du Pont did eventually invest in Remington during the depression, later buying the whole company, only to dispose of it in 1993 to a Manhattan investment company. For the Olins, buying Winchester was a logical step. From their origins making blasting powder in Illinois, they'd moved into manufacturing ammunition and brass fabrication, and now the family was in the gun business. Yet for Franklin, John, and Spencer Olin, purchasing the company in the bleakest of economic times was a bold act, as Edwin Pugsley noted: "Only those who passed through the financial depression can realize the courage of these three men in staking practically their entire fortune upon their judgement."[1]

Once the Olins had made their bet on the future and purchased the ailing arms company, they renamed it Winchester–Western. Franklin and his two sons, who ran the family owned business, were as canny and foresighted as Oliver Winchester and Tom Bennett had been. John Olin in particular is credited with rescuing Winchester and turning it around. As a company official said in his tribute to the Olins many years later,

> It is through their foresight and business wisdom back in 1931 that Winchester has survived. The history of Winchester in time of peace and in time of armed conflict is in a very real sense the history of America, and Olin has played a major part in keeping the legend alive.[2]

Franklin Olin had begun his business with a small black-powder mill at East Alton, Illinois in the late 19th century. This small concern expanded into an empire spanning hundreds of companies, selling everything from explosives to chemicals. The Olins said little publicly about their purchase of Winchester – or indeed any of their business dealings, operating in the belief that it is impossible to put one's foot in a closed mouth. Franklin Olin, who died at 91 after 59 years with his company, never gave a competitor a "good morning" unless the information was in the public domain, reported a 1952 profile of the tight-lipped Olins.[3]

Once the Olins had dug deep to buy Winchester, they had to decide who was going to run it. Spencer Olin was works manager of the East Alton blasting powder plants in Illinois, so he couldn't move to New Haven. His brother John was vice-president of Western Cartridge, and it fell to him to bring Winchester back from the brink. John Olin was appalled by what he found once he'd moved his family East. Winchester did still have world-beating guns – the Model 12 shotgun, the most copied gun on the planet; the Model 52 .22 caliber rifle, which held world records for accuracy; the Model 21 shotgun, considered the finest of all double-barreled guns; and the Model 94, the most popular Western rifle ever made.[4] But Winchester was losing money daily on its line of tools, and the place was overstaffed. "One of the cruel things I had to do was turn 400 superannuated people out on the streets in a single day," recalled John Olin.[5] By the end of 1932, he had cut down on the costly tool line, abandoned the radiators and cutlery, ditched gun models that were unpopular, and doubled the promotion of the top sellers such as the 21 shotgun. John Olin realized that in the talented T. C. Johnson and his design team, there was a wealth of experience and plenty of good ideas for new guns in development, just waiting to be patented. With all these changes, Winchester turned in a remarkable profit of $168,000, after years of being in the red. No more flailing around lamely trying to sell washing machines and ice-skates. The company was back in the gun business. The Olins paid off their loan, though did Franklin have anything to say about his son John's transformation of Winchester's fortunes? "Nothing in particular," John recalled. "He was a New Englander too."[6]

As the dark clouds of war descended upon Europe once again, America opted to stay out of World War II – until the attack on Pearl Harbor. Then the US arsenal was bare, having been stripped of munitions to supply the British during Dunkirk. John Olin was approached by an official from Washington, in search of a weapons manufacturer willing to help take on the Axis Powers. Just as Winchester Bennett had dealt with DC bureaucrats wanting mass production 30 years earlier, so John heard out the administration's pitch for Winchester and Western to provide war-volume rifles and ammunition. Franklin Olin knew expansion had been fatal to Winchester in World War I, and was now 80 years old and wanted nothing to do with government business. Just like Tom Bennett at the outbreak of World War I. However, John and Spencer Olin decided to do what they could for the American war effort– which was considerable. Winchester–Western manufactured 15 billion rounds of ammunition for the Allies during World War II, and developed the US Carbine and M-1 rifle. By the end of the war, Winchester–Western employed 62,000 people, including those at plants operated for the government.[7] Patriotic once again, Winchester was able to emerge from World War II in profit rather than drowning in debt as it had at the end of World War I.

Even before the war began, Winchester had been selected to manufacture the new US service rifle, the M1 Garand, which succeeded the Model 1903 Springfield. The first contract to build the Garands was awarded to Winchester in 1937 – by the end of the war Winchester had manufactured more than half a million of the rifles. Winchester's major contribution came in the design and development of the .30-caliber M1 Carbine, a lighter semi-automatic weapon for those in the Army who wouldn't need to carry the bulkier Garand. After initial trials held by the Ordnance Department in 1941 for a new 5 lb semi-automatic weapon failed to find a rifle which was up to scratch, Winchester officials told the Army that their designer David Marshall Williams had been working on a similar gun. Tied up with building the Garand, Winchester hadn't entered the Ordnance trials. Eager to find a lighter weapon which could be used by mortar men, machine gunners, cooks, and clerks, Army officials asked Winchester to submit the gun for trials on September 15, 1941.

Once more, Winchester in New Haven performed admirably under pressure. As Ed Pugsley recalled:

> By working around the clock, including Sundays, the parts of the new gun were assembled on the afternoon of Friday the 13th of September. On Saturday morning a call from the Ordnance Department informed Winchester that the gun must be in Aberdeen [in Maryland] by the noon of the following day in order to undergo a firing test of 1,000 rounds before being submitted to the Test Board on Monday. It was not until early midnight on Saturday that the gun was operating satisfactorily. Six hours later it was on its way to Aberdeen.

Delivered to the US Ordnance Proving Ground in Aberdeen, Maryland, the new Winchester gun performed handily in the preliminary tests, as Ed Pugsley wrote with pride:

> As the test progressed, the Winchester gun pulled away from the field, and at the end of the test, by unanimous choice, became the now worldwide known U.S. Carbine, Caliber .30, M1 of the U.S. forces and, under Lend-Lease, that of our many allies.[8]

During World War II and the Korean War, an estimated 8 million M1s were produced, more than any other American small arm, and the rifle was considered an important factor in the Allied victory in the Pacific.[9]

David Marshall Williams, designer of the operating principle for the M1 Carbine, was another colorful character in the Winchester tradition, straight out of the Wild West. When he was operating an illegal distillery in North Carolina in 1921, Williams was imprisoned for his involvement in the murder of a law enforcement deputy who happened upon the moonshining. Williams turned himself in for the murder, though he claimed innocence, and the evidence was shaky. While he was whiling away the hours in prison, jail officials noticed Williams mechanical aptitude, and allowed him to work in the machine shop on the premises. There, Williams began servicing the weapons used by the prison guards, and worked on his own ideas for self-loading firearms. It was behind bars that Williams constructed the prototype of his innovation in gunmaking – the short-stroke piston.

Superintendent Peoples of the Caledonia Prison Farm, the kindly jailer who had noticed Williams' knack for fixing battered items, listened carefully as the sandy haired Williams explained how he had reduced the distance between the semi-automatic rifle's barrel kicking back and the point at which it hit the breech mechanism. "I didn't know it then, of course, but what this young prisoner was telling me that night would one day be considered by firearms experts one of the most revolutionary advances since Browning's development of the machine gun,"[10] Superintendent Peoples wrote later. Not everyone was so thrilled by the notion of a convicted cop killer sitting around making weapons, and Peoples had to explain himself in front of the North Carolina prison board. Apparently he stated he was so confident Williams wasn't going to break out of jail that he'd serve the rest of Williams' sentence if he did: a promise he never had to make good on. Word of Williams' genius spread, and by the late 1920s influential figures – including the FBI director J. Edgar Hoover – were lobbying for Williams' early release, and he was pardoned in 1929.[11]

Once he was released, Williams designed guns for Remington and Colt, and tangled with Winchester, accusing them of stealing an idea he had patented. Williams' potential as a gun designer was huge, and Winchester hired him full time as war approached. In New Haven, he worked on the semi-automatic rifle invented by a half-brother of John and Matt Browning. Williams was a combustible figure, who worked at his own pace and fell out with Winchester officials frequently during the pressurized trials for the M1 Carbine. Paranoid about others stealing his ideas, and fed up with Winchester's bureaucracy, Williams was a world-class thrower of tantrums. On one occasion, he threatened to shoot a co-worker who was pressing him to continue with the carbine's development.[12] Others finished the M1 Carbine design that Williams had begun, but he is widely credited with inventing the short-stroke piston that made the gun possible. In 1952, MGM released a movie about his life called *Carbine Williams*, starring Jimmy Stewart.

During World War II, Winchester's bosses and employees threw themselves wholeheartedly into the war effort. "Winchester War Workers Go Into Battle Shoulder To Shoulder With Our Troops," declared *Winchester Life*, the in-house publication for Winchester's staff. Employees on the gun-shop floor were encouraged to think of themselves as "soldiers in overalls," and the production staff signed a pledge to put 25 percent more effort into their work, a commitment forwarded to President Roosevelt in Washington. A huge banner went up over the main Winchester entrance, proclaiming, "Through This Gate Pass the World's Greatest Soldiers of Production."

Winchester Life magazine played the role of propagandist and morale booster during wartime, as this classic example of patriotic writing demonstrates:

> Every man and woman employed in this vast plant realizes that he or she is an integral and vital link in the chain of, not only national defense, but national offense as well. We all know and we are deeply impressed with the fact that before our Army can operate to perfection, we must be the first to go "over the top" and we are proud to announce that thousands of Winchester workers man these ramparts with their skill, courage and inherent sense of patriotism. Winchester workers should be justly proud of their occupation and prouder still to wear their badge where everyone may see that they are the men and women who are turning out the best rifle in the world, and the best ammunition to go with it. General MacArthur's spirit, "to win or die," pervades this entire plant. WE ARE READY AND UNAFRAID.[13]

Winchester's workers responded admirably to this call to arms in New Haven, and in March 1943 all previous production records at the plant were smashed. Every division, whether turning out Winchester Carbines, Garand Rifles, ammunition, or radiators for fighting ships, exceeded its quotas. "There's your answer, Hitler!" proclaimed the text beneath a cartoon of Hitler walking the plank in *Winchester Life*. The in-house journal praised the workforce for their outstanding productivity: "Winchester workers have again proved by sweat and toil that our boys in service shall not surrender to a ruthless enemy or die on some far away battlefield for lack of guns and ammunition."[14]

As well as making guns and ammunition, Winchester's radiator division was a key part of the war effort. There, a mostly female workforce made the cabin heaters to keep flight crews comfortable in the sub-zero stratosphere, and engine cooling radiators that allowed fighter planes to keep their efficiency, thus enabling them to 'down our enemies in the stifling heat of the Libyan desert and over the frozen wastes of Tibet," as *Winchester Life* put it. "Winchester radiators flew with General Chennault's 'Flying Tigers' in China and Winchester radiators are helping Russian pilots to blast Hitler's tanks to pieces," announced a feature on the "pretty young ladies" of the radiator division. Their work was used in nearly every type of military and naval plane flying, in tanks, and in the motor torpedo boats which were credited with "doing such good work in the Pacific against the Japs."[15]

From World War II until the present day, the history of Winchester is one of changing fortunes and ownership. Wartime had changed the composition of the traditionally white, male workforce. With men off at the front, just as in World War I, more and more women were employed by Winchester. This time, though, the women didn't give up their positions on the factory floor once the guns fell silent. *Winchester Life* featured more and more items on hairstyles, fashion tips and cooking to cater to this new audience. Winchester even advertised itself as an equal opportunities employer, long before the Civil Rights Act gave legal equality to African Americans. Labor disputes led to a union organizing drive in 1946, though it was 1955 before the plant became unionized.

As the workforce was drawn from an ever-broader geographical area, the cozy, community feel of the place changed. In 1948, the Connecticut Company ended the streetcar service that had ferried workers to Winchester so reliably for so many decades. *Winchester Life* recognized the passing of the trolley car as the symbol of a changing era:

> our remorse at this passing is deep, and stems from the remembrance of a time when the pace was a little more leisurely

and the trolley car was a giant genii which whisked us gaily to such far off and fabulous places as Lighthouse and Savin Rock.[16]

The most famous postwar advertisement for Winchester rifles was surely the writer Ernest Hemingway. The macho, hard-charging author of *Death in the Afternoon, For Whom the Bell Tolls,* and *A Farewell to Arms* loved target shooting and partying. He owned a pump action .22 Winchester Model 61, which he regarded as ideal for both activities. On his 60th birthday, Hemingway celebrated in style, in Malaga, Spain. As Valerie Danby-Smith, Ernest's secretary who later married his youngest son Gregory recalled, "Mary [Hemingway's wife] rented a shooting gallery from a traveling carnival, and it became the main attraction when Ernest, to the horror and fascination of the onlookers, blasted the ash from Antonio's lighted cigarette with a .22 rifle as he held the butt between his lips."[17] Antonio Ordonez, Hemingway's guest and one of Spain's greatest bullfighters, apparently didn't turn a hair. Hemingway liked to point his Winchester .22 at friends holding cigarettes. On safari in East Africa, to the bemusement of the Masai onlookers, Hemingway blasted the ash off his pal Earl Theisen's cigarette, much to the delight of the photographer from *Life* magazine who captured the event. Theisen was only holding the cigarette in the air, not between his lips, however. Hemingway's third son Gregory, or Gigi, had a natural talent with guns, too. Sailing in the Caribbean with his father as a child, he could hit flying fish on the wing with his Winchester Model 62.[18] Martha Gelhorn, the distinguished war correspondent and third wife of Hemingway, was presented with a brand new Model 21 Winchester shotgun for her birthday. Hemingway wished his wife to share his interests. The next Mrs Hemingway inherited this engraved silver-plated shotgun after Ernest and Martha divorced.

Hemingway apart, the postwar period became one of decline for Winchester. By 1981, after falling gun sales and a bitter, sometimes violent labor strike that stood out as one of the ugliest events in New Haven's history, the Olin Corporation sold the loss-making shotgun and rifle manufacturing operations in New Haven to the US Repeating Arms Corporation. Olin retained the profitable ammunition business, now known as Winchester Ammunition, which is still owned by Olin to this day. John Olin was 89 at the time of the sale of Winchester's rifle operations, honorary chairman of the board of Olin, and the company's largest individual shareholder. After 50 years of owning Winchester, having rescued it from the abyss in the depression years, John reportedly did not want to sell and had apparently been blocking Olin's attempts to rid itself of the arms division for several years.

A group of Winchester executives joined forces with a group of private investors and bought the ailing Winchester Arms division of Olin. Hugh Fletcher, president of the new US Repeating Arms Company, explained Olin's motivation in selling the storied brand. "Olin has been principally a chemical company," Mr Fletcher said. "Their thrust is devoted to chemicals. They evaluated Winchester Arms and it did not meet their criteria for growth and profitability."[19]

So much so, that Olin had encountered some difficulty in even finding a buyer. Only one other gun company, Mossberg of North Haven, another historic Civil War era manufacturer, showed any interest. All the other prospective buyers were investment groups. "The standard way to sell is to approach the top corporate 500," explained Richard Pelton, who had been an Olin executive in the Winchester Division, and became a top official in the new US Repeating Arms Corporation. "But given the dismal results of the firearms business and the fact that it was the firearms business, which scares companies, the only ones interested were investor groups."[20] The consortium that purchased Winchester was comprised of former Olin Winchester executives, and was led by Ronald J. Render, himself a former top official at Sperry Vicker's defense division.[21] The purchase price was $24 million, $4 million in private funds and $20 million financed by the Hanover Trust of New York – and to think that 50 years earlier, when the Olin family bought Winchester, they paid $8.1 million. Not a huge return on the investment, adjusting for inflation, though the Winchester ammunition business, which Olin retained, was still profitable.

The US Repeating Arms Corporation purchased the rights to manufacture Winchester-branded rifles and shotguns under license from the Olin Corporation. Hugh Fletcher was optimistic. A student of business philosophy, he felt Winchester had suffered by being owned by the Olin conglomerate, with its many layers of what he saw as unproductive management. The city of New Haven, which didn't want to lose either the jobs provided by the gun factory or the historic connection, provided considerable incentives for the US Repeating Arms Corporation. Real estate and personal property taxes were abated by 80 percent for five years, and the 25 percent state corporate income tax was abated for ten years.[22]

Winchester's share of the domestic sporting market for long guns had dropped from 20 percent to 10 percent in the few years leading up to the sale in 1981. The new bosses of the US Repeating Arms Company believed Winchester could regain a larger slice of that market, estimated back then to be worth between $600 million and $700 million dollars annually. Shooting sports enthusiasts were the target buyers. On Winchester Avenue in New Haven, the new management created a popular attraction at the entrance to the US Repeating Arms Corporation. A life-size statue of the actor John Wayne, brandishing a bronze replica of the famous Winchester Model '94 used in his Western movies, reminded passers-by of the heritage and cinematic appeal of "The Gun That Won The West." "The key to success is to attract the attention of the guy already attracted to the market," explained Richard Pelton. "It is the multiple purchaser we're going after [...] the guy who already has seven or ten long guns."

Initially, the new management's enthusiasm changed the atmosphere at the old Winchester gun shop. The poisonous relations between employers and workers, which had almost shut down the company during the strike years, improved noticeably. "There's been a complete turnabout. They finally listened when we said that if you treat the people with kindness you get results. It's nowhere like it was with Olin. My God, what a difference. 'Cause Olin didn't care," the president of the Machinists' union Lou Romano declared.[23] John J. McDonald, new vice-president of manufacturing, spoke presciently while taking reporters on a tour of the factory:

This is the honeymoon period. The workers love us, the unions love us, the mayor loves us. It was one thing to attack a mythical corporation, but we're here on the floor every day. They see the managers on the floor. The attitude is so different now. But it's a one-time shot. We have to maintain our credibility.

Despite that assessment, McDonald was upbeat about the company's future. "We got the name. We got the product. We got people who are working hard. We are going to make it."[24]

Times were tough in the rifle business, though. In the 1980s, Americans were buying far fewer firearms than they did in the 1960s and 1970s. Declining crime rates, shrinking space for hunting, tighter gun-control laws, economic hard times for blue-collar workers, and a waning interest from young people in hunting and target shooting led to a slowdown in sales. Everyone who wanted a gun had one, it seemed. The gunmakers of the Connecticut River Valley were hit by layoffs. Richard Pelton of the US Repeating Arms Corporation told the *New York Times* the recession of the early 1980s had not helped the gun industry. "Our buyer is not the high-tech worker," he said. "It's the blue-collar, smokestack employee and the farmer – and these two sectors have been reeling."[25]

The thaw in employer-employee relations at the US Repeating Arms Corporation ended, and before too long the deep freeze had returned to the shop floor. In 1982, the plant was shut for five weeks over Christmas and New Year, because of slumping sales. In August 1983, the management told workers to take two weeks of unpaid leave, blaming sluggish sales. "Honeymoon Ends At Gun Plant, No Bonus, Extended Furlough Sour Union on Management," ran one New Haven newspaper headline. The US Repeating Arms Corporation was still New Haven's largest manufacturer, employing about 740 hourly workers in 1985 – and so it was in a position to bargain for state support. Owing money to lenders, the new company was in dire straits early in 1985. Owing money across the board, the management sought $8 million in loans from city, state, and federal governments.

As the company continued to struggle financially, it explored a merger with another arms manufacturer, Savage of Massachusetts. The two firms announced they planned to merge and build a new firearms plant somewhere in New England, closing their existing plants. Jobs would be lost and costs would be cut. The City of New Haven reacted with understandable disappointment. US Repeating Arms and the old Winchester factory were now located within New Haven's Science Park, an 80-acre industrial and high tech complex jointly owned by the city, Olin, and Yale University. One month later, the shotgun marriage between Savage and US Repeating Arms was called off. It wasn't possible for US Repeating Arms to merge while applying for millions of dollars of federal loans. Meanwhile, the Economic Development Administration, having dragged its feet on the loan, had suddenly come up with the guarantee the rifle manufacturers wanted. As a Hartford business writer observed, US Repeating Arms had just pulled off one of the great coups in sporting arms industry history. By threatening a merger and the loss of much needed inner-city jobs in New Haven, the company alarmed Connecticut politicians who lobbied the Economic Development Administration to come up with the loan, pronto. "There will be no farewell to arms in New Haven," wrote Robert Weisman of the *Hartford Courant*.[26] At least not yet, he would have added, had he been able to gaze into his crystal ball.

The troubles of the US Repeating Arms Corporation weren't over, despite the loan. In November 1985, the management announced it planned to furlough workers from Thanksgiving until January, much to the fury of the unions, which threatened to strike. Richard Pelton, company president, wrote to Louis Romano, the union boss, pleading for understanding:

> The company is struggling to meet its legal financial obligations. We are in no position to obligate our company to pay holiday payments not required by our contractual agreement. I believe you are leading the membership towards an unnecessary and no-win confrontation with their company [. . .] The company is in its darkest hour financially. We are trying to rally the necessary financial support to keep going. All the rhetoric in the world will not change the situation.[27]

There was no reprieve for US Repeating Arms – people were simply not buying rifles in sufficient quantities, labor costs were high, and the unpaid bills were piling up. In January 1986, the biggest manufacturer in New Haven filed for bankruptcy, furloughing most of its 850 workers. New Haven officials immediately announced the start of an intensive jobs training program for the largely African American workforce, many of whom lived in the city's poor neighborhoods of Dixwell and Newhallville. Chapter 11 of the US Bankruptcy Code allows companies to continue operating while they reorganize, and the management of the US Repeating Arms Corporation tried to come up with millions in new capital so they could stay afloat.

By September 1987, the company was onto its second set of owners in six years. A Massachusetts businessman, Peter Alcock, and a group of private investors pumped $6 million into the fragile concern, while the Browning Sporting Arms Group of Fabrique Nationale Herstal, based in Belgium, put up $2 million. In all, $30 million of debt was absorbed by the new owners as part of the deal. "Winchester has enormous potential," said Mr Alcock, known for turning around a shoe-box manufacturing company. "It made its name by making high quality guns affordable to the average guy, and we intend to continue that tradition."[28] Alcock acknowledged he had his work cut out. "Every company has a corporate culture, and in this particular corporation, marketing is completely removed from everybody else. I'm trying to change that. The company, as a result, looked to me like the headless horseman. Everybody has been going in different directions."[29]

The ghosts of gunmakers past collided in this deal. The remnants of Oliver Winchester and Tom Bennett's rifle company were bought out by Browning, made famous by the Mormon gunmaker John Browning. Winchester and Browning had collaborated successfully for more than 20 years, as Winchester patented and sold John Browning's brilliant guns. Then after Tom Bennett refused to pay John Browning royalties for his latest invention at the turn of the 20th century, Browning took his latest creation to Belgium in disgust – and some 80 years later, Browning posthumously triumphed over his rivals as the company created by his genius bailed out Winchester.

Back to the near present, and even under new ownership, problems persisted at the New Haven plant. In 1992, there was more turnover and new management for US Repeating Arms. There were plans for a brand new production facility in New Haven, where Winchesters would continue to be manufactured. But not even a modern factory could save the day. In 2006, the US Repeating Arms Corporation, part of the Belgian Herstal Group, announced that it was closing its Winchester firearms factory. Sales of guns used for target shooting and hunting were declining, and the enterprise wasn't making enough money to survive. Two hundred people were to lose their jobs. The news was greeted with great sadness in New Haven. "It's a part of who we are as a nation, just like it's part of who we are as a city," said New Haven's mayor at the time, John DeStefano.[30]

For the workers at US Repeating Arms, it was a bitter blow. "It's depressing," said 58-year-old David Pallanti, who had worked at the factory for 14 years, packing guns. "Who's going to hire someone 58, 60 years old?" Metal finishers ending their shift stood next to a sign at the entrance of the plant, near a sign that read: "Through these gates pass the greatest craftsmen who make the world famous Winchester firearms." Donald Harris was left cold by the message. "That's just a sign now," he said, before heading back into work to pour acid on steel to rustproof the guns. "It used to mean something."[31]

The closing of Winchester's historic New Haven gun shop was noted as the end of an era, and an example of changing times not only in American manufacturing but the wider culture too. In an elegiac piece, Stephen Hunter, an avid Winchester fan, wrote:

> The gun as family totem, the implied trust between generations, the implicit idea that marksmanship followed by hunting were a way of life to be pursued through the decades, the sense of tradition, respect, self-discipline, and bright confidence that Winchester and the American kinship group march forward toward a happy tomorrow – gone, if not with the wind, then with the tide of inner-city and nutcase killings that have led America's once-proud and heavily bourgeois gun culture into the wilderness of marginalization.[32]

After the New Haven plant closed in March 2006, a succession of gunmakers toured the site, but not one opted to purchase it. A real estate company bought the property and vowed to bring it back to life. The Winchester name lived on, even though the rifles were no longer manufactured in New Haven. Olin, owners of the Winchester brand name, entered into a licensing agreement with Browning, a subsidiary of Herstal, for the manufacture and distribution of Winchester rifles and shotguns. Remember, John Browning had designed some of Winchester's most successful guns ever – and by 2010, hunters could once again buy Browning's Model 1886 and 1895 Winchesters.

Today the Winchester Repeating Arms Company brand name is trading as part of the Herstal firearms group. The guns are made in many locations – as the inscription in the barrel will show. The Winchester Model 70 is assembled in Portugal. Hunters and shooters who would rather buy a rifle made in America are informed by the company's website:

> It would be incorrect to base your decision not to buy a Model 70 from our Portugal plant due to a fear of poor performance. Model 70s made and/or assembled in Portugal have stellar quality, accuracy and overall performance that matches or exceeds any production Model 70s ever in our history.[33]

The Super X Pump Action Shotgun is designed in Morgan, Utah and manufactured in Turkey. There's a link to Winchester's storied past, and the days of Oliver Winchester and Tom Bennett visiting Istanbul to sell rifles to the Sultans. The historic Winchesters – the Model 1873, 1894, and so on – are being manufactured once again, with the design overseen in Utah while the rifles are built in the mountains near the city of Kochi, in Japan. The arms manufacturing business is a global concern, far removed from the days of the Winchester factory in New Haven.

As for Winchester Ammunition, still owned by Olin, the post 9/11 campaign against Al Qaeda and the Taliban in Afghanistan and the American-led invasion of Iraq in 2003 created strong sales of ammo to the US military. The push for stricter gun control laws in the wake of the 2012 Newtown killings of teachers and first-grade students in Connecticut led to an increase in sales of guns and ammunition to consumers, as gun owners feared their ability to buy was going to be curtailed. Congress ultimately failed to pass any legislation. Winchester officials in August 2015 forecast that demand for consumer ammunition would remain strong, explaining that many gun owners have taken up target shooting as a hobby.

Gun sales in America continue to be robust. In June 2015, the National Instant Criminal Background Check System logged almost 900,000 checks, a record high in the 17-year history of the system. Background checks are seen as the most reliable indicator of new gun sales. The continued discussion about gun control laws in the wake of mass shootings appears to be keeping demand for weapons high.

Following the Newtown school killings, the state's legislators passed comprehensive gun control laws, which led to Connecticut's gunmakers and dealers threatening to leave the area. Being in a state seen as unfriendly to their business and the Second Amendment right to bear arms was an incentive to depart. Ultimately, only the gunmaker PTR Industries moved out of the state, to North Carolina. The established gun manufacturers, such as Colt and O. F. Mossberg, long-time rivals of Winchester, are still there, just about. However, Colt filed for bankruptcy in June 2015, warning it needed a quick sale to survive. And Mossberg has expanded its facilities in Texas. "Nobody in the gun business wants to be associated with Connecticut," said Scott Hoffman, president of Hoffman Gun Center and Indoor Shooting Range in Newington. "My family has been in business in Connecticut since 1919, and I can't wait to get [...] out of this state," he told *Hartford Business*. "There are a lot of states in the Union that love what I do."[34] No doubt Oliver Winchester, Tom Bennett, and Ed Pugsley would have felt much the same.

As for the old Winchester factory in New Haven, an eyesore for many years as it fell into disrepair, now it has been transformed into an apartment complex called Winchester Lofts. Where men and women once toiled making guns for the world wars, now there's a 158-apartment community complete with a billiard room and a pet grooming station, that most 21st-century amenity. Thirty-two of the apartments have been reserved for affordable housing, as New Haven tries to revitalize the Newhallville district. The lofts display historic photographs of their gunmaking history, and Winchester memor-abilia – a few of those ill-fated washing machines and roller-skates are a reminder of Winchester's excursion into household goods.

In a sign of how the Winchester Rifle is still so closely associated in the public mind with the settling of the West, news of the discovery of a 132-year-old Winchester found propped against a tree in Nevada created headlines around the world in 2015. The Model 1873 rifle, "The Gun That Won The West," had apparently lain undisturbed for years – its rusty steel barrel and grey woodwork blending in with the juniper tree in the Great Basin National Park. What was the story behind the rifle, found in the middle of the rocky Nevada wilderness? Abandoned in a hurry, forgotten, the property of a lone cowboy riding the range, a prospector, or a Native American? No one will ever know for sure, but the image of the rifle virtually camouflaged by the tree evoked romanticized memories of an era far removed from our own. In another indication of the pull of the past, a novel about the Old West called simply *Winchester 1886*, was published early in 2015, with the tagline "On the American Frontier, Every Gun Tells A Story."[35]

The brutal legacy of the Winchester Rifle out West has not faded with the passing of the years. Indeed, in 2013, Montana legislators rejected a proposal to name the Winchester Model 1873 the official state rifle. Supporters of the measure urged lawmakers to view the weapon as a symbol of a place in time, which played a significant role in the state's frontier history. But Native American legislators said they couldn't honor the weapon that had devastated their ancestors, and slaughtered bison.[36]

As for the descendants of Oliver Winchester, none of us are in the gun business. The last direct descendant who worked for the company, my great-grandfather Winchester Bennett, died in Florida in 1953, faithfully tended to by his wife Susan. Susan survived her husband by 12 years, and with her passing, the last direct link to a generation who had known what it was to be part of the Winchester Repeating Arms Company vanished. Ed Pugsley, who had married into the family, was a larger-than-life character right up until his death in 1975 at the age of 90, celebrated for his expertise in gun design. His grandchildren remember Pugsley's outright opposition to any form of gun control when the matter first came up in the 1970s. The glory days of Winchester have bequeathed to family members a beautiful property in Branford, Connecticut, on Johnson's Point, where some live year-round and others enjoy a stunning summer venue. Built by Thomas Gray Bennett, when Winchester was at the height of its dominance, there are more than a few reminders of the golden years. The elderly wooden boat barn where Tom and Winchester Bennett launched their yachts stores our kayaks now, and barn swallows soar through the cobweb-covered rafters, chattering as they swoop and glide. The brass winch that once hauled the big boats into the boat barn at high tide is rusting now, a relic of the past. The Big House, named Islewood, which once looked out regally over Long Island Sound, is long gone. But the rose garden tended so lovingly by my great-grandmother, Susan Bennett, is thriving – thanks to the care lavished upon it by Lisa Lovejoy, Susan's relative by marriage. Our summer home was once the caretaker's cottage to the Big House, a sturdy granite structure close to the crashing waves and rocks, which has survived many a hurricane. The breakwater is still used for launching fireworks on the Fourth of July, just as it ever was.

As I rake the beach at Johnson's Point for oyster shells, watching the ospreys linger for their unsuspecting prey, I think of my shrewd Yankee forefathers and what their ingenuity and determination achieved. At a time when life in the West was nasty, brutish, and short, the Winchester rifle was a means to conquer, survive, and prosper. Close by in New Haven, the profits from the Winchester rifle continue to aid patients with lung disease, thanks to Sarah Winchester's far-sighted bequest. This would have pleased my grandmother, Molly, daughter of Winchester and Susan, who would refer to her inheritance rather disparagingly – and sometimes with a trace of guilt – as "the gun money." It all began with her great-grandfather Oliver Winchester, the shirtmaker turned arms manu-facturer, whose canny investment in rifles spawned a company whose history was, for a time, the history of America. If I narrow my eyes and look westwards from the beach in Connecticut, I can conjure up a vision of the Old West, and picture Winchester's signature fringed rider on his pinto, galloping across the plains, gripping his trusty Model '73.

Fig. 24 Aerial photograph of Thomas Gray Bennett's summer home at Johnson's Point in Branford, Connecticut. The house was pulled down after the death of the author's great-grandmother in 1965.

NOTES

INTRODUCTION

1   George Madis, *The Winchester Era* (1984), p. 6.
2   McCracken Research Library, Buffalo Bill Historical Center, Cody, Wyoming, Henry Brewer to Edwin Pugsley, July 9, 1934.
3   Harold F. Williamson, *Winchester: The Gun that Won the West* (1961), p. 3.
4   Nicholas Johnson, *Negroes and the Gun, The Black Tradition of Arms* (2014), p. 105.
5   John Greenleaf Whittier, *Snow-Bound, A Winter Idyll* (1866).

CHAPTER ONE: THE DAMN YANKEE RIFLE

1   Dean K. Boorman, *The History of Winchester Firearms* (2001), p. 12.
2   Henry Winchester Cunningham, *John Winchester of New England and Some of His Descendants* (1925), p. 4.
3   Ibid., p. 5.
4   Fanny Winchester Hotchkiss, *Winchester Notes* (1912), p. 3.
5   George Madis, *The Winchester Era* (1984), p. 28.
6   *New Haven Daily Morning Journal*, December 11, 1880, obituary of Oliver Winchester.
7   Baltimore City Archives, newspaper advertisement for O. F. Winchester and Co.
8   Patent application by Oliver Fisher Winchester, 1847.
9   Baltimore City Archives, advertisement for William P. Towles, successor to Oliver Winchester as owner of the Gent's furnishing goods at 145 Baltimore Street.
10 Otto E. Schaefer, *New Haven Water Board History*, Chapter One, "Lifestream for a Region."
11 *Hartford Daily Courant*, October 20, 1848.
12 Schaefer, *New Haven Water Board History*, Chapter One.
13 "A Plain Statement of Facts to the New Haven Public," pamphlet (1850).
14 Schaefer, *New Haven Water Board History*, Chapter One.
15 Madis, *The Winchester Era*, p. 29.
16 Ibid., p. 31.
17 Advertisement for Wheeler and Wilson's Medal Family Sewing Machines, sold by Winchester and Davies, 59 Court Street, New Haven.
18 *Columbian Register*, May 8, 1876.
19 Harold F. Williamson, *Winchester: The Gun that Won the West* (1961), p. 21.
20 *New Haven Daily Morning Journal*, December 11, 1880, obituary of Oliver Winchester.
21 New Haven Historical Society, Festival at the New Haven Shirt Manufactory, June 25, 1852.
22 Ibid.
23 Annual report of the New Haven County Horticultural Society, 1851.

24   McCracken Research Center, Buffalo Bill Historical Center, *Winchester Record*, Vol. 1, February 14, 1919.

25   Ibid.

26   D. H. Veader and A. W. Earle, *The Story of the Winchester Repeating Arms Company* (1918), p. 18.

27   Edwin Pugsley, *Winchesters of the Past* (n.d.).

28   Veader and Earle, *The Story of the Winchester Repeating Arms Company.*

29   Ibid.

30   C. F. W. Behm, late of clipper ship *Stag Hound*, New York, March 10, 1855.

31   *Winchester Record*, Vol. 1, February 14, 1919.

32   Madis, *The Winchester Era*, p. 39.

33   Ibid., p. 36.

34   Pugsley, *Winchesters of the Past,* n.d.

35   McCracken Research Library, Cody Firearms Museum, Buffalo Bill Historical Center, New Haven Army Company, Letter Book, O. F Winchester to E. B. Martin, October 18, 1862.

36   Complainant's Main Case, Morse Arms Mfg. Co. v Winchester Repeating Arms Co., p. 399.

37   Boorman, *The History of Winchester Firearms*, p. 12.

38   R. L. Wilson, *Winchester: An American Legend* (2008), pp. 11–12.

39   Letter quoted in Claud E. Fuller, *The Breech-Loader in the Service* (1965), pp. 199–200.

40   Wilson, *Winchester*, p. 11.

41   Chris Kyle with William Doyle, *American Gun, A History of the U.S. in Ten Firearms* (2013).

42   Quoted in Boorman, *The History of Winchester Firearms*, p. 26.

43   Duncan Barnes, *The History of Winchester Firearms, 1866–1980* (1980), pp. 9–10.

44   Boorman, *The History of Winchester Firearms*, p. 24.

45   John E. Parsons, *The First Winchester* (1955), p. 28.

46   Buffalo Bill Center of the West, Oliver Winchester letter to Brigadier General Ripley, June 24, 1863.

47   Bob Redman, *The Spencer Repeater and other Breechloading Rifles of the Civil War* (n.d.) http://www.aotc.net/Spencer.htm.

48   Madis, *The Winchester Era*, p. 43.

49   Pugsley, *Winchesters of the Past.*

50   Wiley Sword, *The Historic Henry Rifle: Oliver Winchester's famous Civil War Repeater* (2002).

51   Madis, *The Winchester Era*, p. 43.

52   Letter from Oliver Winchester to John W. Brown of Ohio, December 1863.

53   Letter from New Haven Arms Company Secretary to John W. Brown of Ohio, December 30, 1862.

54   Boorman, *The History of Winchester Firearms*, p. 27.

55   Letter from Oliver Winchester to Messrs A. B. Simple and Sons, May 4, 1863.

56   Sword, *The Historic Henry Rifle.*

57   Wilson, *Winchester*, p. 12.

58   Report by Brigadier General George D. Ramsay to Assistant Secretary of War R. C. Wilson, April 5, 1864.

59   Williamson, *Winchester*, p. 35.

60   Ibid.

61   Sword, *The Historic Henry Rifle*, p. 28.

62 Letter from Oliver Winchester to Reverend J. P. Pell, Chaplain of the 12th Kentucky Cavalry, July 6, 1863.
63 Henry catalog, 1865, pp. 24–6.
64 Boorman, *The History of Winchester Firearms*, p. 29.
65 Ibid., p. 29.
66 Henry catalog, pp. 7–8.
67 Charles Minor Blackford III, Letters from Lee's Army, p. 7, 1993.
68 Williamson, *Winchester*, p. 35.
69 Boorman, *The History of Winchester Firearms*, p. 28.
70 Williamson, *Winchester*, notes p. 396.
71 Ibid., notes p. 396.
72 Buffalo Bill Center of the West, Oliver Winchester, letter, November 1862.
73 Buffalo Bill Center of the West, Oliver Winchester, letter, October 1862.
74 Buffalo Bill Center of the West, Oliver Winchester, letter to Judge R. K. Williams of Kentucky, April 14, 1863.
75 Boorman, *The History of Winchester Firearms*, p. 20.
76 Ibid., p. 21.
77 Williamson, *Winchester*, p. 40.
78 Letter from Oliver Winchester to A. B. Simple and Sons, May 4, 1863.
79 Wilson, *Winchester*, p. 14.
80 Oliver Winchester, "The First Requisite of a Military Rifle," pamphlet published by the Winchester Repeating Arms Company, 1870
81 McCracken Research Library, Buffalo Bill Historical Center, *Winchester Record*, November 7, 1919.
82 Ibid.

CHAPTER TWO: THE SPIRIT GUN

1 According to a *Hartford Courant* article from 2006, Edwin Pugsley coined this winning phrase in a 1919 Winchester advertisement in the newspaper.
2 *New York Times*, "Sending out a Search Party for the Western," March 5, 2000.
3 Dee Brown, *Bury My Heart At Wounded Knee* (1971), , plate 49.
4 James Parton, *The Life of Horace Greely* (before 1923), quoted in Herbert G. Houze, *Winchester Repeating Arms Company* (2011), p. 45.
5 US Congress, 49th, 1st session, House of Representatives Executive Document 263, quoted in Brown, *Bury My Heart at Wounded Knee*, p. 14.
6 Harold F. Williamson, *Winchester: The Gun that Won the West* (1961), p. 43.
7 Dean K. Boorman, *The History of Winchester Firearms* (2001), p. 29.
8 Neill C. Wilson, *Treasure Express: The Epic Days of Wells Fargo* (1987).
9 Houze, *Winchester Repeating Arms Company*, p. 23.
10 Ibid., p. 30.
11 Williamson, *Winchester*, p. 46.
12 George Madis, *The Winchester Era* (1984), p. 61.
13 Ibid.
14 Captain E. C. Crossman, "With Captain Crossman at the Big Winchester Factories', *Sporting Goods Dealer* (January 1920).
15 Houze, *Winchester Repeating Arms Company*, p. 43.
16 Ibid., p. 43.
17 Letter from Oliver Winchester to William Saunders, March 17, 1859.
18 *Norwich Aurora*, May 28, 1867.
19 *Connecticut Courant*, January 28, 1865.

20   Edwin Pugsley, *Winchesters of the Past*, (n.d.).
21   Madis, *The Winchester Era*, p. 57.
22   Boorman, *The History of Winchester Firearms*, p. 31.
23   D. H. Veader and A. W. Earle, *The Story of the Winchester Repeating Arms Company* (1918), p. 28.
24   McCracken Research Library, Buffalo Bill Historical Center, Cody, Wyoming, account by Arthur Earle, November 15, 1922.
25   Pugsley, *Winchesters of the Past*.
26   Veader and Earle, *The Story of the Winchester Repeating Arms Company*, p. 27.
27   Ibid., p. 38.
28   Madis, *The Winchester Era*, p 59.
29   Boorman, *The History of Winchester Firearms*, p. 31.
30   Houze, *Winchester Repeating Arms Company*, p. 48.
31   Veader and Earle, *The Story of the Winchester Repeating Arms Company*.
32   Williamson, *Winchester*, p. 52.
33   Houze, *Winchester Repeating Arms Company*, p. 58.
34   Ibid., p. 69.
35   Ibid., p. 63.
36   Williamson, *Winchester*, p. 474.
37   Felicia Johnson Deyrup, *Arms Makers of the Connecticut Valley : A Regional Study of the Economic Development of the Small Arms Industry, 1798–1870* (Northampton, MA: Smith College, 1948)
38   Boorman, *The History of Winchester Firearms*, p. 34.
39   John E. Parsons, *The First Winchester* (1955), p. 66.
40   Boorman, *The History of Winchester Firearms*, p. 34.
41   Parsons, *The First Winchester*, p. 69.
42   Thomas Goodrich, *Scalp Dance* (1997), p. 261.
43   Ibid., p. 261.
44   Brown, *Bury My Heart at Wounded Knee*, p. 294.
45   Goodrich, *Scalp Dance*, p. 252.
46   James McLaughlin, *My Friend the Indian* (1910), p. 175.
47   Goodrich, *Scalp Dance*, p. 262.
48   Doug Scott, quoted by Chris Kyle in *American Gun, A History of the U.S. in Ten Firearms* (2013), p. 105.
49   US Bureau of American Ethnology, Annual Report 1888–9, quoted in Brown, *Bury My Heart at Wounded Knee*, p. 296.
50   Williamson, *Winchester*.
51   Boorman, *The History of Winchester Firearms*, p. 43.
52   Brown, *Bury My Heart At Wounded Knee*, p. 444.
53   Boorman, *The History of Winchester Firearms*, p. 44.
54   Houze, *Winchester Repeating Arms Company*, p. 107.
55   Alexander Rose, *American Rifle* (2009), p. 186.
56   Houze, *Winchester Repeating Arms Company*, p. 110.
57   Winchester Repeating Arms Company Catalog, 1875.
58   Pugsley, *Winchesters of the Past*.
59   Veader and Earle, *The Story of the Winchester Repeating Arms Company*, p. 56.
60   Contracts with the Turkish Government, November 9, 1870 and August 19, 1871.
61   Connecticut Historical Society, letter from Thomas Gray Bennett to Jennie Bennett, December 8, 1877.
62   Ibid.

63 Connecticut Historical Society, letter from Thomas Gray Bennett to Jennie Bennett, December 7, 1877.

64 Williamson, *Winchester*, p. 55.

65 Ibid., p. 64.

66 Veader and Earle, *The Story of the Winchester Repeating Arms Company*, p. 58.

67 Connecticut Historical Society, letter from Thomas Bennett to Jennie Winchester, February 16, 1876.

68 Connecticut Historical Society, letter from Thomas Bennett to Jennie Bennett, April 14, 1876.

69 Connecticut Historical Society, letter from Thomas Bennett to Jennie Bennett, December 8, 1877.

70 Connecticut Historical Society, letter from Thomas Bennett to Jennie Bennett, April 12, 1876.

71 Connecticut Historical Society, letter from Thomas Bennett to Jennie Bennett, March 10, 1875.

72 Rose, *American Rifle*, p. 182.

73 Connecticut Historical Society, letter from Thomas Bennett to Jennie Bennett, April 16, 1876.

74 Williamson, *Winchester*, p. 65.

75 Madis, *The Winchester Era*, p. 66.

76 Connecticut Historical Society, letter from Thomas Gray Bennett to Jennie Bennett, December 14, 1877.

77 Richard T. Trenk, Snr, "The Plevna Delay, Winchesters and Peabody-Martins in the Russo-Turkish War," *Man At Arms*, Vol. 19, No. Four (August 1997).

78 Ibid.

79 Ibid.

80 Richard T. Trenk, Snr,, Man At Arms Magazine, Volume 19, No Four, August 1997

81 Connecticut Historical Society, letter from Thomas Gray Bennett to Jane Bennett, December 5, 1877.

82 Connecticut Historical Society, letter from Thomas Gray Bennett to Jane Bennett, December 21, 1877.

83 The official citation on Tom's decoration of the Medjidie was for "assistance in settling differences between the Porte and English and continental bankers." In other words, he was the go between in the sale of rifles.

84 Madis, *The Winchester Era*, p. 65.

85 *New Haven Daily Morning Journal*, December 11, 1880, obituary of Oliver Winchester.

86 Letter from Frank Schlesinger, Director of the Yale Observatory, to Burton E. Livingston, September 20, 1920.

87 The Institute Library, New Haven. See institutelibrary.org.

88 The Institute Library, 31st annual report of the New Haven Young Men's Institute, May 20, 1857.

89 The Institute Library, *Daily Palladium*, December 16, 1857.

90 The Institute Library, song sung at the opening of the new building of the Young Men's Institute, October 13, 1856.

91 The Institute Library, 31st annual report of the New Haven Young Men's Institute, May 20, 1857.

92 New York Public Library Records, *Columbian Register*, October 14, 1854.

93 *Norwich Aurora*, February 13, 1867, letter from Oliver Winchester.

94 Quoted in the *Norwich Aurora*, April 28, 1866.

95   *New Haven Daily Morning Journal*, December 11, 1880, obituary of Oliver Winchester.
96   Williamson, *Winchester*, p. 77.
97   *New Haven Daily Morning Journal*, December 15, 1880.
98   Ibid.
99   *New Haven Evening Register*, December 15, 1880.
100 *New Haven Evening Register*, quoting E. S. Wheeler, December 28, 1880.
101 *New Haven Morning Journal*, December 15, 1880.
102 "Richest Woman in New England is now Dead," *Trenton Evening Times*, March 24, 1898.
103 *The New Haven Daily Palladium*, March 24, 1898.
104 Mary Jo Ignoffo, *Captive of the Labyrinth* (2012), p. 82.
105 Joe Dobrow, "A Farewell to Arms: Winchester Repeating Arms Company and New Haven, Connecticut," *Journal of the New Haven Colony Historical Society* (Spring 1993), p. 28.

CHAPTER THREE: THE WRESTLER

1   "Winchester Shops Mecca for Six Thousand Persons Daily," *New Haven Union*, February 15, 1914.
2   Reverdy Whitlock, "William Huntington Russell and the Collegiate and Commercial Institute," *New Haven Colony Historical Society*, Volume 18, No 4 (December 1969).
3   Private family collection, Thomas Gray Bennett, diary entry, February 8, 1863.
4   Private family collection, Thomas Grey Bennett, letter home, Pensacola, Florida, December 25, 1862.
5   Private family collection, Thomas Gray Bennett, letter home, Fort Barnabas, March 10, 1863.
6   Private family collection, Thomas Gray Bennett, letter home, Camp Ferris, Barancas, March 28, 1863.
7   Connecticut Historical Society, Thomas Gray Bennett, letter home, Port Hudson, LA, July 16, 1863.
8   Ibid.
9   Private family collection, Thomas Gray Bennett, diary entry October 19, 1864.
10   Private family collection, letter from Edwin Pugsley, n.d.
11   Private family collection, Thomas Gray Bennett, diary entry, March 13, 1865.
12   Connecticut Historical Society, Thomas Gray Bennett to Hannah Jane Winchester, November 28, 1871.
13   Connecticut Historical Society, Thomas Gray Bennett to Hannah Jane Winchester, March 28, 1871.
14   Connecticut Historical Society, letter from Thomas Bennett to Jane Winchester, November 30, 1871.
15   Connecticut Historical Society, Thomas Bennett to Jane Bennett, May 2, 1876.
16   Connecticut Historical Society, letter from Thomas Bennett to Jane Bennett, May 8, 1876.
17   Whitworth Society, see www.whitworthsociety.org.
18   Connecticut Historical Society, Thomas Bennett to Jane Bennett, May 8, 1876.
19   Edwin Pugsley, *Winchesters of the Past*.
20   Harold Williamson, *Winchester: The Gun that Won the West* (1961), p. 94.
21   Ibid., p. 70.

22   Connecticut Historical Society, letter from Tom Bennett to Hannah Jane Bennett, December 10, 1883.
23   Browning Arms Company, *A History of Browning Guns from 1831* (1942).
24   John Browning and Curt Gentry, *John M. Browning, American Gunmaker* (2012), p. 20.
25   Ibid.
26   Connecticut Historical Society, letter from Tom Bennett to Hannah Jane Bennett, December 10, 1883.
27   Browning and Gentry, *John M. Browning*, p. 100.
28   George Madis, *The Winchester Era* (1984), p. 103.
29   R. L. Wilson, *Winchester: An American Legend* (2008), p. 80.
30   Ibid., p. 86.
31   Letter from the Winchester Repeating Arms Company to Missionaries and Salesmen, August 21, 1903.
32   Browning and Gentry, *John M. Browning*.
33   Ibid.
34   Pugsley, *Winchesters of the Past*.
35   Browning and Gentry, *John M. Browning*, p. 140
36   Edwin Pugsley interviewed in 1961 by Browning and Gentry for *John M. Browning*.
37   Browning and Gentry, *John M. Browning*, p. 141.
38   Letter from Winchester Repeating Arms Company to Missionaries and Salesmen, August 21, 1903.
39   Pugsley, *Winchesters of the Past*.
40   Madis, *The Winchester Era*, p. 129.
41   Browning and Gentry, *John M. Browning* – preface.
42   Williamson, *Winchester*, p. 171.
43   Thomas Gray Bennett's diaries, quoted by Herbert G. Houze, *Winchester Repeating Arms Company* (2011), p. 129.
44   Houze, *Winchester Repeating Arms Company*, p. 139.
45   Madis, *The Winchester Era*, p. 76.
46   Ibid., p. 85.
47   Private Pugsley family papers, Edwin Pugsley memoir.
48   Madis, *The Winchester Era*, p. 85.
49   Dean K. Boorman, *The History of Winchester Firearms* (2001), p. 45.
50   Robert A. Carter, *Buffalo Bill Cody: The Man Behind the Legend* (2002), p. 2.
51   Boorman, *The History of Winchester Firearms*, p. 44.
52   *Tombstone Daily Epitaph*, October 27, 1881.
53   R. L. Wilson, *Winchester: The Golden Age of American Gunmaking and the Winchester 1 of 1000* (1983).
54   Chris Kyle with William Doyle, *American Gun: A History of the U.S. in Ten Firearms* (2013), p. 92.
55   Admiral Peary statement circulated by WRAC 1909, "The Rifle that Helped Peary Reach the North Pole."
56   Kyle with Doyle, *American Gun*, p. 107.
57   Ida B. Wells, "Southern Horrors," from *Selected Works of Ida B. Wells-Barnett*, quoted in Nicholas Johnson, *Negroes and the Gun: The Black Tradition of Arms* (2014), p. 110.
58   Johnson, *Negroes and the Gun*, p. 132.
59   Theodore Roosevelt, *Hunting Trips of a Ranchman* (1885).
60   Charles Edward Chapel, *The Guns of the Old West* (1995).

61   Letter from Teddy Roosevelt to the Winchester Repeating Arms Company, July 9, 1908.
62   Letter from Teddy Roosevelt to the Winchester Repeating Arms Company, August 10, 1908.
63   Letter from Teddy Roosevelt to the Winchester Repeating Arms Company, September 16, 1908.
64   Letter from Teddy Roosevelt to the Winchester Repeating Arms Company, December 5, 1908.
65   Letter from Teddy Roosevelt to the Winchester Repeating Arms Company, December 1908.
66   Winchester Repeating Arms Company to William Loeb, Jr, December 14, 1908.
67   Henry Brewer, Historical Notes. Winchester Arms Collection Archives, Buffalo Bill Center of the American West.
68   Charles Edward Chapel, *The Guns of the Old West* (1995).
69   Brewer, Historical Notes.
70   Williamson, *Winchester*, p. 185.
71   *Winchester Record*, April 23, 1920.
72   Ernie Pyle, friend of the Topperweins, quoted in Williamson, *Winchester*, p. 185.
73   D. H. Veader and A. W. Earle, *The Story of the Winchester Repeating Arms Company* (1918).
74   Letter to McKim, Mead, and White from the Olmsted Brothers, May 20, 1902.
75   *New Haven Register*, April 25, 1903.
76   The Community Foundation for Greater New Haven – Legacy of a Winchester Rifle Heiress. https://www.cfgnh.org/About/NewsEvents/ViewArticle/tabid/96/ArticleId/42/Legacy-of-a-Winchester-Rifle-Heiress.aspx.
77   Connecticut Historical Society, letter from Thomas Gray Bennett to Hannah Jane Bennett, July 1, 1915.
78   Connecticut Historical Society, letter from Thomas Gray Bennett to Hannah Jane Bennett, April 4, 1905.
79   Statement by Winchester's board of directors, January 20, 1911.
80   Williamson, *Winchester*, p. 211.

CHAPTER FOUR: LADY OF MYSTERY

1   *New York Times*, March 9, 1881.
2   *Morning Journal and Courier*, March 8, 1881.
3   *The Winchester Mystery House: The Mansion Designed by Spirits*, Official Guidebook (1997), p. 8.
4   Ralph Rambo, *Lady of Mystery: Sarah Winchester* (1967), p. 8.
5   Ibid.
6   Robert Peel, *Mary Baker Eddy: The Years of Discovery* (1966), p. 133.
7   Susy Smith, *Prominent American Ghosts* (1967), Chapter 5: "The Mystery House of the Santa Clara Valley," p. 37.
8   Bruce Spoon, "Sarah Winchester and her House: How a Legend Grows," Master's thesis, San Jose State University (1951).
9   Weldon Melick, "Sevenscore Gables," *Holiday Magazine*, February 1945.
10   Rambo, *Lady of Mystery*, p. 5.
11   Ibid., p. 9.
12   Dean Jennings, "The House That Tragedy Built," *Coronet Magazine*, May 1945.
13   Rambo, *Lady of Mystery*, p. 14.
14   Ibid., p. 15.

15 Frank Faltersack, "The Strangest House in the World," *The Wide World Magazine*, March 1929.
16 Smith, *Prominent American Ghosts*, p. 35.
17 Melick, "Sevenscore Gables."
18 Ruth Amet, "Mystery Novel Atmosphere Dominates Web of Rooms," *San Jose Mercury Herald*, May 27, 1923.
19 *San Jose Evening News*, March 29, 1895.
20 Ruth F. Amet, "Winchester Mystery House Constructed Like Giant Ant Hill," *San Jose Mercury Herald*, May 27, 1923.
21 Letter from Sarah Winchester to Jennie Bennett, May 14, 1898.
22 Jennings, "The House That Tragedy Built."
23 Letter from Sarah Winchester to Jennie Bennett, May 14, 1898.
24 Letter from Sarah Winchester to Jennie Bennett, May 14, 1898.
25 *Oakland Tribune*, August 13, 1915.
26 Letter from Sarah Winchester to Jennie Bennett, June 11, 1898.
27 Lisa L. Selby, *The Inscrutable Mrs Winchester and her Mysterious Mansion* (2006), p. 54.
28 Rambo, *Lady of Mystery*, p. 13.
29 *The Winchester Mystery House*, p. 10.
30 Ibid., p. 14.
31 *The American Weekly*, April 1, 1928.
32 Smith, *Prominent American Ghosts*, p. 38.
33 Rambo, *Lady of Mystery*, p. 8.
34 Ibid., p. 9.
35 Letter from Sarah Winchester to Jennie Bennett, May 14, 1898.
36 Rambo, *Lady of Mystery*, p. 9.
37 Smith, *Prominent American Ghosts*, p. 38.
38 Mary Jo Ignoffo, *Captive of the Labyrinth* (2012), p. 209.
39 Letter from Sarah Winchester to Jennie Bennett, June 11, 1898.
40 Merle H. Gray, "The Workshop of a Woman Architect," *San Jose News*, July 16, 1911.
41 Melick, "Sevenscore Gables."
42 Spoon, "Sarah Winchester and her House."
43 Rambo, *Lady of Mystery*, p. 15.
44 Letter from Sarah Winchester to Jennie Bennett, May 14, 1898.
45 Melick, "Sevenscore Gables."
46 Ibid.
47 Jennings, "The House That Tragedy Built."
48 Rambo, Lady of Mystery, p. 13.
49 *The Winchester Mystery House*, p. 21.
50 Connecticut Historical Society, Bennett family papers, letter from Sarah Winchester to Jennie Bennett, May 14, 1898.
51 Ibid.
52 Ignoffo, *Captive of the Labyrinth*, p. 144.
53 Letter from Sarah Winchester to Frank Leib, August 4, 1905.
54 *The World*, February 13, 1898.
55 Letter from Sarah Winchester to Hannah Jane Bennett, May 14, 1898.
56 Bruce Spoon, "Sarah Winchester and her House: How a Legend Grows," Master's thesis, San Jose State University (1951).
57 Leib Collection, History San Jose, letter from Tom Bennett to Sarah Winchester, April 5, 1918.

58   J. Hasbrouck Wallace, *History of the New Haven Hospital 1826–1958*.
59   Rambo, *Lady of Mystery*, p. 16.
60   Gray, "The Workshop of a Woman Architect."
61   Email from Dr Lynn Tanoue, director of the Winchester Chest Clinic, to the author, July 22, 2015.
62   Ignoffo, *Captive of the Labyrinth*, p. 5.
63   Edith Daley, "Old House at Winchester Place Gives Up Some of Its Well-Guarded Secrets," *The Evening News*, September 16, 1922.
64   Amet, "Mystery Novel Atmosphere Dominates Web of Rooms."
65   Ignoffo, *Captive of the Labyrinth*, p. 209.
66   Ibid., p. 210.
67   Rambo, *Lady of Mystery*, p. 15.
68   Ibid.
69   Dave McNary, "Winchester Mystery House Movie Attracts Spierig Brothers," *Variety*, July 24, 2014.
70   Roger Rule, *Sarah* (2003), p. 382.
71   Bruce Spoon, quoted in the *San Mateo Times*, May 31, 1969.

CHAPTER FIVE: DECLINE AND FALL

1   Pugsley family collection, letter from Edwin Pugsley to "John," undated.
2   Robin W. Winks, *Cloak and Gown: Scholars in the Secret War, 1939–61* (1987), p. 254.
3   Connecticut Historical Society, Susan Silliman Bennett's diary, March 14, 1902.
4   Connecticut Historical Society Susan Silliman Bennett's diary, May 14, 1902.
5   Connecticut Historical Society Thomas Gray Bennett's letter to his wife Hannah Jane Bennett, August 1, 1902.
6   Connecticut Historical Society Thomas Gray Bennett, letter to his wife Hannah Jane Bennett, August 19, 1902.
7   Connecticut Historical Society Susan Silliman's Bennett's diary, December 21, 1902.
8   Connecticut Historical Society, Susan Silliman Bennett's diary, October 16, 1903.
9   oe Dobrow, "A Farewell to Arms: Winchester Repeating Arms Company and New Haven, Connecticut," *Journal of the New Haven Colony Historical Society* (Spring 1993).
10   Herbert G. Houze, *Winchester Repeating Arms Company* (2011), pp. 196–7
11   George Madis, *The Winchester Era* (1984), p. 139.
12   Ibid., p. 139.
13   Connecticut Historical Society, Bennett family papers, Susan Silliman Bennett diary entry, January 20, 1909.
14   Connecticut Historical Society, Bennett family papers, Susan Silliman Bennett diary entry, March 2. 1909.
15   Smithsonian Archives of American Art, Cecilia Beaux diary entry, March 2, 1909.
16   Houze, *Winchester Repeating Arms Company*, p. 223.
17   Linda H. Davis, *Charles Addams: A Cartoonist's Life* (2006), p. 183.
18   Private Pugsley family papers, Edwin Pugsley memoir.
19   Edwin Pugsley, *Winchesters of the Past*.
20   Harold F. Williamson, *Winchester: The Gun that Won the West* (1961), p. 218.
21   Buffalo Bill Center of the West, Cody Firearms Museum, Cody, Wyoming, Winchester Repeating Arms Company collection, contract summations and production schedule for .303 British cartridges, August 4, 1914.

22   McCracken Research Library, Buffalo Bill Historical Center, memorandum by Winchester Bennett, November 15, 1916.
23   *Wilkes-Barre Times Leader*, November 19, 1914.
24   *The Springfield Union*, August 21, 1915.
25   Private family papers, Edwin Pugsley memoir.
26   Ibid.
27   *Hartford Courant*, May 22, 1915.
28   Ibid.
29   Ibid.
30   *The Tablet*, April 29, 1916.
31   "Does Capital Expect Rioting?" *Truth*, Erie, Pennsylvania, May 5, 1917.
32   *Trenton Evening Times*, June 10, 1915.
33   Buffalo Bill Center of the West, letter from Winchester Bennett to Secretary of War Newton Baker, May 6, 1916.
34   Buffalo Bill Center of the West, letter from Secretary of War Newton Baker to Winchester Bennett, May 1916.
35   Williamson, *Winchester*, p. 232.
36   Private Pugsley family papers, Edwin Pugsley memoir.
37   Connecticut Historical Society, Bennett family papers, Susan Silliman Bennett diary entry, June 27, 1910.
38   Connecticut Historical Society, Bennett family papers, letter from Thomas Gray Bennett to Sarah Winchester, April 5, 1918.
39   Private Pugsley family papers, Edwin Pugsley memoir.
40   Ibid.
41   Buffalo Bill Center of the West, letter from the British Inspection Department to the Winchester Repeating Arms Company, February 22, 1917.
42   Buffalo Bill Center of the West, Winchester Arms Collection Archives, war orders contract summation, April 1, 1919.
43   New Haven Colony Historical Society, Winchester catalog, 1916.
44   Williamson, *Winchester*, p. 222.
45   Ibid.
46   Private Pugsley family papers, Edwin Pugsley memoir.
47   Morgan Library and Museum, Kidder, Peabody and Co. document. February 4, 1918.
48   Morgan Library and Museum, letter from Kidder Peabody to J. P. Morgan, February 18, 1916. "We have today purchased of the WRAC $16,000,000 of their Two Year 5% notes at 98.14 [...] and have received from Mr. Thomas G. Bennett [...] an option for ninety days on the majority of the stock of the WRAC, at 2,250 per share."
49   Madis, *The Winchester Era*, p. 143.
50   Ibid., p. 139.
51   Buffalo Bill Center, Cody, Wyoming, Henry Brewer, Testimony to the US Congress.
52   Pugsley family collection, Edwin Pugsley's private papers.
53   Burrelle's Press Clippings Bureau, March 2, 1918.
54   Buffalo Bill Center of the West, Fowler Manning, Winchester's sales manager, bulletin dated August 8, 1917.
55   *New York Sun*, April 5, 1917.
56   Joe Dobrow, "Farewell to Arms: Winchester Repeating Arms Company and New Haven, Connecticut," *Journal of the New Haven Colony Historical Society* (Spring 1993), p. 21.

57   Private Pugsley family papers, Edwin Pugsley memoir.
58   Burrelle's Press Clippings Bureau, February 25, 1918.
59   McCracken Research Library, Buffalo Bill Historical Center, letter from Newton Baker, Secretary of War, to Thomas Gray Bennett, February 19, 1918.
60   Williamson, *Winchester*, p. 239.
61   *New Haven Times Leader*, September 12, 1917.
62   Buffalo Bill Center of the West, letter from John Otterson to the War Department, Office of the Chief of Ordnance, November 24, 1917.
63   Buffalo Bill Center of the West, letter to John Otterson from Henry Brewer, December 1, 1917.
64   Letter from R. C. Swanton to J.E. Otterson, March 1, 1918.
65   Madis, *The Winchester Era*, p. 145.
66   Private Pugsley family papers, Edwin Pugsley memoir.
67   Leader in a New Haven newspaper, December 4, 1917. Database of American Historical Newspapers, New York Public Library.
68   Buffalo Bill Center of the West, Winchester Repeating Arms Company Records, memorandum, August 26, 1918.
69   Letter from Thomas Gray Bennett to Sarah Winchester, August 18, 1918,
70   *Wall Street Journal*, reprinted in the *Hartford Courant*, February 19, 1917.
71   Decisions of the Appeals Section, War Department Claims Board, Vol. 8, p. 690.
72   Private Pugsley family papers, Edwin Pugsley memoir.
73   Ibid.
74   Samuel Merwin, *Rise and Fight Againe: The Story of a Life Long Friend* (1935), p. 146.
75   Private Pugsley family papers, Edwin Pugsley memoir.
76   Nancy McClure, Treasures from our West, Winchester Roller Skates, Buffalo Bill Center of the West, http://centerofthewest.org/2014/11/29/treasures-west-winchester-roller-skates/.
77   McCracken Research Library, Buffalo Bill Center of the West, letter to the stockholders of the Winchester Repeating Arms Company, October 26, 1918.
78   Williamson, *Winchester*, p. 257.
79   *Hartford Journal*, February 22, 1920.
80   Madis, *The Winchester Era*, p. 145.
81   Private Pugsley family papers, Edwin Pugsley memoir.
82   Ibid.
83   Buffalo Bill Center of the West, *Winchester Record*, May 21, 1920.
84   *Hardware Review*, Vol. 26, No. 8 (1926).
85   *Winchester Herald*, July/August 1924, Winchester advertisement.
86   Madis, *The Winchester Era*.
87   *New Haven Times*, May 1920.
88   Buffalo Bill Center of the West, *Winchester Record*, October 22, 1920.
89   Madis, *The Winchester Era*, p. 159.
90   Frank Leib letter to Sarah Winchester, April 6, 1921.
91   Private Pugsley family papers, Edwin Pugsley memoir.
92   Williamson, *Winchester*, p. 333.
93   Madis, *The Winchester Era*, p. 161.
94   Williamson, *Winchester*, p. 341.
95   Merwin, *Rise and Fight Againe*, p. 208.
96   Private Pugsley family collection, Edwin Pugsley memoir.
97   Madis, *The Winchester Era*, p. 151.

98 Connecticut Historical Society, Bennett family papers, Susan Silliman Bennett's diary, November 29, 1946.
99 *Hartford Courant*, August 20, 1930.
100 Madis, *The Winchester Era*.
101 Ibid., p. 8.
102 Ibid., p. 166.

CHAPTER SIX: AFTERMATH

1 R. L. Wilson, *Winchester: An American Legend*, p. 176.
2 Ibid., p. 263.
3 Charles Rotkin, "The Rise of the House of Olin," *Fortune Magazine* (December 1952).
4 Ibid.
5 Ibid.
6 Ibid.
7 Olin Corporation website: www.olin.com.
8 Wilson, *Winchester*, p. 179.
9 Andrew Carroll, "Carolina Moonshiner Helps Win WWII," *American History*, Vol. 49, No. 1 (April 2014).
10 Ibid.
11 Ibid.
12 Herbert G. Houze, *Winchester Repeating Arms Company* (2011), p. 268.
13 *Winchester Life*, 1941.
14 *Winchester Life*, April 1943.
15 "The Radiator Division Reports to Uncle Sam," *Winchester Life*.
16 Joe Dobrow, "A Farewell to Arms: Winchester Repeating Arms Company and New Haven, Connecticut," *Journal of the New Haven Colony Historical Society* (Spring 1993), p. 40.
17 Silvio Calabi, Steve Helsley, and Roger Sanger, *Hemingway's Guns: The Sporting Arms of Ernest Hemingway* (2010), p. 125.
18 Ibid., p. 127.
19 Robert Charm, "Shot That Saved Winchester," *Boston Globe*, October 1, 1981.
20 Ibid.
21 Ibid.
22 Ibid.
23 David Ross, Good Vibes at Winchester, *New Haven Advocate*, April 21, 1982.
24 Charm, "Shot That Saved Winchester."
25 James Brooke, "Sales Decline Jolts Connecticut Gun Makers," *New York Times*, July 9, 1985.
26 Robert Weisman, "Gunmaker Kept Loan in Sights," *Hartford Courant*, September 24, 1985.
27 Letter from Richard M. Pelton, President, US Repeating Arms Company, to Louis Romano, 609 Machinists' Union, October 24, 1985.
28 "Winchester Purchaser Sees Huge Potential," *New York Times*, December 31, 1987.
29 "Firearms Manufacturer Takes New Aim in Marketing to Average Gun Consumer," *New England Business*, March 7, 1988.
30 *LA Times*, January 18, 2006.
31 Stacy Stowe, "A Hard Kick From John Wayne's Gun," *New York Times*, January 21, 2006.
32 Stephen Hunter, "Out With A Bang," *Washington Post*, January 20, 2006.

33   See http://www.winchesterguns.com – in the FAQs section.
34   Brad Kane, "Gun Shy – Firearm Makers Anchored to Connecticut," *Hartford Business*, November 24, 2014.
35   William W. Johnstone, with J. A. Johnstone, *Winchester 1886* (2015).
36   "Gun-Shy in Montana," *Wild West*, Vol. 26, No. 1 (June 2013).

BIBLIOGRAPHY

Barnes, Duncan, *The History of Winchester Firearms 1866–1980* (1980)

Blake, William P., ed., *Report of the United States Commissioners to the Paris Universal Exposition, 1867* (1867)

Boorman, Dean K., *The History of Winchester Firearms* (2001)
—— *Guns of the Old West* (2004)

Brown, Dee, *Bury My Heart At Wounded Knee: An Indian History of the American West* (1971)

Browning Arms Company, *A History of Browning Guns from 1831* (1942)

Browning, John and Curt Gentry, *John M. Browning: American Gunmaker* (2012)

Bruce, Robert V., *Lincoln And The Tools of War* (1989)

Calabi, Silvio, Steve Helsley, and Roger Sanger, *Hemingway's Guns: The Sporting Arms of Ernest Hemingway* (2010)

Carter, Robert A., *Buffalo Bill Cody: The Man Behind the Legend* (2002)

Chapel, Charles Edward, *The Guns of the Old West* (1995)

Colby, C. B., *Firearms by Winchester: A Part of United States History* (1957)

Cunningham, Henry Winchester, *John Winchester of New England and Some of his Descendants* (1925)

Davis, Linda H., *Charles Addams: A Cartoonist's Life* (2006)

Dayrup, Felicia Johnson, *Arms Makers of the Connecticut Valley* (1948)

DeVoto, Bernard, *The Year of Decision 1846* (1942)

Dobrow, Joe, *A Farewell to Arms* (1992)

Edwards, William B., *Civil War Guns* (1962)

Freedley, Edwin Troxell, *Leading Pursuits and Leading Men: A Treatise on the Principal Trades and Manufacturers of the United States* (1919)

Fuller, Claud E., *The Breech-Loader in the Service 1816–1917: A History of All Standard and Experimental U.S. Breechloading and Magazine Shoulder Arms* (New Milford, CT: Flayderman, 1965)

Goodrich, Thomas, *Scalp Dance* (1997)

Hansen, Harry, *The Civil War* (1961)

Hotchkiss, Fanny Winchester, *Winchester Notes* (1912)

Houze, Herbert G., *Winchester Repeating Arms Company: Its History and Development from 1865 to 1981* (2011)

Ignoffo, Mary Jo, *Captive of the Labyrinth: Sarah L. Winchester, Heiress to the Rifle Fortune* (2012)

Inskeep, Steve, *Jacksonland: President Andrew Jackson, Cherokee Chief John Ross, and a Great American Land Grab* (2015)

Johnson, Nicholas, *Negroes and the Gun: The Black Tradition of Arms* (2014)

Johnstone, William W., with J. A. Johnstone, *Winchester 1886* (2015)

Kyle, Chris, with William Doyle, *American Gun: A History of the U.S. in Ten Firearms* (2013)

McCracken Research Center, Buffalo Bill Historical Center, *Winchester Record*, Vol. 1, February 14, 1919.

McLaughlin, James, *My Friend the Indian* (1910)

McMurtry, Larry, *Oh What A Slaughter: Massacres in the American West 1846–1890* (2005)

Madis, George, *The Winchester Era* (1984)

Merwin, Samuel, *Rise and Fight Againe: The Story of a Life Long Friend* (1935)

Parsons, John E., *The First Winchester* (1955)

Peel, Robert, *Mary Baker Eddy: The Years of Discovery* (1966)

Pugsley, Edwin, *Winchesters of the Past* (n.d.)

Rambo, Ralph, *Lady of Mystery: Sarah Winchester* (1967)

Reed, Henry M., *The A.B. Frost Book* (1993)

Redman, Bob, *The Spencer Repeater and other breechloading rifles of the Civil War* (n.d.) http://www.aotc.net/Spencer.htm

Rhea, Gordon C., *Letters from Lee's Army: Or Memoirs of Life In and Out of the Army in Virginia* (1998)

Roosevelt, Theodore, *Hunting Trips of a Ranchman* (1885)

Rose, Alexander, *American Rifle* (2009)

Rule, Roger, *Sarah* (2003)

Schaefer, Otto E., *New Haven Water Board History*, Chapter One, "Lifestream for a Region."

Selby, Lisa L., *The Inscrutable Mrs Winchester and Her Mysterious Mansion* (2006)

Sharpe, Philip B., *The Rifle In America* (1938)

Sides, Hampton, *Blood and Thunder: The Epic Story of Kit Carson and the Conquest of the American West* (2006)

Smith, Mickey C., *The Rexall Story: A History of Genius and Neglect* (2004)

Smith, Susy, *Prominent American Ghosts* (1967)

Sword, Wiley, *The Historic Henry Rifle: Oliver Winchester's Famous Civil War Repeater* (2002)

Veader, D. H. and A. W. Earle, *The Story of the Winchester Repeating Arms Company* (1918)

Wallace, Hasbrouck J, *History of the New Haven Hospital 1826–1958*

Ward, Geoffrey C. and Stephen Ives, *The West: An Illustrated History* (1996)

Watrous, George R., *The History of Winchester Firearms 1866–1966* (1966)

Whitlock, Reverdy, *William Huntington Russell and the Collegiate and Commercial Institute* (1969)

Williamson, Harold F., *Winchester: The Gun that Won the West* (1961)

Wilson, Neill C., *Treasure Express: The Epic Days of Wells Fargo* (1987)

Wilson, R. L., *Winchester: The Golden Age of American Gunmaking and the Winchester 1 of 1000* (1983)

—— *Winchester: An American Legend* (2008)

Winchester Mystery House: The Mansion Designed by Spirits, The, Official Guidebook (1997)

Winchester, Oliver, *The First Requisite of a Military Rifle* (1870)

Winchester Record, house magazine of the Winchester Repeating Arms Company, The, published 1918–1921, New Haven, Connecticut.

Winks, Robin W., *Cloak and Gown: Scholars in the Secret War 1939–1961* (1987)

INDEX